EMERGENCY WRITING

Cultural Expressions of World War II

Interwar Preludes, Responses, Memory

Phyllis Lassner, Series Editor

Emergency Writing

Irish Literature, Neutrality, and the Second World War

Anna Teekell

Northwestern University Press | Evanston, Illinois

Northwestern University Press
www.nupress.northwestern.edu

Printed in the United States of America

10 9 8 7 6 5 4 3 2 1

Library of Congress Cataloging-in-Publication Data

Names: Teekell, Anna, author.
Title: Emergency writing : Irish literature, neutrality, and the Second World War / Anna Teekell.
Other titles: Cultural expressions of World War II.
Description: Evanston, Illinois : Northwestern University Press, 2018. | Series: Cultural expressions of World War II: interwar preludes, responses, memory
Identifiers: LCCN 2017057482 | ISBN 9780810137257 (pbk. : alk. paper) | ISBN 9780810137264 (cloth : alk. paper) | ISBN 9780810137271 (e-book)
Subjects: LCSH: English literature—Irish authors—History and criticism. | Irish literature—20th century—History and criticism. | World War, 1939–1945—Literature and the war. | Modernism (Literature)—Ireland. | Ireland—Intellectual life—20th century.
Classification: LCC PR8755.T44 2018 | DDC 820.9941509044—dc23
LC record available at https://lccn.loc.gov/2017057482

For Walker, about whom I am never neutral

Oh yes, Éire will be neutral, which is only the clearest common sense, politically. But that's beside the point. Little patches of immunity like ours are going to be small consolation for what's coming. Being neutral will be precious little help to the imagination.

—KATE O'BRIEN, *The Last of Summer*

Epic

I have lived in important places, times
When great events were decided, who owned
That half a rood of rock, a no-man's land
Surrounded by our pitchfork-armed claims.
I heard the Duffys shouting 'Damn your soul'
And old McCabe stripped to the waist, seen
Step the plot defying blue cast-steel—
'Here is the march along these iron stones.'
That was the year of the Munich bother. Which
Was most important? I inclined
To lose my faith in Ballyrush and Gortin
Till Homer's ghost came whispering to my mind.
He said: I made the Iliad from such
A local row. Gods make their own importance.

—PATRICK KAVANAGH

CONTENTS

ACKNOWLEDGMENTS

The Emergency in Ireland lasted for six years, which is less than the time it has taken to complete this book. Far from neutral, I happily acknowledge the many allies who have supported me and this project over the years. Phyllis Lassner has believed in this book from the moment I pitched it and has been almost unreasonably gracious with both her insight and her time. From the beginning, Guinn Batten encouraged me to think of my dissertation as a future book and believed in its promise. She doggedly taught me never to settle for easy answers; I am a better writer and thinker for her mentorship. Marina MacKay and Dillon Johnston also supported this project from its inception, and I am grateful to them both. Dillon, I'm sorry that I made you read *Watt* again, but I hope it was worth it.

A number of friends have been kind enough to read chapters in progress, and I'm indebted to them for suggesting correlations, criticism, and new ideas. Thank you, Caleb Richardson, Justin Stover, Greg Londe, Terence Brown, Michael Moir, Ashley Maher, Erica Delsandro, Katie Muth, and Matthew Reznicek. I'm also incredibly grateful to the two anonymous readers for Northwestern University Press, whose insights sharpened my thinking and writing in the book's final stages, and to Trevor Perri, the press's acquisitions editor. I thank my former colleagues Dan Debord, Rebecca Brackmann, and Jacques Debrot at Lincoln Memorial University (LMU), where a Faculty Mini-Grant underwrote a 2014 research trip to examine the newly accessible Frank Aiken Papers archive at University College Dublin. My colleagues at Christopher Newport University (CNU), where this book was completed, have welcomed me and this project, and I want to offer thanks to my department chair, Mary Wright, and to my colleagues, especially Kevin Shortsleeve, Kara Keeling, Scott Pollard, Sharon Rowley, Nicole Emmelhainz, Jason Carney, Trevor Hoag, Margarita Marinova, Pat Hopkins, Andrew Rose,

Jessica Kelly, and Danielle Ward-Griffin. A grant from the College of Arts and Humanities at CNU helped defray copyright permission costs; thanks to Dean Lori Underwood. I've had the pleasure of teaching bright undergraduate students at LMU and CNU, and their ideas have helped drive this work. In particular, I thank the students in my 2014 Twentieth-Century Irish Literature course at LMU and those in my 2016 Modernism's Ghosts course at CNU. One of the challenges in teaching at a small liberal arts college is that library resources can be limited. Thanks to two interlibrary loan specialists for bringing the world to me: Janice McDonnell, formerly of LMU, and Jesse Spencer, at CNU; and special thanks to Kenan Padgett at the library of my alma mater, Rhodes College.

I'm lucky to have many friends in Ireland who have put me up and put up with me for the past decade and a half. Huge gratitude to the incomparable Diego Fasciati, formerly of Rough Magic Theatre Company, for archival material from the 2005 production of *Improbable Frequency*. Many friends have shared their thoughts on neutrality and the Emergency's role in contemporary Ireland. *Go raibh míle maith agaibh* especially to Penny Storey and Neil Ardiff and to Lucy McRoberts and Patrick Clarke.

If an academic conference is an intellectual home, mine is the American Conference for Irish Studies (ACIS). My fellow members of the executive board (since 2014) have been remarkable colleagues, cheerleaders, and exemplars of generous scholarship. Thanks, Mary Trotter, Brian Ó Conchubhair, Tim McMahon, Justin Stover, Kate Costello Sullivan, and especially Nick Wolf. Thanks to other ACIS friends, particularly Paige Reynolds and Kelly Sullivan, who provided support and encouragement along the way. Samuel Beckett once wrote, "I have other friends, but only one Georges Duthuit." Well, I have only one Natalie Spar, and while she knows that "words matter," her friendship matters most, and this text is steeped in it.

None of this would have been possible without the support and love of my family. My grandparents, Jan and Byrum Teekell, have always believed in me and cheered me on. To my extended Hays family, thanks for making me part of the gang. I am so lucky to have for a sister a brilliant art historian, Laura Gray McCann, who always makes me think and laugh harder. My father, Gray Teekell, whose fondness for Churchill's rhetoric may have led me down this path, has been generous and supportive of my career. My mother, Mary Teekell, proofread the entire manuscript. She has strong opinions about commas (not all of which I agree with), but it occurs to me that her punctiliousness about punctuation may, in fact, be the "root of the kernel" of much of my thinking here. Thanks, Mom and Dad, for always making me look it up in the dictionary.

To my husband, Shannon Hays, who has been responsible for the general care and feeding of this author, thank you for putting up with the many "emergencies" engendered by this book, and for being a wonderful parent who made it possible for me to write this without having to worry unduly over the brightness of our homestead or the romping of our sturdy children. To my sons, Walker Grady Hays, who was born the day after I signed the advance contract for this book, and Everett James Hays, who arrived the week I signed the final contract, while this may have been written a bit faster without you, you've made each day so much sweeter and given new meaning to my work. Walker, your glee in life and your love of books and stories and the world around you revitalizes my world daily. This book is for you.

I gratefully acknowledge copyright permissions for the following reprinted material:

Portions of chapter 4 previously appeared in "Elizabeth Bowen's Language at War" in *New Hibernia Review* 15, no. 3 (September 2011), reprinted with permission of the Center for Irish Studies at the University of St. Thomas.

Portions of chapter 5 previously appeared in "Beckett in Purgatory: 'Unspeakable' *Watt* and the Second World War" in *Twentieth-Century Literature* 62, no. 3 (Fall 2016), reprinted with permission of Duke University Press.

Quotations from Denis Devlin's "Lough Derg" (in *Collected Poems of Denis Devlin* [Dublin: Dedalus Press, 1999]) are reprinted by kind permission of the Dedalus Press, acting for the Devlin estate.

The quotations from poems by Patrick Kavanagh are reprinted from *Collected Poems*, edited by Antoinette Quinn (London: Lane, 2004; Penguin, 2005), by kind permission of the Trustees of the Estate of the late Katherine B. Kavanagh, through the Jonathan Williams Literary Agency.

Quotations from Louis MacNeice's *Collected Poems*, edited by Peter McDonald (London: Faber and Faber, 2007), are reprinted with permission of David Higham and Associates.

The quotation from Kate O'Brien's *The Last of Summer* (London: Virago, 1990) is reprinted with permission of David Higham and Associates.

The photo of the EIRE marker at Malin Head is reprinted courtesy of Peter Homer.

The set photo from *Improbable Frequency* is reprinted courtesy of Alan Farquharson.

EMERGENCY WRITING

Introduction

In 1942 and 1943, the government of Ireland commissioned eighty-five stone markers at eighty-two Look Out Posts (LOPs) along its coastline.[1] These markers, clearly stating, "EIRE" in whitewashed stones, served as signals to World War II airmen, alerting them to the fact that they were flying over neutral territory. The country's new legal name, Éire, was inscribed onto the land itself: a warning that the war was not permitted to land there; there would be only what the government termed an Emergency.[2] To land there would be an emergency of its own: belligerents downed in Ireland were interned for the war's duration. The choice of "Éire" over "Ireland" for the coastal markings was not merely a preference for the shorter name but a deliberate assertion of deanglicization, an inscription of a new, defiantly Irish signature. This literal emergency writing has left its traces on the Irish landscape. About two dozen of the EIRE signs, in various states of disrepair, are still visible today.[3] They are coastal curiosities referencing a curious period in Irish history, when a young country, healing from civil war and anxious to become European rather than British, attempted to do so by exempting itself from Europe's major conflict. As Éire had virtually no defense budget, the stone markers denote a period of self-sufficient poverty. They are an example of *sinn féin*, the revolutionary motto of "ourselves alone" that focused the independence movement, rewritten into a wartime "leave us alone." Ground-level skywriting made from the materials at hand: the EIRE signs illustrate the sort of peripheral modernity that is common to

Restored LOP 80 sign at Malin Head, County Donegal, 2014. Reproduced by kind permission of Peter Homer.

postcolonial spaces. Aimed at the sky, they are future oriented. Made from the stone that defines Ireland's emptying rural landscape, they are reminders of the past: geologically, economically, politically. The signs are also contentious: did the LOP markers serve simply as geographic references over neutral territory, or were they clues to a secret aerial corridor over Lough Erne, allowing Allied planes to skim over Irish territory on their way to Northern Ireland?[4] How neutral was this emergency writing?

The concerns made visible by the stones of Ireland's coastal signs, and their enduring traces on contemporary Irish culture, are also the concerns of *Emergency Writing*. As its title demonstrates, this book takes seriously Ireland's euphemism for World War II, asking both what happens to literature written during a state of emergency and what it means for writing to be a response to an emergency. It also considers how this body of writing is itself an *emergent* form, responding to the sociopolitical conditions of a newly independent Ireland as well as to a fully emerged modernism in literature and art. What emerges in Irish writing in the wake of independence, of the Gaelic revival, of Yeats and Joyce, is a body of work that invokes modernism as a set of discursive practices with which to counter Irish political pieties. In this way, the late modernism of Ireland's wartime writers shares with modernism globally a sense of "modernity as crisis," as Joe Cleary has put it.[5] Irish late modernism is both a response to crisis and a linguistic crisis in itself.

In his introduction to the *Cambridge Companion to Irish Modernism*, Cleary notes that "a remarkable but still scarcely conceptualized late Irish modernism begins to appear" (3) when we look at the work of Samuel Beckett alongside that of his contemporaries. These Irish late modernists—in the present volume, chiefly Beckett, Louis MacNeice, Elizabeth Bowen, Flann O'Brien, Patrick Kavanagh, and Denis Devlin—created, in Cleary's words, "a strange (sometimes downright eccentric) art, formally inventive, provocatively and perversely erudite, and—for the most part—politically more vexed than anything else" (10). Their work has not yet been conceptualized as a body because the Irish-British dichotomy in criticism has deterred scholars from sufficiently contextualizing an Irish literature from the death of Yeats to the mid-twentieth century. Taoiseach Eamon de Valera's recoding of the war—just an "Emergency"—seems to have elided critical consideration of its impact on the art produced by Irish nationals from 1939 to 1945.[6] Until very recently, most literary critics have either ignored the literature written in Ireland during the war or ignored the war as a context for the literature. Though scholars like Declan Kiberd, Roy Foster, and Terence Brown have helped to correct this, many of the most important Irish writers of the period—for example, Bowen and MacNeice—continue to be treated as British writers (or in the case of Beckett, sometimes French, often international genius sui generis), in spite of their imaginative engagement with Ireland. Much of what has passed as British literature of the Second World War is also Irish literature of the Emergency. And the "strange," "eccentric," "inventive," and "politically vexed" literature Cleary hopes to anatomize is the result of Irish writers deploying language in the face of the Emergency. This makes Irish neutrality a particularly important context for understanding the strange language of late modernism: a literary period marked by contorted logic, awkward silences, and syntactical strangeness, a literature consciously emergent in the wake of a high modernism that had already been canonized. But emergent spaces are difficult to theorize, and there has been little to no vocabulary for talking about neutrality. There was a joke going around Dublin in 1939: "But who are we neutral against?" Language, as war, adores a binary. Can literature be neutral? Can language function neutrally? These are the questions *Emergency Writing* takes up.

Ireland's neutrality in World War II places Irish writers in a peculiar position vis-à-vis war literature. The relative lack of critical attention to Ireland's literature written during and in response to the war has typically been due to the presumption that, as Edna Longley once wrote, the experience of the Second World War was "alien" to Irish literature, that military neutrality somehow neutralized war content for Irish writers.[7] Because Irish neutrality appeared to invalidate the concept of an Irish literature of World War II, the texts I discuss in *Emergency Writing* have often been classed as either literature of the British Home Front—as with Elizabeth Bowen's London-based *The Heat of the Day* and Louis MacNeice's Blitz poems in *Springboard*—or absurdist work without a wartime context, as in the case of Samuel Beckett's *Watt* and Flann O'Brien's *The Third Policeman*, both written during but published after the war. The poetry of Patrick Kavanagh, like much of the counterrevival realism published in *The Bell*, is often read as parochial and antimodern (a reading Kavanagh encouraged in the 1930s and 1940s), in spite of the poet's real engagement with both European themes and the afterlife of poetic high modernism. Denis Devlin, a diplomat, allied himself with the Agrarian school in America, and as such, formalist, new critical readings dominated his reception, making him appear as a cosmopolitan modernist, though his "Lough Derg" exposes a deep interest in not just a formal response to conflict but also to the politics, prayers, and people of his home country.

In the cases of all these writers, readings of their work in the 1940s tended to either elide or divorce the categories of nationality and form. However, for the generation of writers who came to artistic maturity during the war years, no such tidy divisions existed. Irish literature was certainly not neutral toward the war; instead, it strained to account for the ways in which war and neutrality threw Europe and Ireland into relief and, at times, conflated them. This study integrates the work of Irish wartime writers—many of whom were published primarily in Britain—into the narrative of World War II and mid-twentieth century British literary history, without losing sight of how their Irishness impacted their thinking and writing. It simultaneously reexamines a narrative of Irish literary history that has long ignored major European events in favor of an insular, nationalist story that fails to accommodate newly independent Ireland's cultural and diplomatic relationships with Britain and the European continent. By taking the literature of Ireland from the late 1930s to the 1940s into account, *Emergency Writing* provides a new approach to the literature of wartime neutrality, considering the ethical dilemma of performing neutrality—emotionally, politically, and rhetorically—in a world at war.

In recent years, studies by Marina MacKay, Mark Rawlinson, Patrick Deer, and Thomas Davis, among others, have disclosed the ways in which the political conditions of the Second World War produced acutely self-aware literary forms and have argued convincingly that definitions of modernism must take the literature of World War II into account.[8] In addition, definitions of war literature have been stretched by the work of feminist scholars like Kristine Miller, Gill Plain, Karen Schneider, and Phyllis Lassner, who show how aerial bombardment, particularly in Britain, obliterated the line between front and home front, making war writers out of all writers, combatant and noncombatant, male and female.[9] While such redefinitions of late modernism and the literature of war have productively expanded our ability to read this work, they still need to accommodate the many important writers whose main reading audience was British but whose national identities were unfixed (even as war asked citizens to prioritize national identity over personal identity). Ireland's unusual relationship with the United Kingdom from 1939 to 1945, merely seventeen years into both independence and partition, meant that Irish citizens often seemed to experience war and neutrality simultaneously. A porous and contested border with Northern Ireland, intertwined economies, and a shared and shifting population meant that Irish writers—many of whom published and lived in London—had to negotiate dilemmas of national belonging as they shifted between neutral and belligerent countries.

Neutrality looks, from certain angles, like a liminal, noncommittal position, but Irish neutrality in the 1940s was torn from both sides. In *Ireland and the Problem of Information*, Damien Keane provides a fresh look at the concept, countering the dominant narrative of neutrality as isolationism by arguing that "as a real and dynamic practice, neutrality . . . embodied the response to wartime constraints on independence."[10] Understanding neutrality as practice, not posture, allows us to understand the literature of neutrality as work that embodies ongoing negotiations with language and ideas. By following the literature of the

Emergency inside and outside the island of Ireland, I follow Keane in the exploration of an Irish literature that does not, as he puts it, "assume the congruence of cultural field and national or geographical territory" (5). Keane's book challenges received notions of Irish inwardness in this period by exploring Irish writers' international engagements, particularly in the field of radio. *Emergency Writing* focuses on more canonical Irish writers but shows that even those who stayed in Ireland during the war (O'Faolain, O'Brien, Kavanagh) were acutely engaged with questioning Ireland's role in the international scene.

Irish writers in the 1940s, far from being idly neutral, engaged explicitly with the war. They encountered linguistic problems created by what I call the languages of war—censorship, propaganda, and espionage—by writing works of fiction, poetry, and nonfiction prose that themselves seem encoded, that use language as riddle, that *perform* the contortions of censorship and spy work. The writers in the present work use the war—and Ireland's neutrality in it—as a vehicle for asking questions about what it means to be Irish, to be an Irish writer, in a newly postcolonial state. At the same time, the Irish government was trying to use wartime censorship to provide answers, to define Irishness in ways that did not sit well with all its citizens, many of whom felt stifled by the form of Gaelic Catholicism promoted by their postrevolutionary government. The literature of the Emergency is, then, both literature written in a political state of emergency and literature that speaks out about the *emergence* of a new state. The Emergency necessitated new forms because it exposed lived contradictions that could no longer be comfortably tolerated; Emergency writing comprises a body of texts that perform stylistic shifts that show late modernism to be a particularly vibrant moment in Irish letters.

If anyone has been canonized as the exemplary voice of mid-century Ireland, it is the poet Patrick Kavanagh. Born in 1905 in the Ulster county of Monaghan, Kavanagh chose Dublin as his professional home, but he courted fame by hewing his poetry close to the land, claiming to be a "ploughman poet" for the bulk of his career, then a personal poet for the final decade. His best-known work, the epic poem *The Great Hunger*, was written during the Emergency. Published (and partially censored) in 1942, it hardly nods to the war and focuses instead on the socioeconomic battles waged by Ireland's rural poor. Kavanagh later repudiated the poem and his use of the tragic mode, and his "conversion," as he put it, came in 1955, when he "lost [his] messianic compulsion" and became content to sing the virtues of the everyday.[11] But four years before this conversion, Kavanagh published another "Epic"; this one, wryly titled, is a sonnet, in which the poet revisits 1938 from the perspective of 1951. It is one of Kavanagh's best-known lyrics, usually read as a proclamation of the artistic merit of finding the universal in the local. "I have lived in important places," the speaker declares, "times / When great events were decided, who owned / That half a rood of rock."[12] The poem's titular irony—these events may be "epic," but the form of the poem is not—becomes clear here. The "important places" are important only to the Duffys and McCabes, not to the players in the global world system.

For those looking for a poet in whose work sounds the rural realism extolled by the postrevival generation, Kavanagh's elevation of this "local row" (14) to epic status serves as confirmation of the value of postcolonial parochialism.[13] In the poem's final lines, the "ghost" of Homer tells the speaker that "I made the Iliad from such / A local row. Gods make their own importance" (12–14). Set in "the year of the Munich bother" (9), the poem seems to declare that nations, like gods, make their own importance, too. In reviewing the Munich Crisis from the perspective of the newly minted Republic of Ireland, Kavanagh's sonnet appears to support the state-sanctioned argument that by exempting itself from the war, Ireland would finally claim its own status as an independent nation, just as the boundary dispute between the Duffys and McCabes parallels, according to Homer's voice, the *Iliad*, never mind that Munich "bother."[14] Furthermore, the role of the writer, as affirmed in the sonnet's sestet, is one of elevation: by writing the "local rows" Kavanagh himself can become Ireland's Homer; the emergent Ireland can stake a literary claim that will elevate its modern literature from regional to classical—a claim made possible by the contemporaneous canonization of modernist Irish writers like Yeats, Joyce, and even Beckett.

But Kavanagh's poem, with World War II as its absent center, is less decisive than this standard reading assumes. Paul Muldoon sees in it a "failure of nerve" exemplified by the double emphasis on the word "important."[15] But the real tension in the poem rests in its wayward punctuation, for the sonnet's volta invites two readings. It can be read, as printed, as a question: "That was the year of the Munich bother. Which / Was most important?" (9–10), but the enjambment encourages an alternative reading, the definitive statement "That was the year of the Munich bother, which / Was most important." The sonnet appears to resolve the matter by answering the question—the local, Homer's *Iliad* insists, can manifest universal significance. The standard reading of the poem revises the ironic "important" from the first line to assign "Ballyrush and Gortin" (11) the "importance" of Athens and Troy, affirming the significance of the "local row" to literature.[16] Yet the poem seethes with ambiguity. "Epic," after all, is not an epic but a sonnet. As such (like the epic form itself), it is not a form native to Ballyrush or Gortin but an import, via the imperial English, from Europe. A hallmark of late modernism, the form of the poem itself seems to fight against its interpretation. If Kavanagh inherited an Irish sonnet form from Yeats, it was one that, like "Leda and the Swan," found more business in asking questions than answering them. Kavanagh's title is a joke, but a serious joke.

In "Epic," as in 1938, Ireland's relationship with Europe is blurred. By describing that "half a rood" of rocky Monaghan as a "march" through "a no-man's land" (3, 8), Kavanagh aligns it with imagery of World War I.[17] Like the volta, this comparison invites both an affirmative reading (that the Monaghan conflict merits the importance of the Great War) and a skeptical one (that the Duffys' and McCabes' boundary dispute is no match for the bloody border dispute of 1914–18). As do many poems of the Second World War, "Epic" invokes the Great War to foreshadow the larger war to come, represented in this case by the "Munich bother." Kavanagh's colloquial diction is an indicator of Irish opinion in the late 1930s. That the Munich Agreement of 1938, recognizable at its signing as a foreshock to war rather than a true "peace for our time," is rendered a "bother" reminds the reader that for many, Europe's trouble was not a primary issue in places like Ballyrush and Gortin.[18] (Or, as a character in Kate O'Brien's 1943 novel *The Last of Summer* has it, "It's a long way from Danzig to Drumaninch.")[19] By 1938, de Valera had already made it clear that when war came to Europe, Ireland would remain neutral. Kavanagh's "bother" undercuts the value of the poem's central question by assigning this colloquial pejorative to Munich while painting the Duffys and McCabes with diction of defiance and damnation.

Yet in spite of Kavanagh's diction and Homer's ghost, the syntax of that crucial question, "Which / Was most important?" retains ambiguity. Marooned at the end of the ninth line, the word "which" invites the reader to pause over it, investing it with a stress that seems to support the alternative punctuation and prioritize Munich over Monaghan. The enjambing of the next sentence, "I inclined / To lose my faith in Ballyrush and Gortin," into line ten further encourages this reading, as it teases the reader into inclining toward Munich as well. In this way, Kavanagh's "Epic" implies there might be a different answer from the one offered by Homer. The sonnet hints at an alternative reading but leaves it buried, implying a simmering dissatisfaction with the parochial, a sort of secret skepticism about the state's diplomatic policy to keep its rows local. "Epic" mimics the rhetorical double-dealing that characterized the Irish experience of the Emergency, even as it licenses the emergence of a newly important local poetry.

The skepticism in Kavanagh's poem is contained in both form and content, a gesture that makes the sonnet exemplary of the late modernist period as it has been theorized by critics like Tyrus Miller, Jed Esty, Marina MacKay, Thomas Davis, and others.[20] In *The Extinct Scene: Late Modernism and Everyday Life*, Davis accounts for late modernist artwork by arguing that it is "simultaneously aesthetic and political" (6) and that "the internal dialectics of an artwork disclose for us the contradictions of its historical moment" (19). This is certainly the case in Kavanagh's "Epic," in which the contradictions of the sonnet form actively negotiate the contradictions of a signal political moment in 1938. *Whose* signal moment it is (Europe's or Old McCabe's) is up for grabs, and poetry itself, voiced by Homer, offers to be the deciding factor. For Davis, a key element of late modernism is the way it mediates a collapsing world system through attention to everyday life. In Irish late modernism, as the texts discussed in this book show, attention to everyday life is complicated by questions of nationality. Everyday life in the Emergency was affected by anxiety about the war abroad as much as it was insulated by neutrality at home. If, as Davis puts it, "late modernists render legible their moment of systemic disorder by attending to the particulars of everyday life" (15), the Irish late modernists in this study tend just as much to render their moment *illegible* in ways that are mimetic of everyday life in a country actively practicing an ambiguous neutrality.

Kavanagh's sonnet attends to everyday life in "Ballyrush and Gortin" while leaving the sestet's declaration of local importance just faintly illegible.

The equivocal punctuation echoes the Irish government's equivocal use of language in wartime (discussed in chapter 1). If Kavanagh's local realism elbows international politics, this is because both the local and the international subjects of the poem trade in what Keane calls the "problem of information." James Purdon's *Modernist Informatics* adds to a body of work suggesting that the "government of information" (in both the noun and verb senses) is a key factor in the development of literary modernism.[21] For Purdon, modernism emerges through the aesthetics of information, as information management becomes part of everyday life (11). The management of information is always most evident in wartime—when in Britain, for example, it becomes the name of an official ministry—given the extra pressures put on language use by propaganda, censorship, and espionage. Though these three forms of language control are most often associated with war, I show in this book that they were no less pervasive in Ireland's Emergency; in fact, they underwrote its very existence.

Ireland's neutrality was crafted with a rhetorical sleight of hand, and it was guarded by a state censorship that aimed to prevent "unneutral language" and "unneutral thought."[22] Before declaring, on September 3, 1939, the state officially neutral, the Oireachtas amended the constitutional definition of "time of war" to include "a time when there is taking place an armed conflict in which the State is not a participant but in respect of which . . . a national emergency exists affecting the vital interests of the State."[23] In other words, "war" no longer meant just *war*. The Irish government created its neutrality through a manipulation of constitutional language; concurrently, with the passage of the Emergency Powers Act, the state could rely on the censoring of texts (from weather reports to private correspondence) to manipulate thought as well. The impact of this linguistically created state of emergency ramified in the work of Irish writers because it changed the way that language worked in everyday civic life. With the "neutral" censor subjecting language to war legislation, the meaning and location of war became less and less discernible.

To an "Emergency" characterized (like any war) by euphemism, nationalist propaganda, and censorship, Irish writers responded with work that challenged the meaning of language itself, particularly the confidence with which it could be deployed. *Emergency Writing* shows how in their wartime poetry and prose, as in Kavanagh's "Epic," Irish writers fret and worry about the moral culpability of exempting themselves from the war, and their language frets and worries around the same wartime constrictions of censorship, propaganda, and espionage as the language of writers from belligerent nations. But the Irish literature of the Second World War adds another dimension—one that questions the meaning of national belonging in the face of a global war. All sides are "caught up" (to echo Yeats), and neutrality only highlights the impossibility of escaping war guilt.[24]

If the essential Dublin question was "Who are we neutral against?" this study takes on the ethical problem at the center of the joke, examining how a diverse collection of Irish writing—from the realist poetry of Kavanagh to the metafiction of Flann O'Brien—utilizes and revises modernist literary practices to reveal the ways in which language itself can mask or unmask political and personal intentions. This project is rooted in close readings of published poetry and novels but also analyzes archival material from authors' letters, journals, and manuscript revisions, and from contemporary newspapers, literary journals, and Irish political speeches and legislation. These diverse forms demonstrate how information crosses boundaries, as Purdon suggests, making it difficult to separate public from private, official from unofficial discourse (11), just as Kavanagh's "Epic" conflates personal and international conquest, local and political poetry. My readings of the Irish literature of World War II are attuned to the ways in which writers respond both to historical and cultural circumstance and to their modernist literary antecedents.

If late modernism sees modernism as a body of practices open to reuse and renovation,[25] then Kavanagh's sonnet stages this in its conversation with Yeats. Like "Epic," "Leda and the Swan" is concerned with information, asking if in the moment of her rape by Zeus, Leda "put on his knowledge with his power" (13). Both poems, compressing the epic action of the *Iliad* into sonnet form, ask questions of both political and poetic importance. Both sonnets are concerned with the power not only of personal and political violence but also of the poet as the final arbiter of information. Kavanagh's wry reuse of Yeats's material takes the modernist trope of reinventing classical mythology but ties it into the generically realist concerns of the everyday. If "Epic" does assert that a literature of classical power may emerge in local places, it acknowledges that this cannot happen without its being colored by the greater landscape. After all, if Munich was no more than a "bother" to the farmers of Ballyrush, the *Iliad* is still about a war.

In evoking "Leda and the Swan," Kavanagh connects the subject matter of "Epic" to a different local row as well, since the inclusion of "Leda and the Swan" in *The Tower* (1925) places it among Yeats's most important poems of the Anglo-Irish and Irish Civil Wars. In this way, "Epic" also demonstrates the ways in which Irish late modernist texts cannot be disentangled from Irish national history; they are artifacts of an emerging state as much as of an evolving literary modernism. Kavanagh's own biography underscores the question of an emerging postindependence Irish literature. As he writes in the "Author's Note" to his *Collected Poems*, "I had the misfortune to live the worst years of my life through a period when there were no Arts Councils, Foundations, Fellowships for the benefit of young poets. On many occasions I literally starved in Dublin" (xiii). The emergence of Irish state-funded arts dates to the postwar period; the Irish Arts Council was founded in 1951. By 1955, Kavanagh was benefiting from state aid in the form of a stipended extramural lectureship at University College Dublin. Three years after his death in December 1967, his name became synonymous with a major poetry prize; his papers are held in the National Library; and in 1991 he was elevated to the highest level of recognition in Dublin: public statuary. Kavanagh's transition from literal starving artist to state-commissioned statue embodies the transition of Irish literature from postcolonial product to national asset. If "Epic" depicts the battle between local realism and canonical recognition, it also helps us pinpoint the Second World War as a key moment of transition for literature in the new Irish state.

In *Culture, Northern Ireland, and the Second World War*, Guy Woodward notes that Northern Ireland has been marginalized in accounts of Ireland and World War II because of the focus on neutrality.[26] While the present study includes work by three Ulster-born writers (Kavanagh, MacNeice, O'Brien—along with the Ulster-educated Beckett), my concern is indeed with the practice of neutrality in the twenty six counties of Ireland, and I see the ambivalent sense of national belonging expressed, particularly by Kavanagh and MacNeice, as part of the uncomfortable ambivalence occasioned by Ireland's neutrality. The writers examined in the present work had all reached their teenage years before partition, and thus their sense of national belonging included ongoing negotiations with the impact of Irish revolutionary history. For readers interested in the cultural impact of the war on Northern Ireland, I commend Woodward's work. *Emergency Writing* shows that the strange ambivalence of neutrality was inextricably related to the strange ambivalence of partition, and like partition, Ireland's wartime neutrality has become a signal marker of the contemporary Republic's cultural self-imaging.

In the past decade, debates on the Lisbon and Nice treaties and the way that Ireland's military neutrality impacts its membership in the European Union have prompted a renewed academic interest in the origins of Ireland's seemingly sacrosanct neutrality policy.[27] Aided by recently opened archives, several new histories have reconsidered Ireland's relationship to the Second World War. Brian Girvin's *The Emergency* and Ian Wood's *Britain, Ireland and the Second World War* expand the foundational work that Robert Fisk began with his archivally rich *In Time of War*.[28] These histories demonstrate that the "sacred egoism" of Ireland's neutrality has never been straightforward, and they pave the way for the recognition that World War II is far from "alien" to the Irish experience and to Irish literature. Social and cultural histories of the Emergency, in particular Clair Wills's magisterial *That Neutral Island*, have played an important role in bringing to light the ways in which Irish authors were invested in writing the war experience.[29] As Terence Brown does in *Ireland: A Social and Cultural History*, Wills makes frequent recourse to the voices of Ireland's writers as she explores the cultural landscape of the Emergency.[30]

This study is made possible by the work of scholars like Brown and particularly Wills, who provide the historical and cultural background in which the readings in the following chapters are grounded. With the breadth of historical scholarship available on 1939–45 Ireland, a dedicated consideration of Irish literary responses to World War II is due. Historians of the Emergency have often cited literary texts from the period in order to arrive at a political point or to provide a contemporary commentary on historical events. Ian Wood's offhand citation of MacNeice is typical of this. Wood writes that the Battle of the Atlantic "prompted the poet . . . to make an emotional appeal to his compatriots in the poem 'Neutrality.' In it he tried in vain to convince them that it was the British naval and aircrew members who, in the cold waters of the Atlantic, would pay the real price of Irish neutrality" (19). But MacNeice's poem is far more complex than the historian's treatment of it indicates. MacNeice's grappling with the meaning of neutrality, both for himself and for his countrymen, resulted in a body of poetry whose rhetorical and tropological intricacy belie readings like Wood's, which assigns the poem a straightforward political comment. Like "Neutrality," the literature of Ireland's neutrality in World War II is multivalent. It deserves—and demands—closer scrutiny than historians have provided. This literature has much to tell us about the experience of the war in Ireland and about late modernist language itself. Recently, Damien Keane's study and the edited collection *Irish Culture and Wartime Europe, 1938–1948* have offered first looks at the importance of this period to Irish literary culture.[31] As Keane puts it, "By graphically intensifying the contests between nationalism and internationalism that defined Ireland's relationship to the world, the Second World War upended the modern Irish cultural field" (7). The aim of this book is to provide both broad and close textual analyses of how those "upended" writers responded, with a focus on resituating well-known late modernist texts in their Emergency contexts.

Chapter 1 examines political rhetoric, censorship, and print culture in Emergency-era Ireland, demonstrating the impact of "neutral" rhetoric on everyday language use. I use the term "rhetoric" in its common and Platonic sense as the art of persuasive speech and writing. As Steven Lynn points out, this definition "sounds innocent enough unless you mistrust language and the public—which Plato certainly did."[32] This chapter describes the unique culture of neutral Ireland, examining how the constitutional redefinition of "war" created a slippage between belligerence and neutrality that would trouble daily life in Ireland, where many felt they experienced war and neutrality simultaneously. Neutral Ireland has been portrayed as at once porous—dangerously open to outside influence—and sealed off, like Plato's Cave, from the world at war.[33] In this chapter, I explain how the Irish government crafted its policy of neutrality and how its handmaiden, the Censorship Board, enforced a policy of "neutral language." I argue that this policy, with its implicit presumption that language could be made transparent, failed in its intent to make Irish publications a beacon of clarity by eliminating Allied or Axis propaganda. Instead, much writing either went unpublished or appeared in print so excoriated that even battle results and death notices made little sense. Reading constitutional amendments, de Valera's public comments, Seanad debate records, and previously unpublished Cabinet memoranda, I show how Emergency censorship shifted from a matter of diplomacy to one of dogma: in short, how the Irish government used its wartime neutrality to censor its way to cultural nationalism. Even if de Valera did not know Plato's *Phaedrus* definition of rhetoric as "the art of winning the soul by discourse," his own rhetoric was deeply invested with his vision of the Irish (Gaelic, Catholic) soul.[34] Irish print culture responded angrily—and inventively—to the challenges posed by neutral propaganda and censorship. The chapter concludes with readings of material from the *Irish Times* and *The Bell*, which demonstrate how a direct confrontation with censorship and cultural nationalism shaped the discursive practices of late modernist writers in Ireland.

Chapter 2 focuses on a particularly pervasive element of de Valera's depiction of neutrality: its impact on the nation's soul. The equation of neutrality with peace and piety was often advocated through the claim that Ireland could—as Denis Devlin satirically puts it—"pray [Europe] whole again."[35] In this chapter, the ancient Catholic pilgrimage site, Lough Derg, also known as Station Island and Saint Patrick's Purgatory, serves as a focal point for a neutral island whose wartime existence was commonly referred to as a version of purgatory. In 1942, both Patrick Kavanagh and Denis Devlin wrote poems based on the pilgrimage to Lough Derg. In both "Lough Derg" poems, Station Island becomes both the purgatory that mimes neutral Ireland at its most narrowly nationalistic and the pivot point used to explore its relationship with a war-torn, Catholic Europe. In examining these two poems, part of a tradition of writing about Lough Derg that reaches back to Dante, this chapter demonstrates that neutral Ireland's conception of the war is not, as is commonly assumed, inextricably tied to the state's relationship with Britain but also embraces Ireland's self-identification as European and its shared neutrality with other small, European, predominantly Catholic countries. In their poetry, Kavanagh and Devlin test the propagandistic claim that prayer is the appropriate form of action for the neutral soul. Their poems, both Catholic in concern and formally ambitious, posit prayer as action and poetry as prayer; they offer pilgrimage as a poetic form and as a form of purgation. Though their titles are identical and their concerns intertwined, Kavanagh's and Devlin's poems are formally divergent in their different takes on modernist practice. Kavanagh's long poem of mixed forms (ranging from free verse to a sonnet sequence) is both recognizably realist and attuned to the everyday, while Devlin's "profound and abstruse" poetry (as praised by the equally profound and abstruse Samuel Beckett)[36] is formally precise but narratively confounding. These two poems demonstrate the wide variety in late modernist poetry, but they share an impetus to make their different forms of poetic "difficulty" mimetic of the pilgrim experience. Like the pilgrimages they depict, these "Lough Derg" poems are *almost* successful; the result is a poetry of paradox and irresolution, both in terms of the poems' formal gestures and their suggestions, made in different measures, that venturing to the heart of neutral Ireland does little to clarify, and perhaps complicates, the neutral penitent's relationship with a "shattered" Europe.

Chapter 3 examines the poetry of Louis MacNeice, whose professional peregrinations embodied Ireland's complicated relationship with the wider world. The Belfast-born MacNeice spent the beginning of the war in neutral Ireland and the then-neutral United States and the latter part of the war producing propaganda for the BBC. But, as Yeats wrote, "We make out of the quarrel with others, rhetoric, but of the quarrel with ourselves, poetry,"[37] and MacNeice's three volumes of poetry published during the war are deeply antipropagandistic, to the point that some contemporary readers found them subversive. His best war lyrics question the concepts of neutrality and allegiance, conflating both in a rhetoric of complicity and challenging contemporary definitions of what it meant to be a "war poet." MacNeice's wartime writing is acutely engaged with the high modernist poetry that followed the Great War, and his late modernist struggle with fellow Irishman W. B. Yeats's legacy, including Yeats's own self-questioning as a war poet, is what allows the younger poet to dismantle (while referring to) the oppositional structures that Paul Fussell claims characterize nearly all literature after World War I. For MacNeice in the 1940s, the distinction between friend and enemy, guilty and innocent, is no longer clear. While Kavanagh and Devlin deal in paradox and ambiguity, MacNeice uses complex forms of repetition and reflexive imagery to craft a poetry of wartime complicity. In MacNeice's lyrics of suicide and cannibalism, no one is neutral: everyone is complicit, and even the blaze of German firebombs becomes "enemy and image of ourselves."

Elizabeth Bowen's wartime novel, *The Heat of the Day*, is the centerpiece of chapter 4. It shares with Kavanagh's, Devlin's, and MacNeice's work a deep skepticism about personal complicity with the sins of war. I read the novel in the context of the war's government of information and of Bowen's own participation in intelligence gathering in Ireland for the British Ministry of Information. The notoriously contorted syntactical structures in *The Heat of the Day* are, I argue, Bowen's response to what she experienced as the languages of war: propaganda and espionage. Bowen shares with MacNeice an understanding that language itself is duplicitous and dangerous in wartime; this is woven into the linguistic structure of her novel. An incursion into the spy-thriller genre, Bowen's psychological drama records the eventfulness of language itself, for the plot is driven less by characters' actions than by their words. Like the double agent at the center of the novel, Bowen's dangerous language often appears to mean or be two different things at once. Formally, the novel plays on secret and surprising doubles as it interrogates the imagined space between England and Ireland. Bowen weaves both content and rhetoric from her 1942 history of her family home in Ireland, *Bowen's Court*, into *The Heat of the Day*. By figuratively collapsing the distance between London at war and Bowen's Court at peace, Bowen's novel demonstrates the impossibility of neutral space just as it questions the ability of language to function as a neutral medium.

In chapter 5, I examine two antinovels that interrogate language's ability to convey meaning at all in the face of trauma. Written in wartime isolation, Samuel Beckett's *Watt* and Flann O'Brien's *The Third Policeman* can both be read as black comedic takes on the death of the foundational Anglo-Irish genre, the "big house" novel. Their conscious distortion of that generic heritage makes the two novels exemplary participants in the shift from modernism to postmodernism—a shift typically dated to the Second World War. *Watt* and *The Third Policeman* each concern characters who cannot escape from an isolated, rural Ireland that is both relentlessly illogical and characterized by cyclical movement and linguistic breakdown. These novels, along with Máirtín Ó Cadhain's Irish-language antinovel *Cré na Cille*, cycle chapter 5 back to the thematic concerns of chapter 2 as the novels join the "Lough Derg" poems (and Kavanagh's

The Great Hunger) in the imagining of Emergency-era Ireland as a purgatory of society and language, albeit one with little chance of escape or redemption. In both Beckett's and O'Brien's novels, language and meaning are increasingly impossible to decipher as their protagonists fail to come to terms with traumatic experience. The language of these novels functions as a code for the experience of trauma while also exposing as farce the censor's concept of a totally readable "neutral language" that could represent the war. The protagonists' experiences analogize the trouble of missed trauma in the Emergency. By not dealing with the real trauma of war—by missing, so to speak, the very site of trauma—"neutral language" fails to create meaning at all.

The epilogue examines the role of Irish neutrality in Ireland's European politics—a role that will be further tested by the impact of Brexit. The lasting cultural legacy of the Emergency is borne out by a number of contemporary novels and plays set in the period. Arthur Riordan and Bell Helicopter's 2005 musical *Improbable Frequency* serves here as a lens through which to view Irish cultural memory of the war years. The musical and its popularity highlight ways in which the Emergency was a watershed event in twentieth-century Irish history, a period that has been read, variously, as embarrassing and empowering to the young state. In an increasingly centralized European Union, and an increasingly multiethnic immigrant Ireland, the Emergency remains a historical moment that separates the Irish from Europe and joins them together as Irish. *Improbable Frequency* demonstrates how simmering concerns about the ethics of neutrality are inextricably tied to language use. The most memorable aspect of the play is its linguistic eventfulness: written entirely in verse, it is riddled with puzzles, crossworded with puns—an ebullient mimicry of the late modern literary language of the Emergency itself.

CHAPTER 1

The Rhetoric of Irish Neutrality

Eamon de Valera began setting up the basis of Irish military neutrality in 1936 as a campaign of conspicuous nonalignment in the Spanish Civil War.[1] In a speech to the League of Nations on July 2, 1936, de Valera exhorted small nations "to determine that they will not become the tools of any great power and that they will resist with whatever strength they may possess every attempt to force them into a war against their will."[2] Over time, this argument, based on the embattled sovereignty of small nations, would become the moral doctrine on which Irish neutrality is seen to rest. Neutrality, de Valera encouraged his countrymen to believe, was an ethical stance against the making of war, particularly war with imperial ambitions. In a 1937 article in *Ireland Today*, Michael Tierney summarized what would become the prominent rationale for the policy: "We must be implicated, as far as in us lies, in no more wars to end wars or wars for democracy or for any of the other high-sounding ideals in which war-propaganda is so fruitful. Our course, above all in war-time, must be one of 'sacred egoism.'"[3] The phrase "sacred egoism" had, since 1918, been associated with the republican concept of *sinn féin*, or "ourselves alone." Written pseudonymously by Ernest Boyd, a pioneering critic of the Irish literary renaissance, the 1918 pamphlet *The Sacred Egoism of Sinn Féin* shows the concept of "sacred egoism" to be rooted in the Great War's Irish anticonscription movement. Boyd argues that if the war was an "Allied crusade for the liberation of small nationalities . . . one had been forgotten," and that by asserting their unwillingness to participate for Britain in this gallant act of hypocrisy, Irishmen could assert their independent nationality.[4] Sacred egoism and *sinn féin* come to define, for Boyd, the "tenacious selfishness, without which [small nationalities] must abandon the struggle for life." The echoes of the doctrine of sacred egoism in de Valera's approach to the Second World War are clear: Ireland's unwillingness to participate should be read not as a sign of isolationism but as self-assertion on an international scale. For de Valera's Fianna Fáil government, *sinn féin* made an organic transition from republican motto to rallying cry for self-sufficient neutrality.

After V-E Day, de Valera felt justified enough to defy Churchill's claim that Britain "stood alone" against tyranny,[5] in a radio address that proclaimed Ireland as "a small nation that stood alone, not for one year or two, but for several hundred years against aggression . . . a small nation that could never be got to accept defeat and has never surrendered her soul."[6] The sacred egoism of neutrality, then, also implied sustained purity of soul—or at least of de Valera's fondly imagined Irish, Catholic soul. Not everyone was swayed by the taoiseach's argument. In 1943, Sean O'Faolain noted in *The Bell* that the meaning of *sinn féin* seemed to have undergone a different sort of change: "Self-reliance has taken on the astonishing implication of estrangement from the world."[7] The morality of Ireland's sacred egoism was compromised by the uniquely ethical grounds in which the Allied fight against fascism was couched. Like O'Faolain, many Irish writers and intellectuals worried that the lofty self-sufficiency of neutrality might not be enough to insulate the country from an indictment of moral negligence.

Behind his rhetoric of idealism, de Valera had shrewdly realistic reasons for charting a course of neutrality. For economic and defense purposes, and for the purpose of galvanizing a young country only just healing from the civil war of 1922–23, neutrality was the most practicable option.[8] But its great success as a policy, its continued valuation as a marker of Irish difference, and de Valera's reputation as a statesman rest on the way in which Irish neutrality was couched as a moral choice. Throughout the Emergency, de Valera's public pronouncements relied on diction of morality and justice and a rhetoric that couched neutrality only in positive terms. That Irish neutrality is still generally perceived as an ethical obligation rather than a self-serving policy attests to the power of de Valera's rhetoric.[9] Neutrality was enforced by a deliberate manipulation of language and guarded by a state censorship that shielded the government from any scrutiny that might have revealed just how unneutrally it behaved.

As Ireland's vulnerability in the war decreased, Emergency censorship increased. In a sense, there was less to be frightened of, but more to cover up. De Valera's government was anything but neutral when it came to promoting its image of what Ireland ought to be, and censorship became a primary weapon in making the "morality" of neutrality an essential part of a conservative, Catholic, and insular Ireland. De Valera's famous 1943 "dream" of an Ireland of "happy maidens" and "athletic youths," of "frugal comforts" in "cozy homesteads," "serene" wisdom and "right living" owes something of its imagery to popular interpretations of Gaelic revival ideology.[10] If the literature of the revival aimed to disrupt the aesthetic autonomy of the tired, English, Arnoldian notion of the Celt, de Valera's camp revivalism created a similarly autonomous vision of a conservative Gaeilgeoir's Catholic Ireland. Much of the literature of the Emergency is a response to the government's attempt to legislate aesthetic autonomy, as well as an acknowledgment that if modernist forms are no longer capable of making things new, they are still capable of disrupting dominant cultural narratives.

This chapter examines the political rhetoric of Ireland's wartime neutrality in order to reveal the ways in which Irish late modernism emerged to disrupt it. First, I explore the manipulation of legal language that allowed the Irish government to create a state of emergency in Ireland that it could propagandize as both nationally empowering and morally upright. Next, I show how de Valera's conservative government adapted—or one might say perverted—the nationalism of the Gaelic revival into a rhetoric that could conflate sovereignty with sanctity, and then used the political power of wartime censorship to censor materials for the public's moral "safety" as well as the safety of the body politic in wartime. But as the Fianna Fáil government misread and ossified the revival, Irish late modernists returned in spirit to the revival's disruptive aesthetics while simultaneously eschewing them as the bourgeois clothing of official republicanism.[11] In the final section of the chapter, I read material and manifestos from two dissident periodicals, the *Irish Times* and *The Bell*, in order to show how print culture responded to the cultural, financial, and even verbal constrictions of Emergency censorship to create a late modern stylistics of disruption. While the realism of Sean O'Faolain and Patrick Kavanagh may seem, at first, a far cry from the verbal play of Flann O'Brien and Samuel Beckett, this chapter introduces the conditions that governed what these second-generation modernists have in common: an intention to disrupt the status quo and break through to what is really an adaptation of the high modernist notion of the Real. I add to Mark Quigley's analysis of late modernism in Ireland as a rejection of "the mimetic impulses driving both official nationalism's Revivalist inheritance and a disillusioned postcolonial naturalism that would seek to repudiate it" [12] by pinpointing the Emergency as the period when Irish writers' search for new forms became a genuine aesthetic crisis.

"She Has Invested Her Self-Respect in It": The Rhetoric of Neutrality

Ian Wood articulates what is now the mainstream view of de Valera's diplomatic policy when he suggests that Ireland's position on World War II was "a stance of non-belligerency rather than one of neutrality" because of Ireland's "friendly neutrality" toward the Allies.[13] The Irish government and its intelligence agency, G2, secretly aided the Allies throughout the war, communicating intelligence on German spies, reporting Irish weather forecasts to Britain, "overlooking" the seven-mile "Donegal Corridor" through which Allied seaplanes reached Lough Erne, and repatriating downed Allied soldiers through Northern Ireland while detaining Axis personnel whose planes or ships went down in Irish territory.[14] The extent of this collaboration was not known, however, outside official corridors, and in fact Ireland was broadly lambasted in the British press for being disloyal, fascistic, and ignoble.[15] This characterization suited both governments, since it was cheaper for the United Kingdom to maintain relations with a neutral Ireland than it would have been to protect a largely defenseless ally. The narrow Irish Sea was a far friendlier border than the North Atlantic. But many Irish citizens bristled as the British press accused them of egotism and even fratricide; the majority saw their neutrality in a vastly different light. As an Anglo-Irishwoman working in London, Elizabeth Bowen recognized her value as a cultural go-between and volunteered as an intelligence reporter to the British Ministry of Information, in exchange for the right to travel freely between her homes in London and County Cork. In her November 1940 report to the Dominions Office, Bowen wrote, "It may be felt in England that Éire is making a fetish of her neutrality. But this assertion of her neutrality is Éire's first free self-assertion: As such alone it would mean a great deal to her. Éire (and I think rightly) sees her neutrality as positive, not merely negative. She has invested her self-respect in it. It is typical of her intense and narrow view of herself that she cannot see that her attitude must appear to England an affair of blindness, egotism, escapism or sheer funk . . . I could wish that the English kept history in mind more, that the Irish kept it in mind less."[16] Bowen's characterization of neutrality as Ireland's "first free self-assertion" is accurate; only seventeen years in existence, Ireland used neutrality to make its mark as an independent country. Asserting Ireland's difference from Britain by remaining neutral in the war was the fulfillment of de Valera's rallying cry for small states in the League of Nations. By declaring neutrality, Ireland joined other small, independent European nations, including Belgium, the Netherlands, Luxembourg, Denmark, Norway, Sweden, Finland, Hungary, Yugoslavia, Romania, Bulgaria, Portugal, and Switzerland, as an equal in diplomatic policy. That the policy was so overwhelmingly approved of by the Irish populace indicated the success of what Bowen called its "positive" characterization. As Clair Wills writes, it was only the history of Ireland's long connection with Britain (including the Northern Irish border)—and its economic dependence on its larger neighbor—"which made its neutrality conspicuous" (47).

The return of the Treaty Ports at Cobh, Berehaven, and Lough Swilly from British to Irish control in 1938 cemented Ireland's physical sovereignty over its twenty-six counties and made martial neutrality a legitimate possibility.[17] It was also the cause of tremendous tension between Ireland and Britain when, at the height of the Battle of the Atlantic, Churchill considered taking the Treaty Ports by military force; this included a variety of offers to de Valera that would end partition in exchange for the use of the ports. In May 1941, Louis MacNeice found himself acting as another Anglo-Irish go-between, asking the readership of *Common Sense* to

> remember that the feeling in Éire is now predominantly pro-British (though still opposed to participation in the War), that the

> pro-German minority is extremely small and de Valera's position is agonisingly difficult. Those who propose the application of a strong hand to Éire are forgetting their history, but the other kind of extremist can be equally silly; an example is a recent little book . . . called *Churchill Can Unite Ireland*, [the thesis of which is:] end Partition in Ireland by a fiat and the whole country will automatically throw all its energies into the crusade against Hitler. Whereas what would really happen would be civil war.[18]

Perhaps the real payoff of neutrality was that *it* united the pro- and anti-treaty factions of the Irish population. Though banned by the Irish government since 1936, the Irish Republican Army (IRA) was still an active force creating unrest. The IRA declared war on Britain in January 1939, implementing a deadly sabotage campaign against England in 1939–40 and courting Nazi support throughout World War II. Neutrality was de Valera's surest way to prevent strong pro- and anti-British sympathies from igniting a second civil war, but to enforce it the government resorted to interning IRA members without trial for the Emergency's duration. Neutrality did not mean impartiality or peace; this was a neutrality maintained by force.

If the partition of Ireland and Northern Ireland incited the danger of paramilitarism that threatened neutrality, it was also a major justification for neutrality as a moral stance. In his 1941 Saint Patrick's Day radio broadcast to the (still neutral) United States, de Valera confidently reported, "A small country like ours that had for centuries resisted imperial absorption, and that still wished to preserve its separate national identity, was bound to choose the course of neutrality in this war. No other course could secure the necessary unity of purpose and effort amongst its people, and at a time like this we heed the warning that the house divided against itself shall not stand. The continued existence of partition . . . added in our case a further decisive reason" (454). Partition was, unquestionably, a primary factor in de Valera's moral justification for neutrality. The implication was that if Britain expected Ireland to fight a war for democracy while Britain still occupied Northern Ireland, this was a case of imperial hypocrisy. To fight against Britain would be to fight against Northern Ireland and therefore Ireland's own people, and to fight with Britain was to fight for the imperial occupier. J. J. Lee points out, however, that while partition "was a prime Irish justification, if not reason, for neutrality," it was also "a prerequisite for successful neutrality," because the availability of Northern Irish ports and airstrips for Allied use was the primary thing that prevented a British reoccupation of the Treaty Ports.[19] Without partition, much of the moral superiority of neutrality would have fallen flat, yet partition was the very thing that enabled de Valera to maintain the policy's practicability.

In order to practice neutrality, de Valera's government consistently rallied Irish citizens to self-defense. On April 13, 1941, in a speech commemorating the Easter Rising, de Valera issued a typical rallying cry for neutrality: "Today, in a warring world, the freedom of nations is everywhere in peril. I have many times warned you of the dangers which threaten us here although we wish well to all peoples and have no desire to quarrel with any . . . Still, every day whilst this war continues our dangers will increase. Even to maintain our neutrality will mean for us much hardship and privation. Should we be called upon to defend it, it will mean suffering and death for many . . . If we have to take up arms, we shall know that we are fighting for all that is dear to us, and we shall know that our cause is just" (457). This speech illustrates the difficulty de Valera faced in concocting proneutrality propaganda, which seems almost a contradiction in terms. Ireland's citizens had to face the dangers of invasion and the privations of rationing without the certainties of war or of a common enemy to rally against. De Valera's speeches emphasized the values of danger and suffering, resolution and justice, without a concrete object against which to pitch them. All this was encapsulated in the quip that dominated Irish conversations about the policy: "But who are we neutral against?" In popular memory, the answer might be Britain, in that de Valera's notion of the "just cause" was essentially inextricable from the entrenched rhetoric of Irish nationalism. Practically, Ireland was neutral against Germany, being, as Lee claims of all successful neutrals, "neutral for the power that potentially threatened them most" (244). Rhetorically, in spite of his debts to the language of the independence movement, de Valera emphasized his terms of "suffering and privation" to suggest that Ireland was neutral against everyone (even, perhaps, itself). One of the taoiseach's favored talking points was his dream of a completely self-sufficient Ireland. From 1939 to 1945, he was able to taste that dream—though plenty of people felt it was less a dream than a nightmare.[20]

Before declaring the state officially neutral on September 3, 1939, the Oireachtas rushed through two major pieces of legislation in an all-night emergency session. The first was the first amendment to the 1937 Constitution of Ireland, one of two amendments made during the constitution's transitional period, when it could be amended by law without a nationwide referendum. The passage in question was Article 28, No. 3, stating, "Nothing in this Constitution shall be invoked to invalidate any law enacted by the Oireachtas which is expressed to be for the purpose of securing the public safety and the preservation of the State in time of war or armed rebellion."[21] Though Ireland planned to be neutral, the government would still need to legislate for public safety and state preservation while the small country was buffeted by the war around it. The problem was how to enact war legislation without a war; the solution was to redefine the constitution's sense of "time of war" to include the present conflict. The amendment reads, "In this sub-section '*time of war*' includes a time when there is taking place an armed conflict in which the State is not a participant but in respect of which each of the Houses of the Oireachtas shall have resolved that, arising out of such armed conflict, a national emergency exists affecting the vital interests of the State."[22] The phrase "in time of war" no longer just meant "in time of war." In effect, under this amendment, being at "peace" could legally mean the same thing as being at war. The phrase "national emergency" legalized the government's ability to function under a state of emergency, enshrining de Valera's euphemism into the constitution (which he wrote) while also guaranteeing that although "Emergency" might sound like a benign euphemism for "war," it was in fact the legal name for an extra-juridical state of exception. The rewriting of the constitutional definition of war enabled the Oireachtas to pass the second piece of legislation on September 3, 1939, the Emergency Powers Act, which governed Ireland by decree until after the war ended. Though Ireland's policy of neutrality was designed to claim the conspicuous appearance of autonomy, the legislation enacted the night of September 2/3, 1939, exposed the fact that the duration of the Emergency would be entirely dependent on decisions made by outside powers.[23] Even in its neutrality, Ireland was held legally hostage by other countries' actions. Both the concepts of "neutrality" and "emergency" relied on artful rhetorical constructions to elide the tenuousness of their legality.

Giorgio Agamben calls the state of exception (or, in Ireland's case, Emergency) "the legal form of what cannot have legal form," a "no-man's land between public law and political fact."[24] Conceptually, by redefining "war," the Dáil legislated itself out of existence and Ireland into a state analogous to civil war; as Stephen Morton notes, the state of emergency was less an exception than a rule in twentieth-century Ireland, being the status quo for the first half of the 1920s, 1939 to 1945, and much of the Troubles.[25] The legislation of September 3, 1939, permitted the constitutional normalization of an abnormal legal state. But as Agamben's formulations suggest, Ireland's Emergency was not only legally but literally oxymoronic: an apparently contradictory formulation (not war = war) made true. If war restructures language use, then by virtue of the Irish Constitution, so did the nonbelligerent Emergency.[26]

The impact of this linguistically created state of emergency ramified in the work of Irish writers because it changed the way that language worked in everyday civic life. As Wills remarks, the "state of suspension" created by the constitutional amendment "represented the triumph of euphemism" over clarity.[27] This manipulation of legal language was reinforced by the government's ability, under the Emergency Powers Act, to manipulate the language of Éire's citizens, owing to the act's censorship provisos, which built upon the Censorship of Publications Act passed in 1929. While the Emergency Powers Act of 1939 allowed the government to legislate by decree, to intern citizens without trial, to impose rationing and other regulations on commerce, to take over private property, it is the Censorship, rather than rationing, travel restrictions, and curtailment of civil liberties that retains the strongest hold over Irish cultural memory of the period. This may be best illustrated by a contemporary rhetorical habit—"the Censorship" was always referred to with the definite article and a capital C. Newspapers, novels, poetry, mail, telegrams, telephones, movies, maps—even the weather was censored. In a sense, life as a whole was censored (Elizabeth Bowen memorably called it "a ban on feeling").[28] The government's attempt to control language amounted to an attempt to control thought.

In this sense, Emergency Ireland was little different from its belligerent neighbors; indeed, on an island already divided into belligerent and neutral jurisdictions, the division between war and neutrality would necessarily be unclear. The linguistic slippage introduced into the phrase "in time of war" mirrored the fact that many people in Ireland—especially those living near the border—felt they experienced war and neutrality simultaneously. The meaning and location of war became less and less discernible. Bowen gives vent to this sense of dislocation and "ban on feeling" in her long 1943 story "Summer Night," set in County Cork. Miming the sense of isolation that dominated Ireland during the Emergency, every character in Bowen's story is in some way isolated, or, as one says, "immobilized, God help us, and each so far apart that we can't even try to signal each other."[29] There is a young child, ignored and burning for escape; a pair of adulterous lovers who, when they finally meet, find only a "broken fairytale"; a disaffected bachelor—a likely portrait of Sean O'Faolain—cut off by war from his anticipated holiday in France and staying in the isolating company of his deaf sister (605). Loneliest of all is the spinster Aunt Fran, who, islanded even within her own family, is nevertheless discomfited by the shifting definition of "in time of war." "Each moment is everywhere," Fran thinks, "it holds the war in its crystal; there is no elsewhere, no other place" (599). "Apart" as Fran may stand, the war seems to recognize no personal or geographical boundaries (598).

Fran's isolation is emphasized by her family's habit of censorship. An unwanted accessory to her nephew's household, Fran is kept in the dark about family affairs, like her niece-in-law's adultery, which she senses around her but cannot see. She protests to her nephew: "Whatever *I* see, whatever I hear it's 'nothing', though the house might fall down. You keep everything back from me . . . I am never told, never told, never told. I get the one answer, 'nothing'. I am expected to wait here. No one comes near the drawing-room. I am never allowed to go and see!" (597). Perhaps it is because of her sensitivity to the outside world, the "everywhere" of "each moment," that Fran so viscerally feels the constriction of censorship. She is, in this way, a picture of Ireland in wartime. With the Emergency Powers Act of 1939, the Irish government implemented a strict policy of censorship aimed at eliding the very strain they had placed on the definition of war.

"A Ban on Feeling": Censorship and Neutral Language

While British citizens were asked to accept censorship as a condition of war, Irish Emergency censorship fell under the legal structure of preexisting, peacetime law; the co-option of cultural censorship for national security purposes is part of the legacy of Irish resentment for the Emergency censorship. Seventeen years of cultural censorship, beginning with the 1923 Censorship of Films Act, banning anything "indecent, obscene, or blasphemous," paved the way for political censorship in the Emergency.[30] Article 40 of the constitution itself guarantees freedom of speech and expression only as far as it is "subject to public order and morality": "i. [The] State shall endeavour to ensure that organs of public opinion, such as the radio, the press, the cinema, while preserving their rightful liberty of expression, including criticism of Government policy, shall not be used to undermine public order or morality or the authority of the State. ii. The publication or utterance of blasphemous, seditious, or indecent matter is an offence which shall be punishable in accordance with law."[31] Fearing exactly this—that criticism of neutrality could "undermine public order" in the Emergency—de Valera's government acted swiftly to neutralize dissent in his neutral state. The Emergency Powers Act provided for censorship of any means of communication, including film, radio (though there was no way to prevent Irish listeners from tuning in to programs broadcast from abroad), periodicals, and books, as well as postal and telegraph communication.[32] This had a drastic effect on Irish writers, who, their British sales already jeopardized, had little hope of making a living on Irish sales alone. Being banned could spell financial disaster.

There was no objective necessity for the severity of Irish censorship during the Emergency, according to Lee, but it served two other purposes: it suppressed the potential of internal divisiveness, and it suppressed the truth of Ireland's partiality toward the Allies (266). In *Censorship in Ireland, 1939–1945*, Donal Ó Drisceoil explains, "What must be kept in mind is that the 'neutrality' which the Censorship set out to protect was essentially an illusion, one, indeed, which the Censorship itself helped to create and sustain. Irish policy during the war was partial and it was a function of the Censorship to hide that fact behind a deceptive screen."[33] For example, while weather forecasts were banned from all Irish news outlets—an unimaginable burden on Irish conversation!—Met Éireann supplied forecasts to the British throughout the war, and Irish meteorologists were crucial in planning the D-Day invasion (102). But the degree of Ireland's friendly neutrality was so well concealed that the British press habitually accused the Irish of pro-German sentiment.[34] Not until Fisk's

In Time of War was published in 1983 did the extent of Irish-Allied cooperation begin to be revealed. This concealment was almost wholly due to the Emergency censorship designed and implemented by Frank Aiken. Aiken's title, Minister for Co-ordination of Defensive Measures, was itself a remarkable piece of euphemism. Formerly the Minister for Defense, and for years de Valera's right-hand man, Aiken was technically a minister without portfolio, though he functioned as the highest-ranking member of the cabinet. Aiken's ministry (abolished at the war's end) was directly responsible for management of and recruitment into the Defense Forces and for censorship. Aiken's papers reveal his intense involvement with the Step Together recruitment campaign and a deeply researched interest in self-sufficient agriculture; in 1941, de Valera sent him to America to "gather material and moral support for Ireland's neutrality policy."[35] Effectively, all these tasks fell under a common brief: managing the rhetoric of the state.

Aiken and de Valera's policies emphasized two complementary conceptions of neutral language as the basis for Irish censorship. The first was the implicit message that language could be neutered of war content, made wholly euphemistic—the term "Emergency" being the apotheosis of this neutral language. In his speech in response to the April 1941 Blitz on Belfast, for example, the taoiseach referred to it elliptically as "the disaster in Belfast" (458), avoiding any actual mention of Germans, airplanes, fires, or bombs, as if Belfast had been wracked instead by some cataclysm of nature—an earthquake or an out-of-place tornado. Aiken, then, made a perfect director of censorship; he preferred to call the Battle of Britain "the air battle over Southern England and the Channel in 1940."[36] This neutralizing of language extended even to the symbolic language of the streets. When troops arrived in Ireland on furlough they were required to change into civilian attire; the ports at Dun Laoghaire and Holyhead were stocked with clothing for arriving and departing soldiers. The war became, literally, an invisible presence in the cities and towns of Ireland, censored from view by the policy of neutralization.

The second conception of neutral language relied on the notion that words could function as a neutral conduit, a transparent and unbiased means of communication. This was the justification behind news censorship in Ireland. Because no Irish paper employed foreign correspondents, all war news in the Irish press came from international news agencies, principally the British and American wire services, and was then "neutralized" for Irish publication.[37] While day-late British papers were usually available, particularly in Dublin, for those who cared to read them, most citizens chose to read their customary Irish papers, especially as they were more widely (and timely) distributed. Much of the emphasis behind the censorship was intended to craft a public record of Ireland's neutrality. As such, Irish news censorship aimed to present a balanced and objective picture of war events by eliminating anything the censor considered to be propaganda or propagandist terminology; even the words "Nazi" and "fascist" were considered too inflammatory to print.[38]

Aiken, no semanticist, was convinced of the efficacy of language as a neutral conduit. Speaking before the Seanad on January 27, 1944, he confidently announced,

> There is no other country in the world at the present time . . . where the people have had a better and a clearer opportunity of getting all the news of this war in an unbiased manner. There has not been a single bit of news from the beginning of the war that was worth talking about that has been banned in our papers . . . What we have objected to, and what we have stood firmly against, is our people being oppressed by a barrage of propaganda from one side into taking a completely unbalanced view of what is going on in the world . . . We have allowed all the news to go through but we stopped the propaganda and we have enabled the Irish people to keep their balance during this disastrous war.[39]

To enable Irish readers to "keep their balance," newspapers were required to print side by side the official communiqués issued by belligerents. But "for fear of eliciting unneutral sympathy," reports of persecution and cruelty from across occupied Europe were censored.[40] This meant that the worst atrocities of the war were screened from Irish eyes. In the Irish papers, there were no concentration camps, no massacre at Katyn, no Bataan Death March or Burma Railway, no firebombing of civilian Dresden. Ó Drisceoil reports that "Aiken did indeed know what was happening in the camps, and outside, as details passed through his organization in increasing volume,"[41] but he kept these from the pages of the Irish newspapers as harmful to what he called "neutral-mindedness."[42]

If news was "worth talking about," it was Aiken's organization that made the call. In effect, Aiken was attempting to separate the two elements of what Mark Wollaeger calls the "information-propaganda matrix," when the two, coming as they did from European news agencies, were already practically inseparable.[43] If Aiken's conception of language as a neutral conduit could impart depropagandized information, it was doomed by the "neutralizing" of its terms into euphemism—merely another form of propaganda. In his attempts to purify Irish broadcasts and periodicals, Aiken effectively rejoined information and propaganda in his own fashion by passing off the Irish news as unedited. In a memorandum on the establishment of press censorship in late 1939, he determined that "no indication shall be given to the public where matter has been excised or altered by censorship."[44] From the beginning of the censorship, not only was the news to be censored: the act of censorship itself would be neutralized in print.[45]

Aiken's press censorship demanded a special set of reading practices. Irish readers were asked to weigh equally the words of enemy nations and create for themselves a balanced and neutral understanding of events, an individual parsing of information from propaganda. Speaking before the Seanad in 1940, in response to Sir John Keane's motion that the press censorship exercised "unreasonable" powers in domestic matters, Aiken outlined the concept of balance he would later celebrate: "I think, as the war goes on, [Irish citizens] will become even more accustomed to discerning truth from untruth in regard to domestic affairs. In regard to foreign affairs, they can hear both sides of the story by sitting at the many thousands of wireless sets which are in the country."[46]

When prompted by Keane, "The Minister does not think they [the public] can get the truth that way?" Aiken replied,

> They can split the difference . . . I challenge anybody in this country to spend the whole of the night at a wireless set, listen to the news and views from all the countries in the world, belligerent and otherwise, and then turn to the [Irish] newspapers afterwards to see if he does not get a fair representation of the news from the whole world as well as news of domestic affairs. It is recognised on the Continent and elsewhere that both our newspapers and our wireless station publish the most objective and

> the best reports of the war, taking practically the whole world. There is a lot of flap-doodle and propaganda cut out, but the bones of the news are left, and they can always get at the truth.[47]

But the censor's heavy-handedness actually made it impossible to deduce the body from the bones. Perhaps a judicious reader could get "at the truth," as Aiken suggested, but no closer. As Damien Keane reminds us, the "problem of information"—especially in wartime—is there is always simultaneously too much and too little of it (12). Sorting through "the news and views from all the countries in the world" would have been practically and intellectually impossible. On the other hand, without full reporting of events—particularly of flagrant moral atrocities—Irish readers were left with a news neutralized into meaninglessness. As Elizabeth Bowen put it in the *New Statesman* in 1941, "There is freedom of public speech, but no freedom of reporting. No home criticism of Eire's neutrality, or suggestion that this ever could or should be abandoned, is allowed mention by the press . . . facts are denied moral context. In the cinemas, the omission of all war scenes from the newsreels gives one the feeling of an invented world."[48] In this "invented world," the truth about events was so denuded that after the war many Irish refused to believe that the Nazi concentration camps had even existed, because so stark an atrocity, they felt, could only be Allied propaganda.[49] The truth about censorship was that Aiken intentionally held back material that might have compromised the moral superiority of neutrality's position above "this disastrous war." Censorship not only quashed dissent, it enabled de Valera's characterization of neutrality as righteousness. Meanwhile, in Aiken's search for "balance," the Censorship kept a nation of readers skeptically poised on their toes, trusting nothing.

"The Ideal Ireland": Censorship and Cultural Nationalism

Aiken's conception of what censorship ought to achieve evolved over the course of the war. In early memos, he outlined the "duty of impartiality" of neutrals under international law and spoke about adhering to Hague Convention guidelines when he addressed the Seanad in 1940.[50] His original model was Swiss World War I policy, and his goal was preventing publication or circulation of information and news that might influence relations with foreign countries.[51] Some of the Irish censor's immediate victims now seem laughably trite: the December 1939 censor's report cited "grossly partisan and unneutral comments" in *Irish Golf*.[52] The danger of *Irish Golf*'s inciting unrest or falling into Hitler's hands is perhaps less germane to history than the fact that its readership included a large percentage of (stereotypically pro-British) Protestants. For, as the immediate danger to Ireland decreased over the course of the war, the censor's powers did not. Aiken's 1939 memorandum delicately noted that "the question of the effect that the publication of certain information might have on the state's own internal and political conditions could also arise."[53] And this aspect of censorship—though he still couched it in the language of "balance"—became the most enduring legacy of the Emergency on Irish literature: Aiken and de Valera's use of the censorship provisions of the Emergency Powers Act to legislate cultural nationalism—to craft a monolithic Catholic Ireland into which people like the Anglo-Irish senator Sir John Keane and the readers of *Irish Golf* did not seem to fit.

The Seanad offers a lively public record of the reaction to Emergency censorship, though that record is skewed by the fact that all Dáil and Seanad debates or questions concerning censorship originate in opposition to it.[54] What stands out clearly, however, is that supporters of censorship in almost all cases conflated political and cultural censorship. Senator Martin O'Dwyer's 1942 speech in support of the banning of Eric Cross's *The Tailor and Ansty* is a good example:

> To-day the Government have to meet another danger, that of foreign invasion. Hundreds of thousands of our people are watching along the coast and are ready to lay down their lives to prevent invasion. There is even a greater danger confronting us, the danger of this tide of immorality which is pervading the whole world. It is the duty of the Government to defend the virtue of the Irish people against the immoral literature that threatened to overwhelm it. If these modern ideas, as I call them, got a hold, the virtue of the whole Irish race would be in danger . . . the souls of our people are at stake. It is the duty of the Government not to do away with the censorship, but to extend its powers so that our country is made safe, as far as it is possible to make it. The censorship must be maintained, but it needs to be strengthened.[55]

According to O'Dwyer, the political dangers of foreign invasion were far overshadowed by the spiritual dangers of the invasion of worldly "immorality," in the form of literature. The Emergency censorship was imposed to keep the bodies of Ireland's people safe, but Senator O'Dwyer makes it clear that it is "souls" he is worried about. As far as the government's duty to oversee the safety of its people is concerned, for senators like O'Dwyer, there was no separation between body and soul. And O'Dwyer, like his Fianna Fáil party, was in the majority.

The Emergency Powers Act copperfastened de Valera's government for an indefinite period, and he did not waste the opportunity to promote his agenda.[56] In a 1940 Seanad debate on press censorship, Fine Gael leader Frank MacDermot addressed Aiken: "I do not think the Minister would, in fact, deny the statement that the censorship has got gradually stricter, probably he would say more successful. The appetite for exercising despotic authority inevitably grows with what it feeds upon, and there is a strong tendency all the time to exclude things, not because they are really dangerous to the State, but simply because the Government does not like them."[57] MacDermot's attention to language here—"stricter" versus "more successful"—indicates he well understood that Aiken's project was not just political but cultural. Sharing de Valera's "twin application of 'moral neutrality' and 'moral economy,'" as Bryce Evans puts it (147), Aiken was a thoroughgoing republican (a former IRA commander) who "attempted to use censorship to purge the country of the cultural remnants of Anglo-Ireland, such as place names" (152). In a largely sympathetic history of Aiken, Evans concludes that he "does bear responsibility for some of [what Ó Drisceoil calls the] 'slippage towards authoritarianism' during the Emergency, even if he legitimized his actions by pointing to the horrors of total war and starvation" (152). The question under debate in 1940 was not whether censorship was necessary but whether Aiken was overstepping his bounds in domestic press and literary censorship. Again and again in the debate records, TD's and senators acknowledge the difficulty of parsing domestic from foreign matters where censorship is concerned; again and again, Aiken responds with the difficulty of separating information from propaganda.

Certainly, a vocal minority in the press—writing mostly in *The Bell* and the *Irish Times*—were aware that the government was using the war as an excuse to censor the published image of Ireland as a whole. If Aiken's policy was nominally based on Swiss and Swedish precedents, it did not share with those neutrals their wide tolerance for political and cultural dissent in the popular press. Instead, Aiken's censorship policies did exactly what Senator O'Dwyer hoped for: they conflated cultural and political censorship under the banner of the "safety" of the Irish people.

The famous "comely maidens" paragraph of de Valera's Saint Patrick's Day radio broadcast of 1943, so beloved by scholars and critics of his administration, actually opens with an oft-elided sentence that conflates the ideas of physical and spiritual safety.[58] It begins, "Acutely conscious though we all are of the misery and desolation in which the greater part of the world is plunged, let us turn aside for a moment to that ideal Ireland that we would have" (466). Nationalist retrenchment is, for de Valera, the antidote to a world in misery. Here is his visionary place:

> The ideal Ireland that we would have, the Ireland that we dreamed of, would be the home of a people who valued material wealth only as a basis for right living, of a people who, satisfied with frugal comfort, devoted their leisure to the things of the spirit—a land whose countryside would be bright with cosy homesteads, whose fields and villages would be joyous with the sounds of industry, with the romping of sturdy children, the contest of athletic youths and the laughter of happy maidens, whose firesides would be forums for the wisdom of serene old age. The home, in short, of a people living the life that God desires that men should live. (466)

The *Irish Press* misquoted de Valera's "happy maidens" as "comely maidens," and the address has gone down in history misremembered as the comely-maidens-dancing-at-the-crossroads speech.[59] This revision in itself speaks volumes about how de Valera's policies were viewed by Irish people critical of his cultural project: one in which poverty is a spiritual asset, the citizenry is doggedly connected to the land, and neutrality—cultural and political—could be mobilized as part of a higher aim: living the will of God.

It is important to note that the Censorship of Publications Board, since its creation in 1929, always included a priest. The board was charged with the duty of banning anything it deemed "indecent or obscene."[60] But under the Emergency Powers Act, the board's control was moved from the Dáil to the Ministry for Co-ordination of Defensive Measures, and its powers extended to include material deemed a danger to the state's policy of neutrality, officially conflating political and cultural censorship. By the Dáil's first Emergency sitting on September 27, 1939, Aiken's secrecy had already raised the hackles of several TD's. If the taoiseach had a line on how God desired men to live, his deputy certainly drew the line on what Dev desired men to read. In other words, Emergency censorship in Ireland was designed with a twofold political purpose: one, to keep the government in power, and two, to promote the government's spiritual vision of what the Irish people ought to read.[61]

It was those very "fireside . . . forums for the wisdom of serene old age" beloved of the taoiseach that heated the flashpoint of dissent against Emergency censorship: the 1942 Seanad debate on the banning of several works of literature, notably Eric Cross's *The Tailor and Ansty*, a compilation of fireside chat by Irish-speaking Cork *seanchaí* (storyteller) "The Tailor" Tim Buckley and his wife, Anastasia. Sir John Keane again took up the crusade against what he now called the "literary Gestapo," moving that the Censorship of Publications Board had ceased to retain public confidence.[62] The motion was directed at literary censorship, but this itself was a recognizably coded way of protesting political censorship. The four-day debate became a spectacle. Caleb Richardson's article on the controversy notes that the Government Publications Office actually sold out of the official report, "and clerks advised customers to reserve copies of the next debate in advance" (166).

The Tailor's fireside, at which he sits on his butter box, ruling the world of Garrynapeaka, is a forum for old age, indeed, but serene it is not. The room fills with bawdy jokes (often hinging on the sex lives of livestock), with exclamations of "Bydam!" and "Divil!"; such language was deemed grossly inappropriate by the Censorship Board.[63] For the same reason, Frank O'Connor's translation of Brian Merriman's 1780 aisling poem *Cúirt An Mheán Oíche* (*The Midnight Court*, excerpted in *The Bell* in May 1941, immediately following the three-month serialization of *The Tailor and Ansty*) was banned when it appeared in full in 1945.[64] "The Midnight Court," a political critique couched in a woman's complaint against the unmarriageable men of Ireland, was banned in English, while *Cúirt An Mheán Oíche*, even more risqué *as Gaeilge*, remained an indisputable classic of the national language.

A gap between information and propaganda is glaringly obvious here, especially given the full context of de Valera's "ideal Ireland" speech. For the second half of "The Ireland That We Dreamed Of" is devoted wholly to the promotion of the national language. In celebrating the fiftieth anniversary of the Gaelic League, de Valera revisits the ghost of Pearse to conflate politics and poetry in his own peculiar aisling: "It was the idea of such an Ireland, happy, vigorous, spiritual, that fired the imagination of our poets, that made successive generations of patriotic men give their lives to win religious and political liberty" (466). To achieve this dream vision, the taoiseach inveighs his people to bring the Irish language into daily use, claiming, "The more we preserve and develop our individuality and our characteristics as a distinct nation, the more secure will be our freedom and the more valuable our contribution to humanity when this war is over" (469). If the Gaelic League aimed for cultural sovereignty as a foothold toward political independence, fifty years later, the head of that independent government used the threat that war represented to Irish sovereignty as a prime justification for promoting cultural nationalism.

While most contemporary readers chuckle at the "happy maidens" paragraph, the speech's real irony is in the disparity between de Valera's vision and the reality presented by his government's policies. Connecting language with lifestyle, de Valera explains, "As the bearer to us of a philosophy, of an outlook on life deeply Christian and rich in practical wisdom, the language today is worth far too much to dream of letting it go" (467). Learning the language was easier in 1943 than ever, the taoiseach claims: "Today there is no dearth of books and reading matter and other facilities for those who wish to begin their study or to improve their knowledge" (468). And yet, in two of the most famous censorship cases of the Emergency, de Valera's policies suppressed precisely the texts—translations—that would introduce the language to a modern audience. In the midst of "the present war" (466), de Valera marshals the Irish language as security propaganda: like neutrality, it keeps the nation apart from the destructive and insecure world. It offers a "contribution to humanity" through its trove of wisdom and philosophy. But de Valera (who closes the speech in the national language itself, with a *cúpla focal* of inspired piousness and banality) has dreamed an ideal Irish language to match his ideal Ireland. It is homely and Christian, patriotic and rural. It is decidedly not the language of the Tailor and Ansty or of Brian Merriman: lyrical and pastoral but also ribald, sexy, and acutely critical of the conditions in which its speakers live. (The aisling form, after all, is both a relic of paganism and a political lament.) The language of de Valera's ideal Irish-speaking Ireland would have to be censored into being.[65]

Fondly imagined Tailors of the Gaeltacht, scions of the rural hearth, were praised in the 1940s by taoiseach and TD's alike, their "values" catered to in campaigns, contrasted with the vice-ridden city dwellers; but when translated into English—indeed, when made audible to the majority of the Irish reading public—their fires were snuffed out, their "PQ," in Abbey Theatre parlance, a little too "Peasant" and not enough "Quality." In short, de Valera's "dream" of a conservative, Gaelic Ireland was just that. Confronted with the real thing—at least in print—the Censorship Board swiftly condemned it as blasphemy. The Seanad debates of 1942 and 1944 illustrate, however, that blasphemy against the rural Irish ideal was, during the Emergency, simultaneously blasphemy against neutrality. Or as Senator William Magennis put it, "It is propaganda, to show the English-speaking world what manner of man the Irish peasant is who is the citizen of Éire. It is propaganda, naked and unashamed."[66] So, too, was the censor's erasure of such citizens of Éire—a fact perhaps lost on Magennis because of the seeming impossibility of "neutral propaganda," which is proof, moreover, of just how successful de Valera's propaganda campaign was.

The banning, as Samuel Beckett put it, of "Irish authors deemed from time to time unwholesome" was nothing new, as he complains in 1935 in "Censorship in the Saorstat."[67] In his essay, Beckett lists as banned "O'Flaherty, O'Casey, O'Leary, O Faolain (no apostrophe), Shaw, Clarke and (George) Moore" before remarking ruefully, "My own registered number is 465, number four hundred and sixty-five, if I may presume to say so. We now feed our pigs on sugarbeet pulp. It is all the same to them" (88). Indiscriminate swine aside, by the Emergency, being banned was nearly a sign that a writer had "made it," though the implied critical plaudit was also a financial kiss of death.[68] In the 1942 Seanad debate, Sir John Keane went as far as to say, "There is hardly a modern author of repute who is not represented on the banned list," and after reciting names ranging from Shaw to Hemingway, added, "In addition to those, there were, I think, all the modern Irish writers—Kate O'Brien, Frank O'Connor, Seán Ó Faoláin, Liam O Flaherty and even—would you believe it?—Austin Clark—who, I believe, is recognised by the Church as one of the outstanding poets. There is not a modern Irish writer I can think of that is not on the list. It is especially hard on the Irish writers, as their circulation is, of course, mainly in the country."[69]

Flann O'Brien (pen name of Brian O'Nolan) did not make the list, but his alter ego in the *Irish Times*, Myles Na gCopaleen, summarized the Seanad debates in a "Cruiskeen Lawn" column that simultaneously sent up the Censorship and betrayed his own insecurities as a writer. It concludes, "I will not stand for it, do you hear, I will not stand for this bestial censorship. Take my own books. Who but a madman would dare to suggest that they are not works of genius? I tell you I will not have it, I will not have it do you hear me, I will go and live in Paris and then you will all be sorry, another great Irish artist driven into exile."[70] O'Brien would go on to blame Hitler directly for the poor sales of *At Swim-Two-Birds*, published in 1939 and blurbed by no less a personage than the great exiled artist himself, James Joyce (who read it with a magnifying glass and found it truly funny).[71] But it sold only about two hundred copies, and O'Brien's next published novel (as Na gCopaleen) would be the Irish-language *An Béal Bocht* in 1941.[72] Had it been published in English (it wasn't until 1973), *The Poor Mouth* might well have been banned: it is a perfect send-up of de Valera's imaginary Irish-speaking island—in which the rain never ceases and accuracy of Gaelic (as well as holiness of spirit) grows in proportion to one's lack of worldly goods.[73] The narrator explains that "since [they] had the choicest poverty and calamity" in the parish of Corkadoragha, they speak the best Gaelic as well (436). When Corkadoragha is visited by Gaeilgeoirs, the language enthusiasts eventually retreat in dismay, for "it appeared that . . . the poverty of the countryside was too poor. The Gaelicism of the countryside was too Gaelic [and] the tradition of the countryside was too traditional" (437).

If *An Béal Bocht*, as a parody of the Blasket autobiographies published in the 1920s, is a perfect mockery of the Gaelic revival, it is both because it is written in perfect Irish and because O'Brien's reverence for his source texts (*An t-Oileánach*, *Peig*) is matched by an acute understanding of the way they had been misread and misappropriated by the republican government in power.[74] "If we are truly Gaelic," opines the self-named "Gaelic Daisy," President of the Corkadoragha Feis (the Secretary is "the West Wind" and the Auditor, "the Dative Case"), "we must constantly discuss the question of the Gaelic revival and the question of Gaelicism . . . There is nothing in this life so nice and so Gaelic as truly true Gaelic Gaels who speak in true Gaelic Gaelic about the truly Gaelic language" (440). The names of the Secretary and Auditor and the rest of their colleagues are purely funny, but the president's name is a deliberate jab at the President of Ireland since 1938 and founding President of the Gaelic League, Douglas Hyde, whose Irish pen name, An Craoibhín Aoibhinn, means "The Pleasant Little Branch." In *An Béal Bocht*, O'Brien's imaginary parish of Corkadoragha simultaneously survives on and suffers from the Gaelic revival. Ten years of visiting Gaeilgeoirs bring pittance money to the islanders, but the institutionalizing of the revival leaves them financially and linguistically depleted when "the gentlemen" move on to newly built colleges of Irish in more comfortable Galway (436). Soon mainlanders appear only on day trips to praise the Gaelicness of the Gaeltacht—or to arrest and imprison the Gaels for being unable to make themselves understood.

O'Brien's turn to writing parody in "the learned smooth Gaelic" (i) may have been due to his frustration with his inability to make his English-language novels "understood" by publishers and readers at the outbreak of the war. But *An Béal Bocht* is not just O'Brien "making a poor mouth" at the publishing industry; it shares with *At Swim-Two-Birds* and *The Third Policeman* a criticism of the Gaelic revival in aesthetic terms. Formally innovative, O'Brien's novels have often been read as a simple rejection of the revival. Rónán McDonald summarizes the literary response to the revival as "an Oedipal opposition" in which "those who came after sought to demythologize it, to contrast its investment in legend and folklore to the mess and murk of lived experience . . . There are those who reject the Revival in the name of a harder social realism and those who reject it for avant-garde modernism."[75] O'Brien is generally classed in the latter camp, though *An Béal Bocht*'s travestying of rural poverty plays the role of social realism, too. But it also couldn't have been written *without* the revival, and in this sense Flann O'Brien's writing is an important corrective to the story that Irish modernism stands in opposition to the Irish revival, for the revival, as McDonald argues, "far from the opposite of 'modernism,' is now typically regarded as an incubatory moment of it, its anti-modern ideology of a piece with the modernist disdain for bourgeois values and prefabricated realist forms" (51). The revivalists, after all, were subversive at the core, aiming to upend tired caricatures of the Celt in favor of an "authentic" national literature. To remember the Gaelic revival as nothing but tired clichés in the twilight is to forget the actual rioting it caused and the forces of change that it galvanized.

But as rebels inherit the reins of government, it is their ideology, not their subversive spirit, which becomes law. In a nation whose president was the president of the Gaelic League, revival ideology, not revivalist disruption, became institutionalized, and as Free State and Éire governments ossified the revival, its subversion was subsumed into camp. Under the shrinking of the literary audience and the pressures of nationalist censorship, the Emergency became a moment of aesthetic crisis for Irish writers. Late modernists writing during the Emergency returned in spirit to the revival's disruptive energies while simultaneously eschewing its aesthetics as the bourgeois clothing of official republicanism. The result is a body of texts whose language—even when putatively "realistic" like Kavanagh's and O'Faolain's—incubates the "strange waywardness" of late modernism. Ready to utilize formal techniques of radical disruption and reinvention learned from both the revival and the high modernist movement, Irish late modernists responded to the Emergency's pressures on language use with the urgency of a crisis that was simultaneously political and aesthetic.

"All Our Symbols Have to Be Created Afresh": Aesthetic Crisis and *The Bell*

Elizabeth Bowen and Sean O'Faolain may have seemed unlikely bedmates. Though both were from County Cork, they grew up in two different worlds: she a Protestant, English-educated daughter of the Bowen's Court plantation, he a Catholic IRA fighter in the War of Independence. But before they met, their novels already shared a strangeness of texture; realist on the surface, their fictions were modernist at the core—aiming for newness of form, of image, a new way of speaking. Having read and admired each other's work (and despite both being married) they began an affair in 1937, which continued until the outbreak of the war.[76] The extramarital affair in "Summer Night" is not theirs, but Bowen's depiction of the bachelor Justin Cavey, "a city man, a black-coat," is so like O'Faolain that his dialogue might well be an editorial in *The Bell*.[77] Visiting his sister in Cork, Justin is glad "not to have to face the screen of his own mind, on which . . . the war-broken towers of Europe, constantly stood. . . . In the heart of the neutral Irishman indirect suffering pulled like a crooked knife" (588). The war in Europe—and his isolation from it—ever on his mind, Justin declares, "We should have to find a new form . . . A new form for thinking and feeling" (589). The problem of "living" for Justin is a problem of language, and it constitutes an emergency: "We can no longer express ourselves: what we say doesn't even approximate to reality; it only approximates to what's been said. I say, this war's an awful illumination; it's destroyed our dark; we have to see where we are. Immobilized, God help us, and each so far apart that we can't even try to signal each other. And our currency's worthless—our 'ideas' and so on, so on. We've got to mint a new one. We've got to break through to the new form—it needs genius. We're precipitated, this moment, between genius and death" (590). It's hard to take Justin Cavey seriously as a conversationalist, so urgent is his delivery, but these lines encapsulate the aesthetic energies of Emergency writing. And no writer was more committed to—and instrumental in—finding a new form for Irish art production during the Emergency than Sean O'Faolain.

In *Empire's Wake*, Mark Quigley calls O'Faolain's fictions of the 1930s "republican realism,"[78] usefully characterizing it as more disruptive and less straightforwardly nonmodernist than the standard critical line would have it (a similar critical reinterpretation has invigorated Bowen's reputation in recent years). Revising the standard narrative that O'Faolain's naturalism is an Oedipal reversal of both revivalism and Joycean modernism, Quigley writes, "O'Faolain's more ragged realism can thus be understood as a late-modernist practice that dissolves the stability of bourgeois solidity more effectively and subversively from within" (69). His first collection of short stories, *Midsummer Night Madness*, was banned as obscene by the Censorship Board in 1932. One would look hard to find obscenity in *Midsummer Night Madness*, but the reader quickly recognizes critiques of the Catholic Church, the war for independence, the institution of marriage, and the petty hypocrisies of the Irish middle class. The stories, like the rest of O'Faolain's fiction, are spare, elegant, and realist in a Russian vein (O'Faolain's second novel, *A Nest of Simple*

Folk, takes its title from Turgenev; in later years he would compare the Russian writer to Elizabeth Bowen). Taking his cue from high modernism, O'Faolain hoped to present, as Joyce claimed of *Dubliners,* a nicely polished looking glass, and the Censorship Board—as with Joyce—did not like the reflection they saw. By 1940, with two of his books banned in Ireland, O'Faolain was an established fiction writer, as well as an essayist for the *Spectator* and the *New Statesman.* Inspired by the success of Cyril Connolly's *Horizon* magazine in London, O'Faolain determined to recast his looking glass in periodical form. It would show Ireland as it really was—it would be an opportunity to showcase new and established Irish writers, an opportunity to craft a national identity broader than the one the government was trying to legislate into life. So in October 1940, with contributions from now-canonical names like Elizabeth Bowen, Flann O'Brien, Frank O'Connor, Patrick Kavanagh, and Jack B. Yeats, O'Faolain edited and published the first issue of *The Bell.* It sold out every copy. The magazine would go on to run for fourteen years (six as a monthly under O'Faolain's editorship) and become the most influential periodical in twentieth-century Irish literature.[79]

The Bell carried a whiff of the forbidden anywhere more provincial than Dublin (which meant virtually everywhere). In country towns, it was known to be kept behind the counter by shop owners and newsagents, who held it in paper wrappers for patrons who asked for a copy. The magazine's success, both financially and in its mission to "open a window" into Irish life, indicates the strength of Irish interest in art and literature in this period, in spite of the claustrophobia that government policies appeared to create.[80] Young writers from both Ireland and Northern Ireland, such as Brendan Behan, Donagh MacDonagh, W. R. Rodgers, and John Hewitt, found their way into the pages of *The Bell,* as did established figures like Bowen, W. B. Yeats (posthumously), Louis MacNeice, and Cecil Day Lewis. Many of these writers also published in London journals, such as *Horizon,* which was likewise established as a cultural life support in wartime. Ironically, when *Horizon* published an Irish issue in 1942, it was immediately banned and seized in Ireland on account of "obscenities" in the contributions of Kavanagh and O'Connor.[81] It can be assumed that these two hardened utterers of censorable material toned down their work for *The Bell.* Still, the Irish journal's book reviews, literary essays, and Michael Farrell's regular column on the country theater attest that literary and cultural productivity in Ireland was vigorous—if provincial—throughout the war years.

At a moment when the Fianna Fáil government was censoring its way toward de Valera's narrow vision, *The Bell* aimed to present postcolonial Ireland as not fragmented or hybrid but as diverse and many strained: a polyphonic symphony of writers on such plain, earthy topics as sugawn chairs, orphanages, fisheries, linograph cuts, teachers, slum dwellers, hat factories, country dances, amateur theatrics, and dog races. "The Five Strains: A Symposium" in September 1941 (*The Bell*'s first-anniversary issue) included essays on the Gaelic, classical, Norman, Anglo-Irish, and English strains in Irish culture, "to remind us," O'Faolain says, "of the danger of oversimplifying history" (13). This was a deliberate counter to the comely-maidens-at-the-crossroads view of Irish culture.

O'Faolain rejected the notion that such a person existed as a "typical Irishman" in favor of a rhetoric of experimentalism. His early editorials are rallying cries for the minting of a new "currency" or "form," as Bowen's Justin Cavey would have it. In the first-anniversary editorial in 1941, O'Faolain writes, "We are, to-day, in this emergent Ireland living experimentally, i.e., trying out . . . all those vague ideals and ideas that were, for the last hundred years, the picturesque stock-in-trade of patriotic evangelism."[82] What he hoped his magazine could do was "to demonstrate and help to create, a technique of living . . . One may talk of 'Nationality' until one is green in the face and get no nearer the fact . . . But when somebody makes a chair that is patently an Irish chair, and not a Birmingham chair, that *is* Nationality" (11). "We want," he writes, "to project the theory of the Nation in concrete form" (11).

It would be an experiment. What he wanted, essentially, was a form through which he could take the Irish nation and make it new, and what occasioned this necessity to experiment was the Emergency: an aesthetic crisis precipitated by a political one. In the prefatory editorial of *The Bell*'s first issue, O'Faolain wrote what may be read as the magazine's manifesto. He begins by explaining the title. *The Bell* is, he writes, "a spare and hard and simple word . . . with a minimum of associations . . . We could not have used any of the old symbolic words. They are as dead as Brian Boru, Granuaile, the Shan Van Vocht . . . , Cathleen ni Houlihan, the swords of light and the risings of the moon. These belong to the time when we growled in defeat and dreamed of the future. The future has arrived and, with its arrival, killed them. All our symbols have to be created afresh."[83] But in his attempt to kill the symbols of the Gaelic revival, O'Faolain's rhetoric sounds a little familiar. It's the rhetoric of the modernist project of the London-based world system, now projected onto a more intimate, postcolonial scale. And it is this intimacy that O'Faolain sees as the future of national symbolism: "Men and women who have suffered or died in the name of Ireland . . . have died for some old gateway, some old thistle lag-field in which their hearts have been stuck since they were children. These are the true symbols" (5). And these are what he calls for contributors to write about. If *The Bell* is to be a looking glass, the editor contends, "Only the people can create an image of themselves . . . Here is the belfry, the bell-rope, and the bell. If it does not speak that is because you have not taken the bell-rope and swung out of it. Write about your gateway, your well-field, your street-corner, your girl, your boat-slip, pubs, books, pictures, dogs, horses, river, tractor, anything at all that has a hold on you" (7). What O'Faolain proposed was that "this is not so much a magazine as a bit of Life itself, and we believe in Life, and leave Life to shape us after her own image and likeness" (5). "You will notice," he cautions, "that we do not ask, primarily, for perfection in the craftwork . . . you will see several things whose merit is not chiefly Art but Truth" (8). Truth, Art, Life, here cast as proper nouns: *The Bell* would offer a new form for crafting an emerging Ireland.

In O'Faolain's rhetoric about Life as a proper noun, about searching for a form to represent it, one cannot help but hear an echo of an earlier manifesto: Virginia Woolf's 1919 essay "Modern Fiction." In the essay, Woolf proposes that the realist novel is a form of artistic (and, by extension, political and patriarchal) tyranny. She offers a recipe for a realist novel and concludes, "The tyrant is obeyed; the novel is done to a turn. But sometimes, more and more often as time goes by, we suspect a momentary doubt, a spasm of rebellion, as the pages fill themselves in the customary way. Is life like this? Must novels be like this? Look within and life, it seems, is very far from being 'like this.' Examine for a moment an ordinary mind on an ordinary day. The mind receives a myriad impressions—trivial, fantastic, evanescent, or engraved with the sharpness of steel."[84] Modern fiction, for Woolf, is cast as a rebellion, an escape from tyranny. Vince Sherry argues persuasively in *The Great War and the Language of Modernism* that Woolf, Pound, and Eliot's modernist literary practices are direct responses to the failed political rhetoric of World War I. In other words, Woolf's metaphors of tyranny and rebellion may be read here as more than just metaphorical. A generation later, *The Bell* was responding to the nascent Irish state's rhetorical tyranny in the face of the Emergency.

So how would Woolf escape this tyranny? As with O'Faolain, the goal was to find new ways to record life. To "attempt to come closer to life," Woolf says, "and to preserve more sincerely and exactly what interests and moves them, [writers may have to] discard most of the conventions which are commonly observed by the novelist . . . Let us not take it for granted that life exists more fully in what is commonly thought big than in what is commonly thought small" (161). Here are those gateways, well fields, street corners, the daily impressions of the common reader, the buying of flowers oneself. "Any method is right," continues Woolf, "every method is right, that expresses what we wish to express, if we are writers; that brings us closer to the novelist's intention if we are readers. This method has the merit of bringing us closer to what we were prepared to call life itself" (162).

Quigley claims that O'Faolain's use of the "lyrical vocabulary of the 'old gateway'" and so on is a calculated effort to "redeploy and subvert the sentimental language of 'tradition' so as to challenge a more conservative nationalist rhetoric on its own terms" (112). But in a calculated effort to make it new, O'Faolain's little magazine about capital-*L* Life consistently engages with the tropes and media of high modernism. Rebutting the Celtic Twilight in the year after Yeats's death, O'Faolain yet published stories and drawings by Jack Yeats and, later, by W. B. Yeats himself. Proclaiming realism in the year before Joyce's death, *The Bell* published a warm appreciation of James Joyce written by Elizabeth Bowen—whose own fiction embraces both realist and modernist techniques. The oft-told story of *The Bell* and O'Faolain's other writings as reactionary realism marginalizes the magazine's (and editor's) modernist energies. O'Faolain's manifesto for a new form rings out as a primary example of how Irish late modernists responded to the tyranny of aesthetic autonomy deployed by the government's camp iteration of the Gaelic revival. O'Faolain wasn't revising the revival so much as revising the government's revision. If his call for a new form sounds like an emergency, that's because it was a response to the aesthetic crisis brought by the moment:

the language of war abroad, the ethical conundrum of neutrality, and the censored "neutral language" of the Emergency.

Defying the Tyrant: The *Irish Times* and the Censor

The Bell was outspoken in its opposition to censorship, setting itself up as a magazine that would allow Ireland to "see clearly . . . to have the facts and understand the picture."[85] O'Faolain refused to print articles that had been shredded by the censor, waiting to publish a number of them (such as A. J. Leventhal's "What It Means to Be a Jew") in full form after the war.[86] Several of the journal's features were purposely designed to circumvent or comment upon censorship in the Emergency. In the monthly books section, for instance, books were often reviewed that had been or were likely to be banned in order to create readership for what copies remained in the country. The regular "Mise Éire" (I am Ireland) section invited readers to submit press clippings, offering a book token each month for the best quotation. The winning entry for April 1941, under the headline "The Surgeon's Knife," was a clip from the *Irish Times* demonstrating an amusing effect of the censor's neutered language: "The condition of the survivor is rather serious, as he has been severely burned, and also had a fracture of the limbs. He is being removed to Cork under military guard for further medical treatment. An inquest is to be held later."[87] No doubt this clipping won for the unfortunate juxtaposition of the information about the survivor (one can assume that this burned and battered person is under guard for the unmentionable reason that his belligerent aircraft crashed in Éire) and the prediction about the inquest. Has the *Irish Times* predicted his imminent death? It is likely his fellow passenger might be the subject of the inquest, but the rhetorical fault that makes this funny is also an apt commentary on the atmosphere of deadly stasis pervading Ireland at the time. The headline "The Surgeon's Knife" plays a pithy double entendre: cutting newsprint with a scalpel seems to have killed the patient. Aiken's "bones of the news" were nothing but skeletons.

To face the challenge of censorship, Irish writers set their own traps of deception. None did so with more glee than R. M. Smyllie, editor of the *Irish Times*. Aiken disliked Smyllie and his paper for their pro-Allied (or, as Aiken saw it, blatantly pro-British) bias, and Smyllie called Aiken "the iron man with the wooden head," delighting in attempts to beat the censor at his own game.[88] For example, in a 1941 "Irishman's Diary" column, a pseudonymous Smyllie found a way to circumvent the censor's injunction against publishing the deaths of Irishmen fighting in the British forces. He headed this bit of war news "Nippon Go Brath":

> In his broadcast on Sunday night, Mr Winston Churchill, the British Prime Minister (NB Britain is an island to the east of Éire) mentioned by name nine military and naval commanders who had gained fame recently in North Africa and the Mediterranean. I append the names of the gallant nine:
>
> | | |
> |---|---|
> | General Wavell | English |
> | General Mackie | Australian |
> | General Wilson | Japanese (North Island) |
> | General O'Connor | Japanese |
> | General O'Moore Creagh | Japanese |
> | General Dill | Japanese (North Island) |
> | General Brooke | Japanese (North Island) |
> | Admiral Cunningham | Japanese |
> | Admiral Sommerville | Japanese |
>
> As the venerable member of the Samurai, San Tiok Eli, might or might not have put it:
>
> *"Quae regio in terra non plena laboris?"*[89]

Forbidden to celebrate V-E Day in neutral Dublin, Smyllie printed photos of King George, Churchill, Roosevelt, Stalin, and Allied commanders Eisenhower, Alexander, and (the Anglo-Irish) Montgomery to create a V-shaped pattern across the front page. For his part, Aiken fought back with large cuts and small (though he did not achieve his desire to install an in-house censor in the *Irish Times* offices) and, at the end of the war, invited Smyllie and other editors to an end-of-censorship dinner, which he jokingly called "the liberation of Dublin castle." On Smyllie's invitation, Aiken appended the note, "Dinner jacket optional. Rapier de rigueur. Dagger verboten."[90]

But the most inventive and subversive thing Bertie Smyllie did during the Emergency was to hire Brian O'Nolan (Flann O'Brien) as Myles

Na gCopaleen. "F. O'Brien" had begun submitting letters to the editor on June 4, 1940, and throughout the summer, up to nine bizarre and hilarious letters a day—under an array of pseudonyms—appeared in the paper, most penned by O'Brien, though real correspondents, and Smyllie himself, participated in the imagined "controversy."[91] On September 28, the letters disappeared and the "Cruiskeen Lawn" column by Myles Na gCopaleen began instead. For about a month, the column ran in "almost untranslatable" pun-filled Irish but switched to English as it became the paper's most popular feature.[92] While *An Béal Bocht* caused less of a stir than O'Brien had hoped, no doubt due to the limited readership for Irish, and *The Third Policeman* remained unpublished during his lifetime, from 1940 to the end of the war, "Cruiskeen Lawn" became Ireland's most visible locus of linguistic dissent (that didn't serve porter).[93] The column ran daily and was often given precious column inches of rationed paper at the expense of news copy. As Myles, O'Brien utilized the constraints of both journalistic censorship and the physical format of the paper to break as best he could through the boundaries of the time. His columns are best appreciated in facsimile: he manipulates typeface and symbols, draws arrows to other columns and advertisements, engages in metatextual arguments with the editor, drawing attention again and again to the limitations of his forum, as well as the limitations of his countrymen's imaginations.[94] Readers of the February 15, 1943, column may indeed have wondered if de Valera, somehow missing the satire, wasn't simply plagiarizing "Cruiskeen Lawn" in his "Ideal Ireland" speech a month later. In the column, O'Brien deftly ties Fianna Fáil cultural nationalism to Emergency press censorship, proving, perhaps, that the best way out of aesthetic autonomy may be through it:

> We Irish people actually are simple, unspoiled God-fearing sophisticated mid Europeans, cherishing urbanity like a jewel . . . A humble community of persons drawn together in our daily round of uncomplicated agricultural tasks by the strongest traditional ties, loosely woven on a diminutive leprechaun's loom . . . Our conversation—gay, warm and essentially clean—is confined to the charming harmless occurrences of every-day life and *not*, of course, every-night life, that undesirable Parisian phenomenon. The wild and morbid degeneracy of the outer world does not

> concern us . . . What is called "news" (by which one means the perverted sensationalism of the yellow press) does not concern us. We are not amused. Rumour once had it that a war was going to break out. Nothing ever came of it, of course.[95]

Notwithstanding the marvelous juxtapositioning of urbanity and agricultural life, of Europeanness and isolationism, and that cheeky reference to Paris (traditional home, as Myles so frequently points out, of the exiled Irish artist), the key to O'Brien's satire here is in its absolute deadpan faithfulness to the vision promoted by Ireland's "neutral language" policy: "Rumour once had it that a war was going to break out. Nothing ever came of it, of course."

If, as Justin Cavey says in Bowen's story, "it needs genius" to break through to a new form of expression, Flann O'Brien may have been *the* genius of the Emergency. His central role as a character in the 2005 play *Improbable Frequency* and the popularity of Myles's column attest to his centrality in Dublin letters during the period. But O'Brien was not a lone genius in his tower (he didn't even use a single name), nor was he a great Irish artist in exile; he was a minor civil servant, living through the Emergency on a state salary while dodging the censor whose employer he shared. He was, as he liked to call them in his column, one of the "Plain People of Ireland"—or at least their wiser, wiseacre mouthpiece. And as unique as O'Brien's writings may appear, they share much with the fabric of other Emergency writing in their attempt to break through the twinned aesthetic autonomies of revivalism and high modernism and the political autonomy of the censor's "neutral language" to something inevitably stranger, wilder, more like "Life." Those who wrote in the Emergency wrote in its own language, taking rhetorical evasiveness as their aesthetic and mining it for meaning. Emergency writing constitutes both an ethical and a formal response to the problem of Ireland's neutrality.

CHAPTER 2

Pilgrimage as Poetic Form

Kavanagh and Devlin at Lough Derg

"It is midnight in Dublin and Europe is at war," concludes Patrick Kavanagh's *Irish Times* piece of October 25, 1939.[1] The premise of the essay, opening on a Dublin night when "the radio in the flat above me has stopped forwarding to this address the mixture of blather and jazz which is called propaganda and which is supposed to influence the masses" (39), is a reminiscence of pastoral life. Kavanagh claims, "Being an Irishman I should be abnormal if I didn't dream, think and write of far-past peace and quiet in pastoral fields when everybody else is thinking in terms of war" (39). This seemingly offhand remark about "being an Irishman" is perhaps more telling than Kavanagh intended. His implied claim that the "normal" Irishman would necessarily "dream, think and write" of the peace of the past and the pastoral quiet is itself propagandistic and appears to align the poet squarely with both the official discourse of neutrality and the Gaelic revival—a reminder that Kavanagh's principal champion at the time was Æ (George Russell), who promoted the "ploughman poet" and his 1938 autobiography, *The Green Fool*.[2] In his remark that any ordinary Irishman must dream of pastoral peace, Kavanagh manages to unite a revivalist conception of peasant authenticity with the prevailing Catholic discourse of religious pacifism as grounds for wartime neutrality. Indeed, he sounds a bit like a Fianna Fáil TD on the campaign trail, mustering rural nostalgia and church doctrine in the service of neutrality politics.

After meandering through "an October evening in a country place," Kavanagh's essay returns to Dublin, where he notes, "I remember some wild talk of a war in Europe . . . But I know that beyond the headlines, beneath the contemporary froth and flurry, the tide of humanity flows calm" (43). Here, the country ("real life among real folk") squares with de Valera's vision of it, representing the timeless existence of peace and peasantry (a fabrication that Kavanagh would excoriate three years later in *The Great Hunger*), as opposed to Dublin's noisy metropolis, filled with "propaganda," a step closer to that European war. Yet the essay's closing line, "It is midnight in Dublin and Europe is at war" (43), is a firm reminder that the Irish capital city and the continent are separate spheres. Dublin is a step closer to war than the country, but it is still fundamentally detached from Europe and war.

Neutral Ireland as Purgatory

Dublin, in wartime, was seen by belligerents as a carnival paradise of peace, by those skeptical of Irish neutrality as a whispering gallery for international spies, and by Irish intellectuals as a cultural purgatory. These three principal labels were not mutually exclusive. Upon his arrival in Dublin, the poet John Betjeman, the British cultural attaché (and sometime patron of Kavanagh), listed his first impressions as follows: "Neutrality, harps, art exhibitions, reviews, libels, backchat, high-tea, cold, no petrol, no light, no coal, no trains, Irish language, partition, propaganda, propaganda, propaganda, rumour, counter-rumour, flat Georgian facades, Guinness, double Irish, single Scotch, sherry, Censors, morals, rain."[3] Of the twenty-seven items in this list—not to remark on the four varieties of alcohol—ten are about language, four are definitive negatives, four are definitive pejoratives, and the principal rhetorical device, repetition, suggests that many of the other terms are implied negatives—not least "neutrality" itself. If Dublin represents anything, it's a composite of booze and backchat—a highly rhetorical city—and a city of absence. In spite of the presence, as it appeared to British visitors, of plentiful lights and meat and butter, Emergency-era Dublin was defined by absence: the absence of European connections, the absence of war. These absences simultaneously made present what appeared to be plentiful (goods rationed in Britain) and what was suspected to lurk in the shadows of those un-blacked-out lights: spies and professional listeners. In this sense, the absence of war also made Dublin *more* European. It connected Ireland to other neutral powers on the continent and ensured a diplomatic presence of agents from all nations.[4] The presence of so many delegations could make Dublin feel surprisingly European, and an influx of wealthy refugees on semipermanent "holiday" in Irish country hotels occasionally flavored life even on the west coast. Yet in spite of links to Europe, its absence was severely felt in cultural terms. The sense of cultural stagnation that neutrality and Emergency censorship brought to Ireland was more clearly felt once the war ended. An editorial in the *Irish Times* on May 12, 1945, encapsulates the sense that led F. S. L. Lyons to call Emergency Ireland a Plato's Cave: "We feel as anybody must feel who, having been confined in a dark cell for nearly six years, is released suddenly into the sunshine and blinded by the light."[5]

In *That Neutral Island*, Clair Wills portrays Irish wartime intellectuals as a "static generation, cut off from the real world of the war . . . intensified by the strict censorship of printed news and other media."[6] Experiencing the Second World War through the warped lens of the Emergency made Ireland's island isolation very palpable. The state was cut off from its accustomed supply of imported food, goods, and fuel and cut off culturally by the draconian censorship of books, periodicals, and film. Travel abroad was all but impossible, and middle-class Irish families, accustomed to holidaying in France and Spain, found themselves suddenly grounded, like the disappointed Justin Cavey in Bowen's story "Summer Night," "locked in" to what seemed a stifling milieu.[7] Likewise, families of those who had gone to work in the British war industry were unable to visit or to look forward to customary visits (and goods) from their family across the Irish Sea. Travel restrictions to and from England were particularly hard on the creative class, who relied on English publishers and audiences for their livelihood. Wills reports that "stasis and immobilisation became a standard complaint . . . with educated Dubliners in particular described as a 'paralysed' generation, existing . . . on the margin of world events" (264). To many, the experience seemed a sort of limbo, and hopes of someday reaching an end of wartime isolation meant that the experience was often expressed as a purgatory. In Britain, too, the war was often depicted as purgatory.[8] Sebastian Knowles explains, "The paralyzed waiting suffered throughout Britain during the war pervades its literature [and finds] its most common literary expression in the metaphor of purgatory," but adds that "the Second World War is always both hell and purgatory."[9] With the "hell" of real war just across the sea, Ireland's Emergency would always remain purgatory by comparison.

The idea of Ireland as purgatory became something of a zeitgeist in Emergency-era literature. In his August 1944 editorial in *The Bell,* Sean O'Faolain describes Ireland as "a paradise for the *homme moyen sensuel,* . . . a purgatory for the artist, and a hell for the intellectual," adding that for writers, "Ireland is a place or state of punishment where some souls suffer for a time before they push on somewhere else."[10] Novelistic representations of purgatory by Samuel Beckett and Flann O'Brien are the focus of chapter 5 of this book, which includes a brief discussion of Máirtín Ó Cadhain's prosopoetic novel *Cré na Cille* (*Churchyard Clay*) and Yeats's play *Purgatory*—all written between 1938 and 1945. Kavanagh's epic poem *The Great Hunger,* published as he was composing "Lough Derg," similarly explores the ways contemporary Irish life could feel like a living death, particularly in rural areas. The war filters through only one section of the poem, in a pub scene in which farmers contend they could outwit the generals; in *The Great Hunger,* the sense of isolation is not political but human. The epic concludes with a vision of the death of the farmer protagonist, Patrick Maguire, as a mirror of his life:

> Maguire is not afraid of death, the Church will light him a
> candle
> To see his way through the vaults and he'll understand the
> Quality of the clay that dribbles over his coffin.
> He'll know the names of the roots that climb down to tickle his
> feet.
> And he will feel no different than when he walked through
> Donaghmoyne.[11]

The Great Hunger's penultimate stanza hints that Maguire's final residence is neither Ireland, nor heaven, nor hell, but purgatory: "Patrick Maguire, the old peasant, can neither be damned nor glorified; / The graveyard in which he will lie will be just a deep-drilled potato-field" (89). No longer a fit emblem for a Gaelic national culture, the peasant farmer is left somewhere in between damnation and glorification—neither here nor there, like Kavanagh in "Midnight in Dublin." This sense of stymied in-betweenness dominates so much of the discourse surrounding the Emergency that purgatory became a pseudo-official metaphor for Ireland's situation. For Kavanagh, as for the diplomat-poet Denis Devlin, Station Island at Lough Derg, medieval site of Saint Patrick's Purgatory, an earthly door to the afterworld, would come to perfectly represent this in-between.

Poets at Saint Patrick's Purgatory

Lough Derg, the red lake, is a small natural lake in Donegal, near Pettigo, on the border of Counties Donegal and Tyrone and therefore on the border of Northern Ireland and the Republic of Ireland. The political border, still recent in the 1940s, adds another layer to Lough Derg's identity as a liminal place, for since early Christian times it has been considered a thin space, a door to the afterworld—and it is likely that these beliefs descended from older Celtic otherworld place myths. The name of the lake is largely synonymous with Station Island, its largest island, where, according to legend, Saint Patrick came to fast and pray the stations of the cross, lending the island the nickname of Saint Patrick's Purgatory. Monastic settlements on the island date to the fifth century, and the twelfth-century *Tractatus de Purgatorio Sancti Patricii* is the first of many extant medieval accounts of Lough Derg as a pilgrimage site.[12]

Saint Patrick's Purgatory is one of the most punishing pilgrimages in Christendom. Known colloquially in Ireland as "doing Lough Derg," the pilgrimage requires three days of fasting, an all-night vigil on an empty stomach, and countless stations of the cross, which involve repetitive standing and kneeling, performed barefoot on rocky ground, and often as not in the cold rain. Today, the Diocese of Clogher's official Lough Derg website cautions pilgrims that they must be age fifteen or older and in sufficient physical and mental health even to visit the island.[13] According to J. C. C. Mays, Devlin made the pilgrimage with his mother when he was fifteen or sixteen, but he likely traveled there again before publishing "Lough Derg" in the *Southern Review* in the spring of 1942.[14] Kavanagh went on assignment in 1940 for the *Irish Independent*. He had such a miserable experience that his impertinent article was rejected by the editor. He returned in 1942, this time fortified by clandestine whiskey and sandwiches; the result was the more evenhanded assessment in "Lough Derg."[15] Recounting his 1940 visit, Kavanagh writes, "Although, on paper, St Patrick's Purgatory is not such a terrible punishment, in actuality it almost reaches the limits of human endurance. Most people find the vigil the worst part. For me the worst was the austerity, the prostration of both mind and body that is seldom relieved by any flamboyant life."[16] Indeed, the unrelieved "austerity" of the pilgrimage may be what most aligned Lough Derg with the experience of neutral Ireland for the two poets. As a purgatory, Emergency Ireland was a place between worlds, bearing neither the deprivations of war nor the plenty of peace; it was, instead, and especially for artists, a seemingly unendurable experience of austerity. The pilgrimage to Station Island, by contrast, had the benefit of having a fixed duration. It only seemed endless, while Ireland's Emergency would have an indeterminate duration, fixed not by the Irish government but by the warring powers across the sea. If Lough Derg represents the political and social reality of Emergency-era Ireland, as "a site between worlds, where the metaphysical and physical meet," it is also, as Peggy O'Brien suggests, "a natural conceit for poetry itself."[17] In 1942, Lough Derg offered a site to simultaneously explore purgatories spiritual, political, and poetic.

Descriptions of Lough Derg, one of the best-known medieval pilgrimages, were some of Dante's major sources for the *Inferno*.[18] Other early modern works, such as Pedro Calderón de la Barca's *Purgatorio de San Patrico* (1636), solidified Lough Derg as not just a Christian pilgrimage but also a highly literary one. By the time Kavanagh and Devlin took the pilgrimage in the early 1940s, ten thousand pilgrims were visiting Lough Derg annually (the number is now closer to thirty thousand), and modern Irish literary representations of the pilgrimage already included the famous story "The Lough Derg Pilgrim," by William Carleton, and poems by Thomas Moore and W. B. Yeats.[19] Poets like Kavanagh and Devlin could hardly visit an island with such a heritage without imagining writing it, too.

But in his 1946 review of Devlin's *Lough Derg and Other Poems*, Kavanagh writes, "It is a remarkable fact that Lough Derg does not lend itself to the literary spirit. There has yet to be written a great poem or book on this pilgrimage."[20] The remarkable thing about Kavanagh's comment is that it not only elides the Donegal pilgrimage's centuries-long literary history—dating back to Henry of Saltrey's circa 1180 quest narrative *Tractatus de Purgatorio Sancti Patricii*—but also elides the poet's own history.[21] For he, too, wrote a poem called "Lough Derg" in 1942, the same year Devlin's poem of that name was published in the *Southern Review*. Kavanagh's remark that there had "yet to be written a great poem" about Lough Derg, is telling: he himself had tried and failed to write the very poem. Never harvested from, never revised, Kavanagh's 642-line "Lough Derg," was "completely abandoned," according to Antoinette Quinn, who calls the poem "an ambitious failure rather than a masterpiece."[22] But Kavanagh's claims about the island also exemplify the anxious literary history of Lough Derg, which, like Kavanagh's own unpublished poem, is full of failures and ambivalence, reminiscent of the pilgrim experience itself. From the *Tractatus* to Seamus Heaney's *Station Island*, Lough Derg has again and again offered writers a place from which to explore matters of faith and doubt, but never has "that dim lake" provided such a focal point for political anxiety as in 1942, when both Kavanagh and Devlin were working on their Lough Derg poems.[23]

At first glance, these two poems are as different as the men who wrote them. Kavanagh, a self-educated Monaghan farmer, walked fifty miles to Dublin to meet George Russell (Æ) in 1931, the better to enhance his "peasant poet" credentials; during the Emergency, he scraped by in Dublin as a freelance writer. Devlin was the product of a Jesuit education in Dublin, received a master's degree from University College Dublin, studied at the Sorbonne, and traveled widely in Europe. He joined the Irish Department of Foreign Affairs in 1935 and by the time he wrote "Lough Derg" was serving as first secretary to the legation in Washington, D.C.[24] Kavanagh was a fixture of the poets' pubs of Dublin; published in the first issue of *The Bell*, he practiced a rustic realism learned from Frank O'Connor and Sean O'Faolain. The subjects of his poetry appeared to perfectly answer O'Faolain's call to "write about your gateway, your well-field, your . . . horses, river, tractor."[25] Devlin kept company with Brian Coffey and Samuel Beckett in France and Robert Penn Warren and Allen Tate in the United States; his poetry is tightly formal, international, often polyglot.[26] If Kavanagh was agricultural, Devlin was Agrarian: their poems, perhaps echoing their lifestyles, point to two divergent sides of poetic practice in the late modern period.

Both poems can be classed as "ambitious failures" in different ways. Both attempts to anatomize Ireland via its most famous pilgrimage, Kavanagh's poem seems to suffer from a lack of authorial control, Devlin's from too much.[27] Sean O'Faolain complained to Frank O'Connor (then poetry editor of *The Bell*) that "Kavanagh doesn't wash his poetry's ears," and Kavanagh's "Lough Derg" may seem "unwashed" partly because we read it unedited and unrevised.[28] A miscellany of mixed meter, rhyme, and form, Kavanagh's "Lough Derg" runs on for twenty pages in his *Collected Poems*. By contrast, *The Great Hunger* is of similar length but made taut by anger and revision; its canto structure and seasonally organized narrative are clear and easy to follow. "Lough Derg" has a loose narrative structure that follows three pilgrims, Robert, Aggie, and a defrocked priest called "the monk" as they make their pilgrim rounds, but while the detached, first-person speaker ("the poet") slips in and out of view, his own faith journey is the poem's real focus—though the poem's dips into omniscience (transcriptions of other pilgrims' prayers, ventures into Aggie's and Robert's minds) make the poet-speaker's pilgrimage difficult to follow. The effect is one of both confusion and mimesis: the poet simply cannot concentrate on his own pilgrimage amid the din of his fellow pilgrims. In the poem, as on the island, too much seems to be going on, and Kavanagh's poem seems unable or unwilling to restrain its focus.

If Kavanagh's "Lough Derg" errs on the side of transparency, Devlin's errs on the side of opacity; one seems to explain too much, the other too little. To Kavanagh's 642 lines, Devlin's nineteen pentameter sestets, rhymed *ababcc*, cover four pages. If Kavanagh's form is miscellaneous, Devlin's is deeply historical: derived from Shakespeare's *Venus and Adonis*, the stanza was frequently used by Wordsworth, whose constant reach for transcendence seems to echo in Devlin's words. But in spite of—or rather because of—its prosodic precision, the content of Devlin's poem is obscure. The reader struggles against baroque diction, punctuation, and enjambment to uncover even a basic narrative underpinning the poem. "Known to be a difficult poet when nothing else is known of him," as Dillon Johnston puts it, Devlin revised his "Lough Derg" incessantly from first to collected publication, and the poem is perhaps overloaded with such authorial "difficulty."[29] Randall Jarrell famously accuses him of being overly "rhetorical, unevenly assertive, and sophisticated" and prone to "too much conscious and jagged 'brilliance.'"[30] Rhetorically, Devlin and Kavanagh appear to be opposites, but their 1942 "Lough Derg" poems share a dominant trope of ambiguity, which gives readers satisfaction and frustration in equal measure.

For both Devlin and Kavanagh, ambiguity serves as a response designed to undercut political, spiritual, and poetic certainties. Ireland in the Emergency was overdetermined by prescribed cultural certainties. While the government invested in crafting an autonomous aesthetic of "Irishness," Devlin and Kavanagh responded by tracking conventional pieties down to their source and writing poems—Devlin's formalist, Kavanagh's realist—that refuse to uphold either the aesthetic certainties of the revival, the spiritual certainties of Catholicism, or political certainties about neutrality. In a climate where the black-and-white answers promised by propaganda could be treated only with suspicion, the religious pilgrimage offered the suggestion that answers might arrive from a higher authority; Kavanagh's and Devlin's "Lough Derg" poems dangle hope of such answers, but ultimately refuse to offer them.

During the Emergency, Lough Derg itself functioned as an ambiguous space, in that it served as a dual register: it was at once the purgatory that mimed neutral Ireland at its most narrowly nationalistic and an ancient link between the newly independent Irish state and a greater, Catholic Europe. Both poets engage Lough Derg in penitential terms, seeking to understand both the writer's—and his country's—role in a war-torn Europe. While most of the discussion of Irish neutrality in literature has focused on the Irish-British relationship, often oversimplified on a Catholic-Protestant binary, Devlin and Kavanagh turn their sights to the Catholicism that connects Ireland to the Continent. Their Lough Derg poems demonstrate that neutral Ireland's conception of the war is not, as commonly assumed, inextricably tied to the nation's relationship with Britain but also concerns Ireland's self-identification as European and its shared neutrality with other small, European, predominantly Catholic countries. Considered from ancient times to be an earthly door to the afterlife, Station Island in Lough Derg is a thin space, and Kavanagh's and Devlin's poems are formally marked by the site's betweenness, using it as a way to explore the strange indeterminacy of Irish neutrality, conceptualizable as both isolationist and Europeanist. At Lough Derg, the pilgrimage experience both collapses personal identity into the "anonymous mass of pilgrims" and isolates the individual as he seeks, repents, and confesses in the solitude of his own spirit.[31] As a space that both joins and sunders, Lough Derg functions as a mirror for neutral Ireland and its place in Europe. At the same time, the pilgrimage's particular and historical Irishness serves the poets as a mirror for the ways in which state "bureaucracy" (in both poets' words) inflects or infects both individual spirituality and self-image in postindependence Ireland. As a genre, the pilgrimage narrative offers its writer the promise that he may achieve enlightenment by the end of the pilgrimage, but Kavanagh's and Devlin's pilgrimage poems are both occasionally ambivalent and intentionally ambiguous. As the "key to the lock" of Irish neutrality—to borrow from Kavanagh's poem—neither pilgrimage makes for "a reasonable document."[32] But before turning to those documents, it is useful to unlock the key connection between Catholic piety and Emergency bureaucracy.

Soldiers of Christ: Irish Neutrality as Catholic Pacifism

The pivot between war and peace, city and country, Europe and Ireland is a binary schema that appears in several of Kavanagh's lyric poems of the Emergency period. The persistence of this scheme suggests how pervasive was the situational ambivalence of neutrality. Taking its title from the "Midnight in Dublin" essay, the short lyric "Beyond the Headlines," published in the *Irish Times* in March 1943, is a more complex engagement with the divide between "contemporary froth" and "the tide of humanity":

> Then I saw the wild geese flying
> In fair formation to their bases in Inchicore,
> And I knew that these wings would outwear the wings of war,
> And a man's simple thoughts outlive the day's loud lying.[33]

In the image of the wild geese, Kavanagh locates—and militarizes—a rural element in the Dublin suburb of Inchicore while simultaneously alluding to the "wild geese" of Irish history, the term traditionally accorded to Irish mercenary soldiers who served in European conflicts from the sixteenth through eighteenth centuries. Irish "wild geese," more than one hundred thousand of them, would fly again into World War II, but the poem's third line reasserts the avian connotation, making the case that the timeless natural world "outwears" the modern political one with its propaganda and "loud lying."[34]

In the second stanza, Kavanagh asserts the immortality of not the natural world but of the religious one:

> Don't fear, don't fear, I said to my soul:
> The Bedlam of Time is an empty bucket rattled,
> 'Tis you who will say in the end who best battled.
> Only they who fly home to God have flown at all. (5–8)

Political, modern "Time" is presented as mere madness, and it fades in comparison with God's time, as the geese's wings fade into those of the speaker's presumed heavenly ascension. But what is this "fear" that nags at the speaker's soul? The discourse of war and wings suggests that it is a fear about the soul's proper sphere of battle. If the "best battle," the poem concludes, is a spiritual one, the alternative must be the actual battle that the speaker, no wild goose, is avoiding by remaining in Dublin. The allure of the peaceful, neutral countryside is not quite enough to calm nerves about the morality of exempting himself from the war. Sitting it out, the poem implies, has struck fear into his soul.

Another 1943 poem, "Peace," begins in a similar state of doubt. "And sometimes I am sorry" (1), the speaker opines,

> That I am not the voice of country fellows
> Who now are standing by some headland talking
> Of turnips and potatoes or young corn
> Or turf banks stripped for victory.
> Here Peace is still hawking
> His coloured combs and scarves and beads of horn.[35]

Here, Kavanagh counterpoises Northern and southern Ireland, twinned images of belligerence and neutrality, with apparent favor toward the North. Speaking on RTÉ in 1962 about his departure from Monaghan, Kavanagh said, "I came to Dublin in nineteen-thirty-nine. It was the worst mistake of my life. The Hitler war had started. I had my comfortable little holding of watery hills beside the Border. What was to bate it for a life? And yet I wasted what could have been my four glorious years begging and scrambling around the streets of malignant Dublin."[36] Kavanagh liked to claim that he could have made a fortune on the black market had he stayed a Monaghan farmer: "I could have done my smuggling stint" (307). However, the lyric "Peace" is more complex than Kavanagh's grouchy hindsight posturing. The speaker is sometimes "sorry" not to be the "voice of country fellows," not, that is, to be the authentic mouthpiece of the peasant. But in this case, those farming fellows are digging for victory. Their efforts, colored by the fertility of their youth and fields, seem decisive against the gimcrack wares of neutral Dublin. The "coloured combs and scarves and beads of horn" that Peace is "hawking" makes him a bit of a gypsy, a charlatan, a dealer in trinkets rather than permanence.

But "Peace's" imagined wares are also reminders of Kavanagh's more positive views of Irish Catholicism. Kavanagh was a devoted, though often conflicted, Catholic, and during the Emergency, he made a series of reports on native pilgrimages for the Catholic *Standard*. As Quinn notes, "the less severe the pilgrimage, the more he liked it," and Kavanagh much enjoyed trips to places like Knock, where colorful rosary beads and medals and trinkets were sold and traded as souvenirs.[37] After the annual pilgrimage to Croagh Patrick, Kavanagh was delighted: "Croagh Patrick is flamboyant and colourful as some warm-faithed corner of medieval Christendom."[38] "Peace," in the poem, appears to be hawking not just festival wares but the festal wares of Catholic pilgrimage sites, subtly allying the notion of peace with the practice of Catholicism.

By the middle of the Emergency, a rhetoric of religious pacifism had become firmly intertwined with de Valera's neutral propaganda. Devlin's line, in "Lough Derg," that "With mullioned Europe shattered, this Northwest, / Rude-sainted isle would pray it whole again," though not without a twinge of sarcasm, was a serious matter to many Irish Catholics at the time.[39] Pacifism as a Catholic practice was an entrenched part of de Valera's neutral rhetoric, in spite of the fact that Catholic Europe was embroiled on both sides of the war. Wills writes that "in the public mind . . . neutrality and pacifism tended to become aspects of a single Irish identity and perspective on the world" (359). An editorial in the *Donegal Democrat* proudly cited Ireland and other neutral nations as moral saviors: "True to Catholic traditions, Ireland, Spain and Portugal may yet be the salvation of the world. [Europe] will ruefully wish for a return to simpler things and find that solace is only to be had in the discipline of devotion" (quoted in Wills, 256). The notion that solace might be harder to come by under Franco and Salazar is conveniently omitted, and the sentiment is echoed in Agnes Farrelly's 1941 essay in the Irish-Ireland periodical *The Leader*:

> Here in our little island we may be saved—indeed, I firmly believe we shall be saved the woe that is the lot of so many of our fellow men. But if we are immune from the struggle that does not save us from responsibility . . . In these days of brute force a nation as small as ours can only make itself felt on the moral plane. Let us think peace, for thoughts fly thither and thither to find nesting places in the soul of man. Let us speak peace—not the ill-considered peace of unreasoned and unreasoning pacifism but the just peace of the Christian—the only peace likely to lead to stability and happiness.[40]

Farrelly's attitudes echo those voiced by the Fianna Fáil majority in the Dáil and the Seanad. If "Peace" in Kavanagh's poem is a hawker, he is hawking more than just black-market scarves and silk stockings; he is hawking a Catholic worldview that accommodated neutrality as a justifiable moral stance.

Kavanagh's qualms, as expressed in lyrics like "Peace" and "Beyond the Headlines," are more fully addressed in "Lough Derg," which uses the lake island's natural setting to explore the (often spurned) connections between the natural and spiritual worlds while testing the validity of prayer as a response to the war. In both Kavanagh's and Devlin's poems, the pilgrim's journey is a response to a crisis of confidence brought on by Ireland's nonparticipation in the war. The poems question the easy platitude that Ireland could "make itself felt on a moral plane" through pacifist prayer by sending their speakers—and by extension, their poetry itself—on pilgrimage.

Publicans and Prayer Warriors: Lough Derg Pilgrims as the Faces of Neutral Ireland

Lough Derg has long been something of an omphalos to Irish Catholicism. "All Ireland's Patricks were present on Lough Derg" (420), Kavanagh claims in his poem. If, according to Kavanagh, the "normal" Irishman dreams of pastoral peace, Lough Derg represents a place where he can be found at his most intensely Irish. The pilgrimage site, he argues in his 1940 article, "is typical of what may be called the Irish mind."[41] According to legend, it was to that lake in the farthest northwestern reach of the island that the national saint came to pray and center himself. For more than a thousand years since, Irish men and women have journeyed to Lough Derg to do the same. But by the twentieth century, Peggy O'Brien explains, "St Patrick's Purgatory, a putatively spiritual place, has been . . . overly determined by culture . . . the monolithic icon of a gradually merged nationalism and Catholicism" (xx). In short, by 1942, Lough Derg had become for Kavanagh and Devlin a "synecdoche for an island nation idealized and sanctified as 'Holy Ireland'" (xix).

Yet this "Holy Ireland" is populated primarily by the "smug too-faithful," as Kavanagh describes them.[42] Lough Derg, in this sense, mimes a particular middle-class Catholic spirit of Ireland during the 1940s. In the article rejected by the *Independent*, Kavanagh describes the crowds as "one enormous creature," whose "mind" holds "no contemplation, no adventure, the narrow primitive piety of the small huxter with the large family."[43] By 1942, both Kavanagh and Devlin point to this pilgrimage as a place where politics meets piety, where outward sacredness appears to be a cover-up for inward egoism. The pilgrims Devlin and Kavanagh describe are seeking salvation as well as salaried jobs, asking God for personal favors as they progress through a putatively depersonalizing pilgrimage process. Kavanagh's poem seethes with Yeatsian bitterness against pilgrims from the middle class: "Solicitors praying for cushy jobs, / To be County Registrar or Coroner" (19–20). If "sacred egoism" was the basis for Irish foreign policy, Kavanagh suggests that the domestic economy overrides international concerns. Here, "Shopkeepers [are] threatened with sharper rivals / Than any hook-nosed foreigner" (21–22). Kavanagh's pilgrims are largely unconcerned with the world outside their own doorsteps. They are, instead,

> Mothers whose daughters are Final Medicals,
> Too heavy-hipped for thinking;
> Wives whose husbands have angina pectoris,
> Wives whose husbands have taken to drinking. (23–26)

Throughout "Lough Derg," Kavanagh's rhyme and repetition serve to undercut the sincerity of the pilgrimage, highlighting egoism at the expense of sacredness. As with this pairing of "thinking" and "drinking," Latinate heart disease and colloquial alcoholism, Kavanagh uses the same tactic to mock Saint Patrick himself, rhyming "Ireland's national apostle" with "Opposite the men's hostel" (103, 105). Such rhetorical maneuvers prevent Kavanagh's poem from venturing too far into the lyrical sensitivity that is his poetic strength. Critics have, for this reason, called the poem uneven or inconsistent, but a better assessment may be that it is indecisive.

As "a fragment of the Middle Ages set / Into the modern masonry of the conventional Basilica" (80–81), Lough Derg itself is a place of inconsistencies. This shows up in Kavanagh's poem in moments like this:

> The lake waves caught the concrete stilts of the Basilica
> That spread like a bulldog's hind paws. A Leitrim man,
> With a face as sad as a flooded hay-field,
> Leaned in an angle of the walls with his rosary beads in his
> hands. (74–77)

Far from its medieval European counterparts, the Basilica at Lough Derg, for Kavanagh, resembles nothing more than the hind end of a bowlegged dog, yet the poet's depiction is occasionally peopled with portraits as sympathetically drawn as this Leitrim farmer's—banality side by side with lyrical beauty. Quinn suggests that this indecisiveness of tenor is due to Kavanagh's own financial and professional circumstances in 1942 and to his fraught relationship with his Catholic faith, but it is symptomatic of more than just Kavanagh's personal situation. There is an apparent indecisiveness at the heart of neutrality, and Kavanagh's construction of the Lough Derg pilgrimage as an extension of state bureaucracy—penitents look "like young police recruits being measured / Each pilgrim flattened backwards to the wall" (84–85)—is evidence that he sees the "Irish mind" itself as fundamentally not made up. The betweenness of Lough Derg echoes the political indeterminacy of policy in a nation whose official piety was belied by the unofficial worry that turned record numbers of people into pilgrims.

The opening lines of Kavanagh's poem foreground the economic situation in Ireland. Here, one sees Kavanagh in sympathy with the pilgrims:

> From Cavan and from Leitrim and from Mayo,
> From all the thin-faced parishes where the hills
> Are perished noses running peaty water,
> They come to Lough Derg to fast and pray and beg. (1–4)

But by the end of this first stanza, the speaker's attention shifts from the damage done by economic hardship in independent Ireland to the damage done by Irish Catholic conservatism. Dogmatic piety, which Kavanagh will go on to align with the puritanical theology of Jansenism, leads these pilgrims to "push closed the doors that God holds open" (7). Suspicious of bodily pleasure, they are hostile to natural beauty: "Love-sunlit" in June, and "flowers and light . . . to shopkeepers and small lawyers / Are heresies" (8–10). In other words, the same cultural pieties that led the Irish government to condone censorship and attempt to legislate on behalf of the citizenry's souls send pilgrims on their quest while preventing them from achieving transcendence (Kavanagh may be at his most transcendentalist in "Lough Derg").

Key moments in Kavanagh's poem invite double readings, particularly when he alludes to religious and social problems in 1940s Ireland. If Kavanagh flirts with a revivalist notion of the peasantry in 1938–39, by the Emergency settings of *The Great Hunger* and "Lough Derg," his visions of "pastoral peace" have been replaced by pastoral stasis. The cultural pieties of de Valera's neorevivalism are excoriated along with the religious pieties of the "smug too-faithful." It is his use of poetic ambiguity to attack nationalist certainties that unites Kavanagh's poem with other late modernist Emergency writing. For example, when Kavanagh's pilgrims kneel before the "iron crosses and the rutted Beds, / Their feet are swollen and their bellies empty" (60–61), readers familiar with the social criticism of *The Great Hunger* will recognize that Kavanagh plays here on "rutted" beds and empty bellies as a reference to both the uneven ruins of Station Island's monastic settlements—the saints' "beds" around which fasting pilgrims pray—and to the empty wombs of Ireland's aging, single female population, whose beds are fundamentally unrutted and who have come to the island to pray for marriage. At moments like this, Kavanagh's voice rises above indecisiveness to utilize a multivalent language. Here, his late modernist techniques meet his historical time.

Another aspect of Kavanagh's indecisiveness in "Lough Derg" is the poet-speaker's relationship to his subjects. His combination of sarcasm and sympathy, as seen in the opening stanza, is due to the speaker's own position as a "half-pilgrim," the breed he calls "the true / Spirit of Ireland" (35–37). Though it is one hundred lines before Kavanagh's speaker establishes definitive kinship with the other pilgrims, he does so in one of the poem's most moving passages, remarking that "the middle of the island looked like the memory / Of some village evicted by the Famine" (110–11), and concluding that

> So much alike is our historical
> And spiritual pattern, a heap
> Of stones anywhere is consecrated
> By love's terrible need. (118–121)

Writing on Devlin's poem, Terence Dewsnap remarks, "Ireland's bizarre pilgrimage is true to Ireland's history, martyrdoms, famine, narrowness of conviction and guilt, being all of a piece" (103). This is equally true for Kavanagh, and it is telling that the intersection of national history and emotion is where he chooses to establish kinship with the other pilgrims. By the end of the poem, Kavanagh's speaker is able to admit, "He too was one of them . . . and the half untrue / Of this story is his pride's rhythm" (632, 634–35).

Like Kavanagh's poem, Devlin's "Lough Derg" opens with an invocation of Station Island as Ireland in microcosm. Devlin's opening reminds us that "the poor in spirit on their rosary rounds" are often as not poor in material goods as well: "jobbers with their whiskey-angered eyes" (1–2). Devlin's poem, too, is voiced by a speaker who is simultaneously a pilgrim and an observer, both sympathetic to and critical of his fellows. His "poor in spirit" may include the smug bourgeoisie—"the pink bank clerks, the tip-hat papal counts"—but they also include "drab, kind women" whom the papal counts' "tonsured mockery tries / Glad invalids on penitential feet" (3–5). Paradox, such as "glad invalids," is a device at the heart of Devlin's poetics, and the intentional ambiguity that he courts throughout the poem keeps it precariously "balanced," like the Gospel "thief and saint" (12) in the second stanza.[44] In Devlin's poem, indecision is a (paradoxically) intentional device, both in the formal elements of the poem and in its content. The second stanza concludes, "Europe that humanized the sacred bane / Of God's chance who yet laughed in his mind / And balanced thief and saint: were they this kind?" (7–12). Here, God himself appears to laugh, capriciously choosing saved from sinner at the Crucifixion (in this reading, Christ becomes no sure thing, but God's "chance"). The question of "kind" recalls the "drab, kind women" of the previous stanza. Devlin plays on dual connotations of the word: are these sinners the same *type* of person as the women pilgrims? Or are they "kind" as in compassionate? Is this a compassionate God or a capricious one? Are the Irish pilgrims neutral thieves or neutral saints? Devlin's poem raises more questions than it answers.

Though his own devotional stance as a pilgrim is not made clear until the poem's nineteenth and final stanza, Devlin's speaker claims kinship with the Lough Derg pilgrims in the third line of the third stanza, after he describes the lake itself. In one of the poem's most prettily visual passages, in stanza 3, Devlin departs for the first notable time from his dominant iambic pentameter. The shift in meter signifies a shift in the speaker's attitude:

> Low rocks, a few weasels, lake
> Like a field of burnt gorse; the rooks caw;
> Ours, passive, for man's gradual wisdom take
> Firefly instinct dreamed out into law; (13–16)

As with Kavanagh, nature and the sense of place seem to ignite the speaker's feeling of kinship to Lough Derg and its pilgrims. But by the end of the stanza, Devlin's speaker seeks distance again: "The prophets' jeweled kingdom down at heel / Fires no Augustine here. Inert, they kneel" (17–18). The "inert" pilgrims become separate from the speaker as *they* kneel, and the following stanza explains, "All is simple and symbol in their world, / The incomprehended rendered fabulous" (19–20). Though the lake, weasels, rooks are "ours," the speaker differentiates himself from the "Clan Jansen" that he sees in contemporary Irish Catholicism (23).[45] Throughout the poem, Devlin's use of pronouns is puzzling to the point, almost, of being erratic. His fluid switching from first to third person highlights the difficulty in identifying not with the form of his pilgrims' faith—that he shares, as a pilgrim himself—but with its seemingly Jansenist content.[46]

Kavanagh, too, criticizes what he sees as the overly puritanical moralizing, or Jansenism, of his compatriots: "The sharp knife of Jansen / Cuts all the green branches" (567–68). In Devlin's take, for Jansenists, whose dogmatic fear of the flesh is part of a neo-Calvinist focus on man's sinful nature, "Sin teases life whose natural fruits withheld / Sour the deprived nor bloom for timely loss" (21–22). These Jansenists are the "passive" kneelers of line 15, whose beliefs contradict the doctrine of works as a means to salvation. The Jansenist streak in Irish Catholicism is at its most vivid on Lough Derg, where pilgrims must renounce the world, the flesh, and the devil, and by identifying Jansenism as the core of this form of spirituality, Devlin raises the question of the relationship between faith and work—or more particularly, between neutrality and prayer: "With mullioned Europe shattered, this Northwest, / Rude-sainted isle would pray it whole again" (7–8). If Jansenism questions the role of work as a means for salvation, Devlin implies that the same question can be asked of the typical propagandist claims that war is itself salvific: war to save civilization, war to end all wars, war to defeat fascism, war to free Europe for democracy, war to bring about a new economic order. If the "work" of war cannot save, what about abstinence from it? Devlin's pilgrims would not fight but pray to save Europe, but his poem questions what was by then a commonplace that Europe could, indeed, be prayed whole by a neutral Ireland.

Dante in Donegal: Lough Derg on the Map of European War

If Europe might be "prayed whole" by the pilgrimaging Irish, the concept raises the question of what sort of wholeness the Irish may have sought. Certainly, there was an active minority of pro-German Irishpeople: the IRA, though banned by the state, was officially at war with England and unofficially allied with the Nazis. But in spite of a common conception in Britain that Ireland was rife with Nazi sympathizers, public opinion in Ireland was vastly on the side of the Allies, prodemocracy, and antifascist.[47] Ireland, after all, had only recently gained independence from a colonial power, and most Irish people showed no sympathy for imperialism of any kind. They also spurned Communism, particularly for its antireligious bias. Above all, in 1942, the "Irish mind" was religious; de Valera's dream of a holy island was certainly not his alone. As O'Brien writes, "Catholicism, the cultural force that, particularly with Irish independence, came to center and epitomize a constructed Irish identity in the twentieth century, is, ironically, also the force that links insular Ireland intimately with the larger and more diverse continent" (xiv). If the Irish envisioned a "whole" Europe, it was a Roman Catholic one.

In Kavanagh's poem, "All Ireland's Patricks were present on Lough Derg, / All Ireland that froze for want of Europe" (420–21). This "want" speaks to the cultural connections mourned by *The Bell* coterie and other, generally Dublin-based, intellectuals. Lough Derg signifies, for both Kavanagh and Devlin, the historical dimension of the connection between Irish and European Catholic culture. It is after all, as Devlin writes, "where Dante smelled among the stones and bracken / The door to Hell" (55–56). While Lough Derg in 1942 was a particularly Irish pilgrimage, the "Lough Derg" poems remind the reader that it is also, historically, a truly European one. Medieval accounts of Lough Derg were produced in France, Spain, and Italy, notably paving the way for Dante's rendering of hell. By 1492, the far-northwestern lake was sufficiently important to merit inclusion in Martin Behaim's world map.[48] It is, in fact, the only Irish site included in the map, suggesting that Lough Derg, specifically, located a connection between Irish and European medieval and renaissance cultures. This pilgrimage site is where Devlin's "mullioned Europe" and the "Northwest / Rude-sainted isle" have, for hundreds of years, met (7–8).

The endless enjambments of Devlin's poem—across lines and across stanzas—serve to riddle the connections between Ireland and Europe. In the eighth stanza, Devlin questions the validity of the pilgrims' penance as "the sacrifice

> Of dearth puffed positive in the stance of duty
> With which these pilgrims would propitiate
> Their fears; no leafy, medieval state
> Of paschal cathedrals backed on earthy hooves
>
> Against the craftsmen's primary-coloured skies (46–50)

Linking the pilgrims' "fears" directly with the great medieval cathedrals of Europe (now targets for bombers), Devlin's semicolon both joins and separates these Irish pilgrims and the Catholic Europe for which they would offer their penance as sacrifice. What is it that the pilgrims fear? It is, Devlin suggests, that same fear that shakes Kavanagh's speaker in "Beyond the Headlines": the fear that in exempting themselves from the war against fascism, the Irish are bankrupting their souls. The "dearth" of three days' penance at Lough Derg is an attempt to mime the deprivations of the home front or even of soldiering: soldiers of Christ standing in for a fighting army. In spite of Lough Derg's medieval heritage, Devlin finds it, like Kavanagh, thoroughly and banally modernized. Ireland, in 1942, is "The prophets' jeweled kingdom down at heel" (17). Though "built / Part by this race when monks in convents of coracles / For the Merovingian centuries left their land, / Belled, fragrant," contemporary Irish Catholicism is reduced, in Devlin's eye, to "Spirit bureaucracy" (61–63).

The bureaucracy of the Irish state, having committed itself to a near theocracy, committed itself to neutrality and isolationism with the same zeal. Devlin's poem, however, probes the ineradicable cultural lines that still crossed the Irish Sea. In her chapter on "The Static Generation," Wills wonders, "Concern for Europe could find verbal (or privately prayerful) expression—but could this ever be enough?" (308). Devlin asks the same question of those who might reach out in prayer to Europe:

> And if hands touch, such fraternity sags
> Frightened this side the dykes of death disturbed
> Like Aran Islands' bibulous, unclean seas:
> *Pietà*: but the limbs ache; it is not peace. (99–102)

Indeed, neutrality—especially in its sometime guise as tolerance—is never the same as peace, and the neutral heart, Devlin suggests, may be frightened or disturbed but not peaceful. If the dykes of death—reminiscent of the trenches of the Great War—seem safely across the water, Devlin reminds his reader that these seas are "unclean." In fact, they are crowded with casualties of the Battle of the Atlantic—as Louis MacNeice writes in "Neutrality," crowded with mackerel that "are fat—on the flesh of your kin."[49] *Pietà*, "pity": in one word, Devlin conflates Irish Catholicism and its dominant Mariolatry with the continental war. For if *pietà* is a depiction of the Virgin Mary holding her dead son's body, in this context Mary becomes the mother of Europe's fallen sons as well. Devlin suggests that the Irish, trapped across their unclean seas, may be capable of only pity: death "is not peace." Nor, it seemed, was neutrality.

Kavanagh's poem, too, frets over what meaning the Irish pilgrims' actions may have in a world at war. Halfway through "Lough Derg," the speaker breaks away from the central narrative about "the ex-monk, the farmer and the girl" as thoughts of war break in like a news bulletin from the wider world:

> Then there was war, the slang, the contemporary touch,
> The ideologies of the daily papers.
> They must seem realer, Churchill, Stalin, Hitler,
> Than ideas in the contemplative cloister.
> The battles where ten thousand men die
> Are more significant than a peasant's emotional problem.
> (356–61)

The war must "seem" realer, the speaker asserts—but to whom? The assertion that battles are more significant than wedding banns is undercut by the speaker's diction. After all, war here amounts to "slang," to a "touch" of historical color. The indecisive speaker, so committed to his Irish subjects, cannot quite commit to the significance of those across the sea. One stanza before, the speaker rationalizes, "A man's the centre of the world, / A man is not an anonymous / Member of the general public" (349–51), and adds, "God the Father is the Father / Of each one of us" (354–55). This is tenuous; since the stanza on war's significance follows, it suggests that the speaker does not quite believe his own lines. Indeed, war is glossed as a sort of wide-angle pan, "The battles where ten thousand men die," while "Lough Derg" follows what Quinn calls Kavanagh's cinematic method of moving between views of the pilgrims en masse and intense portraits of individuals.[50] Kavanagh's close-ups are bound by their specificity to be more moving than a hypothetical battle he mentions but does not show. Lough Derg is a particularly apt place for exploring the differences between the individual and the crowd, because the pilgrimage format encourages self-abnegation in the service of the soul's private business. Again and again, in the midsection of Kavanagh's poem, the idea of war troubles the primacy of the single pilgrim:

> Lough Derg overwhelmed the individual imagination
> And the personal tragedy.
> Only God thinks of the dying sparrow
> In the middle of a war. (338–41)

"Only God and Kavanagh!" (186), Quinn quite rightly exclaims. But more poets than just Kavanagh share these divine thoughts; English war poetry in the twentieth century is particularly steeped in Arcadianism. Kavanagh's "God, the poet" (344) might as well be a Rupert Brooke, who wrote from the Great War trenches that

> We have found safety with all things undying,
> The winds, and morning, tears of men and mirth,
> The deep night, and birds singing, and clouds flying,
> And sleep, and freedom, and the autumnal earth.[51]

Great War poets like Owen, Rosenberg, and Sassoon would go on to travesty Arcadianism's promise of comfort, but the power of such imagery was not lost by World War II.[52] For Kavanagh, his concern for the sparrows of Lough Derg aligns him with "God, the poet," who memorably cares for the "birds of the air" in the Gospels (Matthew 6:26), and it also foreshadows his own poetic turn to the parochial. But, as if foreshadowing the speaker in "Epic," Kavanagh's speaker in "Lough Derg" seems to know that his parochial focus can't but feel misplaced during wartime.[53] Eventually, though unsurely (beginning a sentence defensively with "But"), he makes the claim, "But wars will be merely dry bones in histories / And these common people real living creatures in it / On the unwritten spaces between the lines" (362–64). It is telling that the following line shows "a man throw[ing] himself prostrate" (365) in prayer. The juxtaposition leaves the speaker appearing desperate, like the praying man, for some consolation that he is right to privilege local concerns above the war. This desperation suffuses both Lough Derg poems. It is the reason for each poet's pilgrimage: both poems depict searches for a version of faith that could withstand not war but neutrality.

Prayer as Purgation and Pilgrimage as Poetic Form

Kavanagh and Devlin followed the Irish masses on pilgrimage to Lough Derg, but in so doing they also followed a long literary tradition. Current publicity materials for Lough Derg tout the pilgrimage as "bringing you the gift of hope."[54] But hope and consolation have proven hard to come by for many of the pilgrims who sought them at Saint Patrick's Purgatory. The medieval Irish poet Donnchadh Mór O Dhálaigh complained in 1244,

> Truagh mo thuras ar loch dearg
> a Rí na gceall is na gclog
> do chaoineadh do chneadh's do chréacht
> 's nach faghaim déar thar mo rosg.
>
> Vain my journey to Lough Derg,
> O King of the cells and bells;
> I came to mourn your sufferings and wounds,
> but no tear will cross my eye.[55]

In fact, the tradition of writing about Lough Derg is riddled with more failures than successes. Kavanagh was particularly familiar with two accounts of the pilgrimage: William Carleton's 1828 story "The Lough Derg Pilgrim" (made famous in *Traits and Stories of the Irish Peasantry*) and Yeats's "The Pilgrim," published in *New Poems* in 1938. In Carleton's story, his narrator sets off for Lough Derg "in the middle of my nineteenth year—of quick perception—warm imagination—a mind peculiarly romantic—a morbid turn for devotion, and a candidate for the priesthood."[56] In spite of his first "souvenir" of the island—a cold, from sinking to the bottom of a pond while attempting to walk on water, in imitation of a reputed Lough Derg miracle some years before—Carleton's hero sets off, well dressed, valiantly barefoot, and in high spirits, only to end up robbed of his hat, coat, waistcoat, and the contents of his purse: "In this trim did I return to my friends—a goose stripped of my feathers; a dupe beknaved and beplundered—having been almost starved to death in the 'island,' and nearly cudgelled by one of the priests" (818). Failed miracles, lost money, lost pride: these appear to be the island's legacy to nineteenth-century literature.

Yeats's poem is just as bleak in its assessment as Carleton's story. Nineteen-thirty-eight was a dark year, and it should be no surprise that the elderly poet would imaginatively visit Lough Derg as he was ruminating over his own mortality and the great shift in the gyres that seemed to be under way. His biding interest in purgatory and reincarnation may have spurred this poetic excursion, but like the old man in his play *Purgatory*, Yeats's pilgrim fails to learn from his experience:

> Round Lough Derg's holy island I went upon the stones,
> I prayed at all the Stations upon my marrow-bones,
> And there I found an old man, and though I prayed all day
> And that old man beside me, nothing would he say
> But fol de rol de rolly O.[57]

Like the old man's response, "The Pilgrim" is dark with nonsense. The diction, such as "Because the fires of purgatory have ate their shapes away" (13), is pure Hiberno-English, and the poem's form—a fourteener, which harks back to sixteenth- and seventeenth-century ballads—is in perfect keeping with the revivalist insistence on finding meaning in traditional culture. Yet the refrain, a sort of imitation Celtic twilight ditty, uses linguistic "Irishness" to reject this quintessentially Irish pilgrimage. This relentlessly nonsensical refrain courts the pilgrim tradition, only to send it off as meaningless. And so the poem ends where it begins, in the pub:

> Now I am in the public house and lean upon the wall,
> So come in rags or come in silk, in cloak or country shawl,
> And come with learned lovers or with what men you may
> For I can put the whole lot down, and all I have to say
> Is fol de rol de rolly O. (21–25)

Robert Welch notes that Yeats's refrain "lurches up to not knowing, to not being able to say anything with any certainty."[58] It uses the very "Irishness" of the pilgrimage to question its validity; consistent with Carleton's and O Dhálaigh's accounts, Yeats's poem suggests that the journey to Lough Derg is vain indeed. But not for lack of trying: in each of these literary pilgrimages, the speaker sets off in full hope that the pilgrimage will offer some sort of miracle, knowledge, or succor.

It is this thread of hope in the pilgrimage's promise that links together the literary tradition of Lough Derg and enables Devlin's and Kavanagh's use of pilgrimage as poetic form.[59] In these two very different assays at anatomizing the pilgrimage in verse, Devlin and Kavanagh employ poetic ambiguity as a reaction against both the aesthetic certainties of revivalism and the artistic confidence of high modernism. In both poems, the speaker is inextricably intertwined with the poet's own voice, and in both poems, the speaker moves from contempt of to compassion with his fellow pilgrims. Though this may seem like a miracle won from the "rosary rounds" of faith, in each poem the pilgrimage falls short of the miraculous, for the sympathy is only half won and spiritually ambiguous; neither achieves empathy with the pilgrims. These are both indecisive poems, but they mutually investigate the form of the Lough Derg pilgrimage—its repetition, its descent into darkness, and its yearning for insight—as a possible way to fashion a poetry of solace for the worried neutral soul. In both cases, the speaker endures the pilgrimage, survives the night vigil, but by the rising of the sun, only the natural world "lightens"; the pilgrim's burden of guilt does not (Devlin, 112).

Ambiguous Form and Content in Devlin's Pilgrimage

If poetry is, as Peggy O'Brien suggests, an attempt to approach the divine through language (107), it follows that the pilgrimage poem is a magnified version of this attempt. Devlin mimes the pilgrimage's "rosary rounds" with the poem's formal regularity. The *ababcc* sestets and dominant iambic pentameter of "Lough Derg" suggest a false sense of resolution, offering, through those rhyming couplets, to sum up each stanza, when in fact he frequently enjambs not only lines but also stanzas. The effect is one of hope offered, then disrupted, again and again, as in a pilgrim's prayers.

Devlin's poem continually references spaces of perdition, as if to test Lough Derg's purgatory against alternative versions of hell, earthly or supernatural. As pilgrims arrive at the island, Devlin writes,

Water withers from the oars. The pilgrims blacken
Out of the boats to masticate their sin
Where Dante smelled among the stones and bracken
The door to Hell (O harder Hell where pain
Is earthed, a casuist sanctuary of guilt!). (55–59)

The reference to casuistry exposes the selfishness of these pilgrims' prayers: the pilgrimage is, perhaps, more a justification or payment for continuing in guilt than a real attempt at repentance, simply chewing over sins as Lough Derg's dry bread. Devlin's curious use of prepositions, however, prevents this from being an easy accusation. One expects a "casuist sanctuary" *from* guilt. If the "harder Hell" of buried pain is a "casuist sanctuary *of* guilt," perhaps, Devlin suggests, the attempt at rationalization is itself a prison of pain: in the sanctuary of rationalization (as in neutrality), buried guilt burns quietly.

Several stanzas later, Devlin offers another definition of hell: "Hell is to know our natural empire used / Wrong, by mind's moulting, brute divinities" (79–80). The wrongfulness of empire building is, of course, at the political heart of the Second World War, and here Devlin reminds the reader that making war is a special act of hubris. Hell is to know that war is a nightmare of human making; the result is the inferno of invasion and bombardment (not to mention the special hell of genocide that marks World War II). This more typical wartime invocation of hell concludes the stanza: "Kent is for Jutes again and Glasgow town / Burns high enough to screen the stars and moon" (83–84). No casuistry, Devlin goes on to imply, can atone for the casualties of war. Devlin writes, "Say it was pride that did it, or virtue's brief: / To them that suffer it is no relief" (89–90). If Lough Derg is purgatory, Devlin's pilgrims can reach only the "door to Hell"; the real hell of war is located across the Irish Sea.

The final two stanzas of Devlin's poem return explicitly to the "rosary ring" of Station Island, remarking caustically on an Irish unwillingness to look the war in the face:

Then to see less, look little, let hearts' hunger
Feed on water and berries. The pilgrims sing:
Life will fare well from elder to younger,
Though courage fail in a world-end, rosary ring. (103–6)

This "world-end" is another of Devlin's rich ambiguities. Death, the thin space of Lough Derg, and world war have already been invoked in the poem as possible ends of the world. The "rosary ring" of Lough Derg's stations mimes cyclical history and the life cycle, but it also belies the pilgrims' song. Life does not always fare well from elder to younger, of course, for it is the younger who are disproportionately affected by war. Devlin goes on: "Courage kills its practitioners and we live, / Nothing forgotten, nothing to forgive" (109–10). The final stanza continues the sentence: "We pray to ourself" (111). The false hope offered by the rhyme scheme in the penultimate stanza makes Devlin's final stanzaic enjambment particularly ambiguous. If there is "nothing to forgive" the living neutrals for (though practitioners of courage die overseas), then the stanza ends on a comforting note. But this apparent statement is, the final stanza reveals, merely a prayer. Moreover, according to the next sentence, it is a "form of prayer without content" (113). The sentence, and the poem, conclude *with* that prayer: "Whitethorn lightens, delicate and blind, / The negro mountain, and so, knelt on her sod, / This woman beside me murmuring *My God! My God!*" (112–14). But if this is what "we pray to ourself" in the stanza's opening line, it is a prayer couched in a strangely antithetical combination of pronouns. Here is the final moment when the speaker identifies directly with his fellow pilgrims, as the praying voice is first person plural—the voice, perhaps, of congregated pilgrims praying in unison. But this "we" prays to "ourself," an arresting corruption of grammar: the singular form suggests that no prayer can truly be shared, that each petitioner can stake only his or her own soul. This could simply be a depiction of silent prayer. But the phrase also suggests something theologically troubling: if "we" pray to "ourself," then, implicitly "we" are not praying to the divine. A prayer to oneself is the selfish prayer of the troubled mind, the mind that worries that "nothing to forgive" may not indicate absolution but omission, that no forgiveness is available.

The night vigil at Lough Derg beneath the "metal moon" relies on the pilgrim's repeating prayers and stations of the cross, over and over, almost into meaninglessness: intended to numb the mind and body to purify the soul. This, the stanza claims, relies on prayer's form rather than content. But the poem "Lough Derg" does not rely merely on form; its careful ambiguities rely on sometimes contradictory combinations of form and content. Attending to Devlin's meticulous diction, for example, reveals that this "prayer without content" is also an accusation of the pilgrimage's failure to provide solace, the "we" of the poem remaining uncontent with the absence of clear absolution. If the prayer that concludes the poem, "*My God! My God!*" is read as a prayer without content, its repetition suggests the quintessence of the pilgrim's quest: a desperate reaching for the divine. Most critics read this line as a moment of poetic transcendence,[60] but the content of this prayer—murmured rather than clearly heard—is itself inconclusive. Repetition is the instinctive expression of uncertainty. Is this exclamation plaint, praise, or apology?

It is certainly an allusion to the final lines of Gerard Manley Hopkins's most ambivalent of the "terrible sonnets," "Carrion Comfort." In the sonnet, Hopkins's speaker wonders whom to "cheer" now his heart has "lapped strength, stole joy" from the "carrion comfort" of "Despair."[61] Should it be "the hero whose heaven-handling flung me" or "me that fought him? O which one? is it each one?" (12–13). The sonnet doesn't offer an answer, but instead concludes with its own allusion to a key moment of Biblical ambiguity, Jacob's wrestling with the angel: "That night, that year / Of now done darkness I wretch lay wrestling with (my God!) my God" (13–14). The speaker's dark night of the soul, akin to the night vigil at Station Island, is "done" but far from conclusive. The sense that his joy is stolen hints at a moral negligence in the way he has overcome a Despair described as a devouring darkness, a bone-bruiser that the speaker is "frantic to avoid . . . and flee" (8). The echo in Devlin's "Lough Derg" is implicit in the pilgrims' desire to atone for avoiding, via neutrality, the "dykes of death" in wartime. But in neither poem is it clear that such relief (as with the angel's blessing of Jacob) has been granted by man or by "*My God! My God!*" Hopkins's conclusion echoes in Devlin's only to intensify the conundrum. The poem—like the pilgrimage—offers no concrete answer.

Kavanagh and the Hope of a "Reasonable Document"

Kavanagh's poem shares this failure to arrive at an answer. In *Isle of Daemons* Terence Dewsnap remarks that Kavanagh "wrote a simpler poem than Devlin or Heaney but his is the most directionless. There is nowhere to go, which possibly explains why he failed to publish the poem"

(130). A sense of directionlessness is an inescapable part of the Lough Derg pilgrimage, with its repetitively encircled stations and beds. Kavanagh's own repetition highlights the monotony: "They knelt and prayed and rose and prayed / And circled the crosses and kissed the stones," repeating "a hundred decades / Of rosaries, until they hardly knew what words meant" (192–93, 189–90). In his attempt to mimic the form of the pilgrimage, Kavanagh chooses to write a linear narrative marked by grammatical repetition. But the resultant trudge through the island can be stultifying. A few hundred lines later, even the speaker is affected: "O the boredom of Purgatory, / Said the poet then" (456–57). And the reader is bored, too, following the plight of Kavanagh's unheroic protagonists.

But, like breaks in the clouds, occasional moments of spiritual insight lighten the narrative. "Something," the speaker claims, "that is Ireland's secret leads / These petty mean people" (62–63) to occasional revelation:

> For here's the day of a poor soul freed
> To a marvelous beauty above its head.
> The Castleblayney grocer trapped in the moment's need
> Puts out a hand and writes what he cannot read . . .
> News from a country beyond the range of birds (64–67, 73)

This "something," however, appears to stem more from the natural world than from the pilgrimage itself. Implicitly pitting contemporary Catholic piety against the island's pagan heritage as a thin space, Kavanagh writes an ancient natural Irishness that seems at odds with bureaucratic "Irish" piety. What works in this pilgrimage is less the rounds of the pilgrims' prayers than the rounds of the earth itself. When dawn breaks after the all-night vigil, Robert and Aggie stand by the water's edge, *almost* close enough to hold hands:

> They watched the lake waves clapping cold hands together
> And saw the morning breaking as it breaks
> Over a field where a man is watching a calving cow.
> New life, new day.
> A half-pilgrim saw it as a rabbiter
> Poaching in wood sees
> Primeval magic among the trees. (289–95)

For Robert and Aggie, the primeval moment of dawn is not quite enough to draw them together: "She only knew that she could hold his hand / If he stood closer" (279–80). If this "new day" were to dawn for Robert, he would have to take it with the knowledge that Aggie is not the virtuous woman he imagines. "You don't need to tell me anything, you could not," he says, "for your innocence is pure glass that I see through" (285–86). In fact, Robert refuses to see Aggie as an ordinary, sinful human; he has too firmly idealized her to break through the "glass" of his own self-image. So the actual "new life, new day" that dawns is a pagan one, "poached" or stolen from the edge of the pilgrims' lake, and the lyricism that lifts the reader out of Kavanagh's uneven narrative is not born of Catholic grace but is the lyricism of the irreligious landscape—Kavanagh's own descriptive strength—of nature itself.

The trouble with these pilgrims, in Kavanagh's speaker's eyes, is that—with the exception of that mystic grocer from Castleblayney—their Jansenism (as the spiritual manifestation of cultural pieties) prevents them from seeing God's poetry in the everyday—those "flowers and light" that they read as "heresies" (9–10). In this diagnosis, one seems to hear the voice of the poet himself, eager to disassociate himself from the masses. Not "we" but "they come to Lough Derg to fast and pray and beg / With all the bitterness of nonentities, and the envy / Of the inarticulate when dealing with an artist" (4–6). Here, the poet-speaker, himself just a "half-pilgrim," betrays his own self-importance—the same attitude he will condemn in the pedantic pilgrim Robert.[62] But this is a poem that, as Quinn says, "begins contemptuously and ends compassionately" (179), and if God is an artist, by the second day of the pilgrimage Kavanagh allows art to the pilgrims as well. After Aggie reveals her tale of "birth, bastardy and murder" (398) to the unsuspecting Robert, the speaker dispenses with the couple and with the defrocked priest who completes the trio of named characters. There is not exactly a plot here, no proper narrative beyond a sketch of the pilgrimage's daily outlines, but Robert's pedantry is punished by Aggie's brutal story, and he is left voiceless: "He only heard rocks crashing distantly / When John Flood rang the midday bell" (399–400). At this juncture, the poem takes a sharp turn:

> Now the three of them got out of the story altogether
> Almost. Now they were not three egotists

> But part of the flood of humanity,
> Anonymous, never to write or be written. (401–4)

The poem subsumes their individual egoism into their communal sacredness. Having punished the character most reminiscent of the judgmental speaker, Kavanagh here abandons what passes for the poem's narrative and instead turns to the elevation of the "inarticulate" "nonentities" from the opening of the poem into artists themselves. Evening falls, and, quite literally, "prose prayers become / Odes and sonnets" (465–66). No surprise, perhaps, that the liminal hours of morning and evening find Kavanagh's pilgrims magically transformed. What happens is that the poet's increasing "boredom"—and, yes, the reader's, too—disappears as Kavanagh (or perhaps God) transmutes his plain pilgrims' confessions into a series of four Shakespearean sonnets.

They are, indeed, lovely sonnets; they elevate the "banal / Beggary" (541–42) of the poor into the English language's most celebrated form. First, a young man, "an engine running / Light down the narrow-gauge railway of life," petitions Saint Anthony, "for Mary Gunning / Of Rathdrumskean to be my wife" (493–96). Next transmuted is a similar petition from the other sex:

> St Anne, I am a young girl from Castleblayney,
> One of a farmer's six grown daughters.
> Our little farm, when the season's rainy,
> Is putty spread on stones. The surface waters
> Soak all the fields of this north-looking townland. (499–503)

The girl asks, in the sonnet's final couplet, "O Patron of the pure woman who lacks a man, / Let me be free I beg of you, St Anne" (511–12). If the content is banal—the next poem belongs to a young man looking for a working wage and a woman—Kavanagh performs the work of God here. If "God, the poet" "hears in the voices of the meanly poor / Homeric utterances, poetry sweeping through" (345, 544–45), Kavanagh appears to be trying the hand of the poet, a God. These plain people's petitions come the closest in "Lough Derg" to the spirit of *The Great Hunger*, for they lyricize the landscape of poverty while pointing out its injustice. One asks the "Sacred Heart of Jesus" merely for "a job so I can settle down and marry; / I want to live a decent life" (513–15). "And through / The flames of St. Patrick's Purgatory" (515–16), the pilgrim explains,

> I go offering every stone-bruise, all my hunger
> In the back-room of my penance I am weaving
> An inside-shirt for charity. How longer
> Must a fifty-shilling-a-week job be day-dreaming? (517–20)

It is the transmutation of these prayers that forms the poet's own penance when he casts aside the speaker's superiority to find poetry in the ordinary pilgrims' needs. If pilgrimage is a poetic form, for Kavanagh casting these prayers into formal poetry is itself a form of pilgrimage. In a long poem that wavers, like the pilgrim experience, between the very personal nature of a pilgrim's quest and the impersonality of the Station Island pilgrimage, Kavanagh's most powerful claim is the spirituality of the poetic enterprise itself. By the end of the poem, Robert, Aggie, and the monk vanish into the crowd,

> Where only God, the poet,
> Followed with interest till he found
> Their secret, and constructed from
> The chaos of its fire
> A reasonable document. (345–49)

What is hinted at here, though not explicitly claimed, is that "Lough Derg" itself could be the "reasonable document" constructed from the chaos of the pilgrimage in 1942. This date is not to be so easily dismissed, despite the seeming timelessness of Station Island. After all, the sonneteers' requests are couched in the contemporary social and economic realities of the Emergency: job scarcity, late marriage, stifled trade, poor farms.

As the poem concludes, boats queue up to row the pilgrims back to the mainland, and Kavanagh's cinematic technique pans out with a journalistic note.

> All happened on Lough Derg as it is written
> In June nineteen forty-two

When the Germans were fighting outside Rostov.
The poet wrote it down as best he knew. (625–28)

And how? Because "he too was one of them" (632). Here, the tale of "St Patrick's Purgatory in Donegal, / Christendom's purge" (616–17) is explicitly placed in time—in wartime. The reference to the Eastern Front, as far as Europe can get from Donegal, connects the pilgrims to that Continent "for want" of which "All Ireland's Patricks" are frozen.[63] The final stanza contrasts the journalistic report of fighting in Russia with the landscape of a nation pointedly *not* at war: "The turnips were a-sowing in the fields around Pettigo / As our train passed through" (636–37). So, what solution has Kavanagh been offered by his pilgrimage? The poem concludes, explicitly naming places on both sides of the Irish border,

By Monaghan and Cavan and Dundalk
By Bundoran and by Omagh the pilgrims went;
And three sad people had found the key to the lock
Of God's delight in disillusionment. (639–42)

These last two lines, like the final line of Devlin's poem, are frustratingly ambiguous: Have the "three sad people" become, themselves, disillusioned, thus unlocking access to divine delight? Or is the "delight" God's own—a delight in the disillusionment of humanity, of bringing clear-sightedness to individuals blinded by egotism? With no clear answer, Kavanagh's poetic pilgrimage to Lough Derg remains potentially vain.

Near the end of the poem, the boats bring newly arrived pilgrims with a "ridiculous cheer / That breaks, like a hole in pants, / Where the heroic armies advance" (549–51). In this moment, Kavanagh undercuts simultaneously the neutral pilgrims and the "heroic" armies of World War II, aligning them both—an embarrassing gibe—with a hole in the pants.[64] Neither soldiers of Christ nor soldiers of war seem to get a vote of faith from the speaker. This odd, prosaic simile may encapsulate the whole pilgrimage: indecisive, unheroic, a "smothered" cheer (449). Like Devlin's poem, Kavanagh's "Lough Derg" is perhaps only a halfway "reasonable document." Though the poet finds a form to elevate nonentities into artists, no certain spiritual awakening emerges in the end, and the pilgrimage so clearly dated "nineteen forty-two" unites and separates the island from a world at war without offering a "key to the lock" of the ambiguity of neutrality.

At the "thin space" of Lough Derg, Ireland's neutrality can be seen as a "thin" construct as well. But rather than a mystical portal to peace, this was a neutrality torn from both sides: connected to Europe by an ancient faith but separated by war and water. Told to marshal their thwarted martial instincts into prayers for peace, Irish Catholics made the Lough Derg pilgrimage in large numbers during the Emergency, in spite of a fuel shortage that would have made transportation to the remote lake difficult. In a country so often described as purgatorial, Saint Patrick's Purgatory served Devlin and Kavanagh as an ideal locus to explore what was troubling the "Irish mind" in 1942. The act of pilgrimage makes an emergency of the faith journey, but neither poet's emergency writing manages to find clear resolution. This is consistent with the "vain" history of Lough Derg as a literary site, and Devlin's and Kavanagh's choice to use the Lough Derg pilgrimage as poetic material constitutes a formal decision. The form of the pilgrimage would structure their poems, but in both cases it would fail to vouchsafe enlightenment. Tentative late modernists, the messianic compulsions of high modernism dead in the water, neither poet commits to revelation, instead teasing their readers with ambiguous endings. This is perhaps as much as could be expected from the conundrum of neutrality. Paradox, irresolution, and unresolved guilt prove, as the next chapter shows, to be the poetics of neutrality.

CHAPTER 3

The Enemy Within

Louis MacNeice's War Poetry

"Up the Rebels, To Hell with the Pope, / And God Save—as you prefer—the King or Ireland."[1] So Louis MacNeice rebukes the binary rhetoric of his native Belfast (one man's "hope / The other man's damnation") in canto 16 of his 1938 *Autumn Journal* (29–30). Critical of loyalism and nationalism alike, MacNeice casts his eye on Ireland and declares, "I hate your grandiose airs . . . / Your assumption that everyone cares / Who is the king of your castle" (109, 111–12). "Castles are out of date," the poet determines: "Put up what flag you like, it is too late / To save your soul with bunting" (113, 115–16). MacNeice's pithy remark is not merely a barb at the North but also a knowing commentary on the Irish tendency to conflate politics with religion. As Kavanagh's and Devlin's "Lough Derg" poems demonstrate, the rhetoric of Irish neutrality leaned heavily on the discourse of the soul, with de Valera promising neutrality as salvific, while the poetry indicates extreme spiritual disquiet. Made in 1938, under the cloud of the Munich Crisis, MacNeice's assertion that a flag decal can't get you into heaven anymore would only increase in relevance once war—or neutrality—broke out the following year.

The vitriol of MacNeice's rhetoric and the precision with which he strikes out at the pieties of contemporary Ireland have made canto 16 of *Autumn Journal* one of the most frequently cited examples of Louis MacNeice's so-called "Irish" poetry.[2] While MacNeice himself never called his own Irishness into question, much ado has been made of it in the criticism. Decades of nationalistic canon formation that aimed to push Protestant writers out of an Irish canon, or to co-opt MacNeice into a narrative of English poetry as a sort of sub-Auden, have cited what Heather Clark has named "that strain of Englishness which led him to remain in London and write BBC propaganda during the Second World War" as a key strike against MacNeice's credibility as an Irish poet.[3] For this reason, Clark argues that the younger generation of Northern poets, including Heaney, Mahon, Muldoon, Carson, and Longley, in claiming MacNeice as the godfather of Northern Irish poetry, "have turned away from the MacNeice of 1938 to 1945 to the lyric, nostalgic, and apolitical MacNeice" (78). "The rush to repatriate MacNeice" ignores what Clark reads as his "loyalty [to England], evident in his anger over Ireland's neutrality and his willingness to sacrifice his creative freedom for the war effort" (78). While Clark's influential assessment of the recasting and re-collecting of the late MacNeice into an icon for the Ulster Renaissance is apt, her labeling of "the MacNeice of 1938 to 1945" as a loyalist Brit synthesizes a number of common critical misreadings: one, that national identity operates on a binary; following that, that MacNeice's work for the Allied war effort required an abdication of his Irishness; that he was angry over neutrality (indeed not; he was critical but understanding of it); and that MacNeice's work for the BBC implied a sacrifice of creative freedom as a poet. None of these claims are borne out in MacNeice's wartime work in poetry, prose, or radio drama.[4]

In fact, his lyric poetry of the Emergency era is the very poetry in which MacNeice is most engaged with ideas of what it means to be an Irish poet, specifically in time of war. If Belfast poets looked to MacNeice to galvanize their poetic tradition in the 1960s, MacNeice in the 1940s was wrestling with an Irish poetic tradition headlined by William Butler Yeats, and in fact, MacNeice's work between 1938 and 1945 is more suffused with Yeatsian imagery and form than any of his other work. Recent critics have productively explored the intersections of Yeats's and MacNeice's work. Tom Walker devotes a chapter to "Yeats's MacNeice" in *Louis MacNeice and the Poetry of His Time*, but the study's focus shifts with the death of Yeats in 1939, just when, as Walker puts it, "as the long-feared world war arrived, it was MacNeice who turned his own 'brainwork' to Yeats."[5] Contrary to Clark, Walker sees the 1940s as MacNeice's *most* Irish period, and his chapter on this decade focuses on MacNeice's interactions with his Irish contemporaries in Dublin and Belfast. Terence Brown, Richard Danson Brown, and Michael Moir have written on the influence of Yeats on MacNeice's wartime poetry, arguing that Ireland represents a place of political escape or forgetfulness that simultaneously seduces and repels the younger poet.[6] But MacNeice saw Ireland and its neutrality, for all its soul-trading politics, as a more complex location than most critics allow for. Danson Brown finally determines that MacNeice's "commitment to the Allied cause is at odds with Yeatsian nationalism" (126), but as I show in this chapter, MacNeice's own sense of "commitment" was equivocal, and he wasn't in the business of saving his soul with bunting. England was not his nation, though London was his city. MacNeice went to London to fight fascism and to keep from "missing History" rather than to support the United Kingdom; it was the decision of an Irish cosmopolitan.[7] In Ireland, de Valera's rhetoric strongly equated neutrality with nationalism, but MacNeice saw nationalism as problematic from the start. His distaste for political binarism makes the critical enterprise's commitment to it all the more ironic. Readings of MacNeice as a poet of "commitment" elide the complex machinery of his poems. In fact, MacNeice's wartime poetry hews closer to the *Oxford English Dictionary*'s first definition of neutrality: "an intermediate state or condition, not clearly one thing or another." A poetry of reflexive images, refrains, and uncanny doubles, it shows a consciousness of war that renders his speakers neither one thing nor the other.

In 1918, in the middle of Ireland's revolutionary decade, Yeats wrote, "We make out of the quarrel with others, rhetoric, but of the quarrel with ourselves, poetry."[8] MacNeice's wartime work follows Yeats's in illustrating this maxim. Like the Yeats of *The Tower*, MacNeice in *Plant and Phantom* (1941) and *Springboard* (1944) quarrels with himself about the place of the poet and the unpoetic realities of war. But as early as *Autumn Journal* he takes up his quarrel with Yeats as well, seeking in his poetry an example of writing the "terrible beauty" of his predicament. For the BBC, *Common Sense*, and the *Partisan Review*, among others, MacNeice worked as a rhetorician, but for himself he worked as a poet, and the quarrels in his wartime poetry dismantle the system of binary oppositions that tend to characterize war writing.[9]

Not Clearly One Thing or Another: MacNeice and the In-Between

Louis MacNeice's Irish birth and English education were, for several decades after his death, a problem for critics of his poetry. Like so many

Anglo-Irish writers, MacNeice found himself "too English for the Irish and too Irish for the English."[10] Although his reputation suffered from this predicament in the past, making critics unable to pinpoint MacNeice either as an English "Thirties Poet" and acolyte of Auden or as an inheritor of Yeats who could stabilize an Irish national poetry, contemporary readers like Fran Brearton find that MacNeice's "failure to express fully either English national sentiments or Irish national aspirations . . . becomes a creative strength and a political virtue."[11] What is most arresting about the body of MacNeice criticism, however, is its repeated insistence on reading the poetry in dualistic terms, English-Irish being a common starting point. The English-Irish debate is, as Dillon Johnston has noted, ultimately "an extraliterary question,"[12] but it has helped to shape a criticism that consistently relies on such terms as "dialectical," "ambivalent," and "paradoxical."[13] MacNeice's interest in writing poetry of "flux" and "tension" dovetails conceptually with his long-term location in a canonical limbo, and so the primary location for MacNeice has been "between": between England and Ireland, between public and private affairs, between two wars (*Autumn Journal*, an epic of betweenness, has always been MacNeice's most-discussed work).[14] "Between," from the famous line "There is more than glass between the snow and the huge roses," in "Snow" (1935), to the end of his career, is a word of "crucial ambiguity in MacNeice's metaphysic," according to Edna Longley, who asks, "Does it separate or join?" (127). This sense of betweenness links MacNeice's concerns with those of Kavanagh and Devlin, and like them, MacNeice found neutrality to function as an ambiguous—and valuable—pivot point amid dialectical approaches to thinking about the war.

In *Sceptical Vision* (1975), the first book-length study of MacNeice, Terence Brown calls MacNeice's "sceptical faith" "a complex conception, basically a dialectical view of life."[15] Brown finds that in MacNeice's wartime poems, like "The Trolls" and "Brother Fire," "Non-being, death, the illimitable, the unknown, permanence, are all possibilities which when considered can convince us of the values of their opposites: being, life, limit, the known, change. These paired opposites form a dialectic which renders life valuable" (87). It is unsurprising that a dialectically minded reader would find this mode visible during World War II; it is *the* event of the twentieth century whose history demands that sides be taken. Wartime suggests the antithetical structure a dialectic requires, but MacNeice's World War II–era poetry consistently complicates a dialectical mode of interpretation. Like many writers and intellectuals, MacNeice saw the war as "a choice of evils."[16] In 1939, the war was by no means the obvious good fight that nostalgia, history, and the revelation of German atrocities have made it. In an April 1939 letter to his new love interest, the American novelist Eleanor Clark, MacNeice makes very clear that for him the "choice of evils" is a mandate to stop the "Hitleris[ation of] the rest of Europe" (318). Clark herself was a Trotskyite, and MacNeice (a socialist but never a Communist) is careful in the letter to position himself in favor of political change, though he is clear that "this impure War" is no proletarian revolution, even if it may afterward lead to something like it. He tells Clark that if this is a war to stop fascism, then "the only logic for me is to go in with it (history after all has been mainly a choice of evils & one can't be Utopian about it)" (319). For MacNeice, the decision to support the war would compromise leftist revolutionary politics, and it was further complicated by his nationality. He wondered to Clark if he might "keep out of things until I can choose some course which is directly & definitely good" (319), and in fact he spent the first year of the war in neutral countries, Ireland and the United States. Neutrality offered MacNeice the apparent choice of opting out, of giving him "time for thought," as he writes in "Dublin," a city that was able to "poise the toppling hour" when he composed the eponymous poem in 1939.[17] In 1939, at a loss for what to do, tired of his job at Bedford College London, and at the end of his affair with Nancy Coldstream, MacNeice applied for the professorship of poetry at Trinity College Dublin. In December, MacNeice wrote to his friend and mentor E. R. Dodds that H. O. White had got the post at Trinity, and he was going to "try America" instead.[18] Since a spring lecture tour in the United States, MacNeice had become more and more serious about Eleanor Clark, and taking a temporary lectureship at Cornell University offered him a chance to have "a bout of irrationality," as he described the deepening affair to Dodds in a February 1940 letter (376). Under the influence of this "romance," MacNeice predicted that he was "going to write (at least I hope so) quite new kinds of poems. After which, no doubt, the deluge" (376).

The deluge came in the shape of the Blitz. Writing from Cornell in May 1940, MacNeice confessed to Clark, "I can't stop thinking about the war . . . I am utterly appalled by it, feel like jumping off a bridge . . . It gives me two crazy impulses, both of which represent sheer defeatism. One is to run away by going back to England, ceasing to be myself any more, letting things just happen to me—jumping down into the machine. The other is to run away over here by giving up entirely . . . the effort to hold on to the things I think valuable" (391–92). The problem for MacNeice was that neither running away nor being conscripted into the war machine seemed like a viable choice, though ultimately he allowed the latter, the inevitable, to happen. MacNeice returned to London in December 1940, having recovered from a near-fatal bout of peritonitis and willing at last, as he told his father, "to crash in on the B.B.C.," but "in the meanwhile I want to finish a book" (416). MacNeice would stay in London for the war's duration, but the book in question—*Plant and Phantom* (1941)—illustrates that he did not stop analyzing his decision.[19] The legacy of MacNeice's grappling with the idea of neutrality is a body of wartime poetry that complicates the friend-enemy dualism of war by contemplating the friend-enemy dualism within the self. At the conclusion of a letter to Clark, MacNeice asks, "Did you ever hear about the Asiatic (I think) tree which only blossoms in a forest fire? I feel one might blossom like that at any moment. Or burn. Or perhaps both. But if one really blossomed it would be worth it" (392). In MacNeice's wartime poetry, the answer seems to be *both*.

His critical engagement with Yeats, including his writing *The Poetry of W. B. Yeats* in 1939–40, helped MacNeice shape his response to this long-dreaded conflagration. Ireland's neutrality in the conflict placed the country outside the traditional dialectic of war, giving MacNeice a ground from which to ask whether all nations and individuals are implicated in conflict, even if they are not active participants. The poet answered with a poetry of reflexive language, which problematizes the linguistic construction of the singular self by continuously doubling, circling, repeating, and even consuming it. MacNeice's wartime poems are characterized by rhetorical schemes such as refrain and repetition, which enact the poetry's suspicion of the self as singular and intact. A dominant trope in the poems is the reflexive, or "self-inwoven,"[20] simile or metaphor, which loops back onto itself, as in the line in "Carrick Revisited," "Memories I had shelved peer back at me from the shelf."[21] As William Keach writes of Shelley, reflexive tropes and imagery like those employed by MacNeice "make the reader aware of the mind's ability not only to perceive relationships but to create them in a context of unity and identity."[22] The net result, in MacNeice's wartime poetry, is the collapsing of the simple oppositions of self/other and friend/enemy into a poetics of the wartime guilt that inhabits the minds of even pacifists and neutrals, suggesting that in a world war, no soul is an island (and no island can save its soul through isolation). In 1946, an American critic disparaged this as bad war poetry—that is, bad propaganda—writing that "MacNeice cannot see the beam in his enemy's eye for the mote in his own."[23] Indeed, for MacNeice, remembering the mote in the eye of even a just warrior was an important part of the moral accounting of war, in which even the neutral nations must be tallied.

Writing from and about an Ireland that was, in multiple ways, both inside and outside the war zone, MacNeice's wartime poetry reminds readers that there are no easy oppositions—not public and private, not the self and the other, not even belligerence and neutrality—between war and apparent peace. MacNeice's Ireland intervenes in the war narrative to drive a poetry that dismantles the war poet's and the modernist poet's authoritative voice and speaks of a total war in which (far from de Valera's soul-saving promises) every self is complicit, even the neutrals.

"The War Came Down on Us Here": MacNeice and Yeats in the Neutral Zone

One might be forgiven for thinking that canto 16 of *Autumn Journal* was written later than 1938, for it sounds like a portrait of Emergency Ireland. Unable to stay away after his 1935 "Valediction," MacNeice tries to answer why he is so compelled to return to his home country. One reason, he suggests, is that Ireland makes a "tiny stage" on which a person might "do local work which is not at the world's mercy" and even "see the end of one particular action" (70–72). The question hangs with literary freight; after all, Yeats seemed to do just this with the Irish National Theatre ("Kathleen ni Houlihan" visits the poem in this canto), and indeed a writer could make a national name in Ireland while remaining anonymous in an England that had fifteen times the population. But MacNeice swiftly dismisses the notion, saying, "It is self-deception of course; / There is no immunity in this island either" (73–74). As

Britain's smaller neighbor, Ireland is "a cart that is drawn by somebody else's horse / And carrying goods to somebody else's market" (75–76). MacNeice casts Ireland's isolationism as self-defeating:

> Ourselves alone! Let the round tower stand aloof
>   In a world of bursting mortar!
> Let the school-children fumble their sums
>   In a half-dead language;
> Let the censor be busy on the books; pull down the
>   Georgian slums;
>   Let the games be played in Gaelic. (79–84)

If *sinn féin* was to be government policy, the result, to MacNeice, was unappealing. And yet MacNeice cannot stop asking, "Why should I want to go back / To you Ireland, my Ireland" (105–6). The allure is made clear by the haunted canto 15, in which MacNeice begs for hedonistic "sensations" (21) to distract himself from the familiar-looking ghosts ("someone at Gallipoli or in Flanders / Caught in the end-all mud?") (51–52) that cast a constant specter over politics and daily life. As canto 15 ends with the acknowledgment that the ghosts "are still there" (84), canto 16 begins, "Nightmare leaves fatigue: / We envy men of action / Who sleep and wake, murder and intrigue / Without being doubtful, without being haunted" (1–4). It is the intransigence of "my own / Countrymen" (5–6) that he envies most; MacNeice is, he tells us, "reading the memoirs of Maud Gonne" (9). It's clear that the specter really haunting MacNeice in this canto is W. B. Yeats. From references to Gonne to the allusion to *Cathleen ni Houlihan*, MacNeice's "envy" echoes part 5 of Yeats's *Meditations in Time of Civil War*, "The Road at My Door," in which the poet finds he must "silence the envy in my thought" after visits from both Irregulars and National soldiers bring the war to his doorstep.[24] In *Meditations*, Yeats vividly interrogates the value of his role as poet in the face of war, concluding section 7 with, "I turn away and shut the door, and on the stair / Wonder how many times I could have proved my worth / In something that all others understand or share" (33–35). Only "the abstract joy, / The half-read wisdom of daemonic images" must "suffice" (37–39) the poet who is not a man of action. Concluding his reading of *Autumn Journal*, Tom Walker remarks that "Yeatsian technique became a resource" for MacNeice, "a means to confront reality rather than escape it" (42). And when the year 1939 came "with bombs," as *Autumn Journal* predicted, Ireland and Yeats's poetry again seemed to offer MacNeice a form of escapism, but one that may have been foreclosed from the start; MacNeice already knew that in Ireland, neutral or not, there was "no immunity."

In September 1939, Louis MacNeice was in Galway, gathering material for *The Poetry of W. B. Yeats*, when war was declared in London, where he lived and worked. That fateful autumn was, for MacNeice, suffused with Yeats's presence, and that presence was a crucial force in shaping his responses to the war. Those responses would ultimately be published in prose as *The Poetry of W. B. Yeats* (1941) and in verse as the sequence poem "The Closing Album," which first appeared as "The Coming of War" in *The Last Ditch*, a limited edition published in 1940 by the Yeats sisters' Cuala Press. *The Poetry of W. B. Yeats*, commissioned by Oxford University Press, was the first book-length critical study of the poet since his death in January 1939. MacNeice, whom Edna Longley has called "the major Irish poet after Yeats who follows him in broad cultural orientation" (28), was an inspired choice, and much of the study still merits scholarly reading today. But ultimately, *The Poetry of W. B. Yeats* tells us more about MacNeice at this critical moment than about Yeats. In the study, MacNeice found himself at once appraising his elder and defending him, revising his own poetic philosophy in the process.[25] MacNeice's particular sounding board in the book is his friend W. H. Auden, whose decision to emigrate to the United States in 1939 was punctuated by two statements of artistic philosophy that take aim at the recently deceased Yeats.[26] Lines from Auden's famous elegy "In Memory of W. B. Yeats,"

> You were silly like us: your gift survived it all;
> The parish of rich women, physical decay,
> Yourself; mad Ireland hurt you into poetry.
> Now Ireland has her madness and her weather still,
> For poetry makes nothing happen: [. . .][27]

prompted the following rejoinder from his Irish friend MacNeice: "Many people, however, exaggerate Yeats's 'escapism'. He was neither so simple-minded nor so esoteric nor so dilettante a poet as he is often represented. I have met people whose attitude is: 'Yeats was a silly old thing but he was a *poet*'. This is a foolish attitude. No silly old thing can write fine poetry . . . Yeats, contrary to some people's opinion, had a mind."[28] The timing of this comment is significant, because in engaging with Yeats's alleged escapism, MacNeice had to silently engage with his own predilection for the same. Both in life (the poems in "The Coming of War" are explicit about how remaining in Ireland at the war's outbreak gives MacNeice "time for thought") and in his work, MacNeice's penchant for surface brightness ("the dazzle on the sea, my darling") might be seen as an escapism of his own.[29] Refuting escapism meant MacNeice would have to reformulate his ideas about poetry as a whole. The introduction to *The Poetry of W. B. Yeats* places the poet-critic at a crisis of meaning—at a moment in which Yeats would be his vehicle to reassess the meaning of poetry in time of war:

> I had only written a little of this book when Germany invaded Poland. On that day I was in Galway. As soon as I heard on the wireless of the outbreak of war, Galway became unreal. And Yeats and his poetry became unreal also. This was not merely because Galway and Yeats belong in a sense to a past order of things. The unreality which now overtook them was also overtaking in my mind modern London, modernist art, and Left Wing politics. If the war made nonsense of Yeats's poetry and of all works that are called 'escapist', it also made nonsense of the poetry that professes to be 'realist' . . . For war spares neither the poetry of Xanadu nor the poetry of pylons. I gradually inferred, as I recovered from the shock of war, that both these kinds of poetry stand or fall together. War does not prove one is better or worse than the other; it attempts to disprove both. But poetry must not be disproved. (17–18)

Yeats's poetry and his own response to war in volumes like *The Tower* (1925) would stand or fall as an example to the younger poet facing another conflict (and its inevitable calls for poetry). MacNeice concludes his book with a telling critique of Auden's essay in the *Partisan Review* in the spring of 1939, a mock debate called "The Public v. the Late Mr.

William Butler Yeats."[30] In his speech for the defense, Auden counters arguments that Yeats's political worldview and mystical interests disqualify him from being a "great poet," arguing, "who . . . will care a button whether the deceased was right about the Irish Question or wrong about the transmigration of souls? But because the excitement out of which his poems arose was genuine, they will . . . be capable of exciting others" (6). The case for the prosecution, Auden writes, "rests on the fallacious belief that art ever makes anything happen" (7). This, of course, is also the gist of Auden's elegy for Yeats. MacNeice complicates the argument in another passage in *The Poetry of* W. B. *Yeats* that merits quoting at length:

> Auden, however, as was natural in a poet who had abruptly abandoned the conception of art as handmaid of politics for the conception of art as autotelic, overstates his case; he says that the case for the prosecution rests on the fallacy that art never makes anything happen. The case for the prosecution does rest on a fallacy but it is not this. The fallacy lies in thinking that it is the *function* of art to make things happen and that the effect of art upon actions is something either direct or calculable. It is an historical fact that art *can* make things happen and Auden in his reaction from a rigid Marxism seems in this article to have been straying towards the Ivory Tower. Yeats did not write primarily in order to influence men's actions but he knew that art can alter a man's outlook and so indirectly affect his actions. (192)

This conclusion has real implications for the poet as critic. If MacNeice determines through Yeats that poetry can make things happen, it is no surprise that he turns to Yeats as a model for what kind of poetry he himself might begin to make in this new war. Yeats's focus on Irish politics, and particularly the *Meditations in Time of Civil War*, positioned his as the voice to reckon with. MacNeice's response to September 1939 would be a poem sequence of his own, one that began life as the premonitory "The Coming of War" but, when republished by Faber midwar, gained its final title, "The Closing Album," which evokes the sepia-toned finality and photo-album nostalgia of MacNeice's last excursions into this prewar, Yeatsian West of Ireland. "The Closing Album" is allusive with Yeatsian diction and meter, but it is not an homage or pastiche. Yeats spoke in an authoritative voice, from the top of his tower, and MacNeice believed in the poet as the voice of the *vulgus*, the people.[31] His war poetry would be democratic, colloquial, a riposte to the certainties of Yeatsian and Eliotic high modern verse. With Yeats, MacNeice found attractions on personal and stylistic levels, but to put them into practice, he had to follow his own prescription: "The spiritual lesson that my generation . . . can learn from Yeats is to write according to our lights. His lights are not ours. *Go thou and do otherwise*" (197).

MacNeice put his own injunction into practice in the poems that became the 1941 Faber volume *Plant and Phantom*. Eight of the poems (including three sequence poems) that appeared in *Plant and Phantom* were first published by Lily and Lolly Yeats, the poet's sisters, in the 1940 Cuala Press volume, *The Last Ditch*. Though MacNeice altered several poems and dropped some from the sequences for the Faber volume (which is the edition I discuss here), the presence of the Cuala volume in the Faber one is part of a presence of Yeats and Ireland that lurks within MacNeice's first volume of poetry published in wartime Britain. As critics like Brown, Longley, and McDonald have noted, Yeats's presence is most firmly felt in "The Closing Album."

"The Closing Album" is one of MacNeice's few deliberately date-marked poems. He marks the sequence as "August–September, 1939," the period of his Yeats research and road trip with Ernst Stahl chronicled in *The Strings Are False*. The first poem in the sequence, "Dublin," is written largely in what one might call Yeats's Dublin trimeter from "Easter, 1916." As "Easter, 1916" (also a deliberately dated poem) remembers an event in a city from which the poet was absent, "Dublin" remembers a city in which the poet is absent from the happening of historic events elsewhere. Dublin is described first in terms of its architecture, "Grey brick upon brick," and its public statuary: "Declamatory bronze / On sombre pedestals— / O'Connell, Grattan, Moore" (1–4). Next, the city comes to life: "And the brewery tugs and the swans / On the balustraded stream" (5–6), and then MacNeice brings life and history together in rhyme and vision:

> And porter running from the taps
> With a head of yellow cream

And Nelson on his pillar
Watching his world collapse. (10–13)

These opening lines consciously evoke Yeatsian imagery: the swans, the river, the heroes of Irish independence listed epitaph-style as Yeats lists the Easter 1916 martyrs. Like Yeats, a poet rather than a revolutionary, MacNeice's speaker (who throughout the sequence is synonymous with the poet himself) is as helpless as the effigy Admiral Nelson watching his world collapse.[32] The poem is built, "brick upon brick," as it were, by a series of repetitions and parallelisms. At sixty-four lines of mostly dimeter and trimeter, the poem is tall and narrow, like the Georgian townhouses typical of Dublin. Its final line, "And brick upon grey brick," stacks repetitively upon the first, "Grey brick upon brick," but "Dublin" is able to "poise the toppling hour" of collapse through balancing its own difficult history: "She is not an Irish town / And she is not English" (39–40). Not Irish and not English (like critical views of the poet himself), MacNeice's Dublin refutes a dualistic definition: Dublin is not either/or but neither/nor, a palimpsest of conflicting identities. Above this town of dangerously doubled histories, MacNeice finds,

And the mist on the Wicklow hills
Is close, as close
As the peasantry were to the landlord,
As the Irish to the Anglo-Irish,
As the killer is close one moment
To the man he kills,
Or as the moment itself
Is close to the next moment. (31–38)

The poem's parallel syntax, with its insistent anaphora, calls attention to the ways in which proximity indicates distance and murder may be man's most intimate act. The past is as close, the logic of this syntax reveals, to the present as peace is to war in this city whose "seedy elegance" recalls the "terrible beauty" of which it is capable. Dublin, as in Kavanagh's claim, "It is midnight in Dublin and Europe is at war,"[33] is separate from the world at war, which never enters the poem. Yet the lines are suffused with the city's violent past and with the knowledge that perceived opposites (peasant/landlord, victim/murderer, neutrality/war, Ireland/Europe) are often more intimately connected than they seem.

Across the Shannon, facing the opposite coast of the island, is the "Galway" of the final place poem in "The Closing Album." Galway, with its proximity to Connemara and the myth-suffused West of Ireland, is Yeatsian territory.[34] The city is county seat for Yeats's Tower, Thoor Ballylee, and MacNeice's "Galway" echoes Yeats, with its "hundred swans / Dreaming on the harbour" (12–13). "Galway" systematically calls up and strikes out Yeatsian imagery in each of its three seven-line stanzas, and it does so in that most Yeatsian manner—a refrain. Galway's poverty, its salmon, its swans, its moon—all are called up in turn then canceled out by, "The war came down on us here" (7). The refrain cancels the escapist charge, makes Galway real, not mythical. The trimeter of that refrain has also a Yeatsian echo: "A terrible beauty is born." For in MacNeice's Galway, "September dawned / Upon willows and ruins: / The war came down on us here" (19–21). By the end of the poem, the refrain has altered the implications of this pairing, "willows and ruins." As the poem opens among the "hollow grey houses" of this still-impoverished place, the willows and ruins appear natural features of the western Irish countryside, pocked as it has been for centuries with the terrible beauty of hundreds of ruined castles and cottages among its fields. The poem's insistence on the presence of war, however, reminds the reader that ruined castles are the souvenirs of war and aggression. Ireland's picturesque willows and ruins suddenly weep into the willows and ruins to be deposited across Europe in the wake of this new conflict. September 1939 and the new war return meaning to the ruins of Yeats country, so that the war that comes down on us *here* is two things at once: the ghostly presence of the wars that lurk in Galway's own ruins as well as the beginning of World War II coming down, insistently "here," deneutralizing even dreamy Galway.

"The Same Again, but Different": Repetition, Refrain, *Springboard*

Most critics who have written of the Yeatsian echoes in MacNeice's wartime work have limited themselves to a handful of poems like "The Closing Album" sequence and "Neutrality." But Yeats's influence is heard throughout both *Plant and Phantom* and *Springboard*, and being attuned to this allows one to tease out the complexities of these poems. Nowhere is this more evident than in MacNeice's use of refrain. Neil Corcoran suggests that MacNeice's "own practice [of refrain] was at least sanctioned by Yeats."[35] It was also sanctioned by historical circumstance. As MacNeice asks in the opening lines of, "Carrick Revisited," "Back to Carrick, the castle as plumb assured / As thirty years ago—Which war was which?"[36] In many of MacNeice's poems of the 1940s, the First World War shadows the Second, as it did for many writers who lived through both wars.[37] If World War II can be read as an altered repetition of World War I, a historical refrain, it is easy to see why MacNeice found refrain to be a congenial rhetorical device for his poems.

In *The Poetry of W. B. Yeats*, MacNeice takes special care to examine Yeats's use of the device. Yeats uses refrain in every volume of poetry across his fifty-year career; in his chapter on the "Crazy Jane" poems, MacNeice notes that "it is worth considering the principle of refrain at some length because refrain in the twentieth century was in many circles for a long time under taboo. [It] is argued that in the modern world [refrain] must seem an affectation . . . This argument is based on the assumption that a complex, unmusical world demands—in all cases—complex, unmusical poetry—an assumption which Yeats never made" (145–46). MacNeice never made that assumption either, which may be one of the reasons that Yeats's aesthetic appealed to him above the more "unmusical" verse of other first-generation modernists like Pound and Stein. It is perhaps also the reason behind critical comments like Anthony Thwaite's assessment of MacNeice as a "very readable . . . never boring" craftsman of verse of a "general lightness" and other contemporary critiques that MacNeice's poetry is all surface brightness and no substance.[38] But Terence Brown has asserted that MacNeice is really "a technical virtuoso . . . a professional poet."[39] A rigorously trained classicist, MacNeice applied rigorous classical methods to his verse, utilizing the full range of schemes, tropes, rhymes, meter, and form.[40] This makes his poetry sometimes surprisingly difficult. If rhetoric is often derided as style without substance, MacNeice's rhetorical flair—the true substance of his style—may account for oversimplified readings of his poems. Poetry, the native home of rhetorical language, is made more complex, not less so, by such formal craft.

MacNeice employs refrain in more than a dozen poems in *Plant and Phantom* and *Springboard*, most memorably in "Galway" ("The war came down on us here") and the haunting "*Come back early or never come*" in "Autobiography." Refrains are, of course, another form of doubling, particularly in "Autobiography," which contains its own epanaleptic echo in the repetition of "come" at the refrain's beginning and end. Sometimes, a slight variance between stanzas (as in Yeats's "The Stolen Child" or MacNeice's "The Trolls") effects an eerie sense of displacement, of the semblable's not-quite-exactitude. Like an uncanny double, a refrain is its own self, but different. MacNeice remarks in the chapter on Yeats's "Crazy Jane" poems, "If you know what my whole self and my only self is, you know a lot more than I do. As far as I can make out, I not only have many different selves but am often, as they say, not myself at all. Maybe it is just when I am not myself—when I am thrown out of gear by circumstances or emotion—that I feel like writing poetry" (146). This sense of not always being quite one's—or *one*—self pervades modern poetry in general and MacNeice's wartime poetry in particular. It is fundamental to Yeats's poetics, for example, in his doctrine of the mask. That MacNeice notes this modernist schizophrenia in his section on refrains indicates that he was also applying such conceptions at the level of his craft. The refrain is the voice of the multiplied self—often in MacNeice it is the self shattered by war's disruption of public and private spheres, and it is just as often the neutral self, the self in an "intermediate state or condition, not clearly one thing or another."[41] From Yeats's refrains to MacNeice's one hears an echo between the two wars, this second war itself a sinister refrain.

MacNeice's 1943 poem "Nuts in May" may indeed have roots in the poet's interest in Yeats's similarly songlike "Crazy Jane" verses, and it provides a telling example of MacNeice's use of refrain to simultaneously highlight similarities and differentiate concepts. Borrowing the title and meter from an English nursery rhyme often sung as a coupling game, MacNeice distorts a familiarly innocent melody into something sinister, just as he uses refrain to both couple and divide peace and war, one spring and another. The poem opens with a driving anaphora:

> May come up with bird-din
> And May come up with sun-dint,
> May come up with water-wheels
>   And May come up with iris. (1–4)

The play on the word "May" gives this quatrain an incantatory quality, as though the month of May is a prayer that spring "may" arrive. No less so does the repetition in this stanza suggest a third meaning: the verbal "may" of potentiality, which, highlighted by the *i* sounds and spondaic slant rhymes of "din," "dint," and "iris," takes on an ominous sheen, as though this little rhyme is suggesting a "May" that may or may not happen. The tension is fulfilled by the portentous second stanza, which intensifies the first stanza's combination of nursery-song meter and rhyme scheme with threatening content:

> In the sun-peppered meadow the shepherds are old,
> Their flutes are broken and their tales are told,
> And their ears are deaf when the guns unfold
>   The new philosophy over the wold. (5–8)

Here, MacNeice deliberately calls up the imagery of quintessentially English Arcadian poetry—shepherds and meadows and wolds—in order to deny the validity of its succor. Arcadian poetry was important to the Georgian poets of World War I, who, schooled in its lyrics throughout their boyhoods, used Arcadian imagery (often ironically) both to counterpoint the horrors of the trenches and to provide imaginative landscapes for temporary escape.[42] For MacNeice, this pastoral form is old, broken, and deaf, without music in the face of the "new philosophy" and noise of guns.[43] And so the poem's third stanza repeats the first, with a difference. Instead of "bird-din," "sun-dint," "water-wheels" and "iris," May now "come[s] up with" "pollen of death," "cordite," "a chinagraph" and "a stopwatch" (9–12). Now pollen is the explosive powder of a cordite bomb, and the temporal progression of the season is a stopwatch ticking down the minutes to—instead of blossom—explosion. The sixth and penultimate stanza in this symmetrical poem is the only one to break the dominant tetrameter scheme of these *aaaa* quatrains, in which the double couplets repeat rhyme to the breaking point:

> Yes, angels are frigid and shepherds are dumb,
> There is no holy water when the enemy come,
> The trees are askew and the skies are a-hum
>   And you have to keep mum and go to it and die for your life
>   and keep mum. (21–24)

Here that anapestic nursery-rhyme rhythm breaks down, for instead of falling silent after the propagandist dictum, "keep mum," the line continues with an off-the-rails energy through a second propagandistic cliché ("go to it") into the strange paradox of "die for your life" (a phrase reminiscent of both the energy and philosophy of the same volume's "Prayer Before Birth") before tumbling back out into another reminder to "keep mum," here given a second, talismanic repetition.[44] The ironic repetition of "keep mum" in this line manages to upset the stanza's form and keep the stanza's rhyme scheme at the same time. Though the rhyming word is "mum," visually and metrically the stanza ought to end with "die" (the fourth stressed syllable), so it feels as if a fear of death keeps the line reeling from its expected finality. The formal simplicity of the rest of the poem enhances the impact of this renegade line. MacNeice's use of unexpected forms of repetition here works to disrupt simple oppositions of war and the pastoral, birds and bombers, while the run-on line attacks the impersonal mandate of propaganda (the speaker cannot, after all, "keep mum," no matter that the rhyme scheme demands it) and undermines the paradoxical statement "die for your life" by metrically ending with "die."

The final stanza of "Nuts in May" uses two different forms of repetition, the anaphora of lines 25–27 and the anadiplosis in lines 27–28, to suggest that perhaps what the Second World War presents is an altered repetition, something that is both familiar and unfamiliar, perhaps less divorced than uncanny. Once again, there's a return to the pastoral: "May come up with fiddle-bows, / May come up with blossom" (25–26), but it's undercut by the ominous final lines, "May come up the same again, / The same again but different" (27–28). Peace and war, like May 1939 and May 1940, and even war and war—like the two world wars—are doubles of each other, in which the second incorporates the meanings of the first and adds to it, "the same again but different." This maps onto the ways in which, in "The Closing Album," neutral Ireland and wartime England are the same, but different.

If "Carrick Revisited" asks "which war was which," MacNeice's original "Carrickfergus," with its description of the town during the Great War, its "mill girls, the smell of porter, the salt-mines / And the soldiers with their guns" (43–44), reminds the reader of a fundamental difference in the way the two wars mapped out. For in "Carrickfergus" MacNeice notes the ubiquitous "maps above the fireplace / With flags on pins moving across and across" (35–36): the entrenched cartography of the war. Nothing was so conceptually tidy about the space of World War II. If those "flags on pins" were the Great War civilian's means of bringing the war into the home, the bombs of the Second World War literalized the metaphor.

The Great War's bloody geography of trenches ensured that many representations of the war would follow the same lines: self/other, us/them, a face-off. According to Paul Fussell, the deployment of binary structures is typical of Great War poetry. Fussell traces the "gross dichotomizing . . . a persisting imaginative habit of modern times" to the "actualities of the Great War."[45] Prolonged trench warfare, he argues, "establishes a model of modern political, social, artistic, and psychological polarization. The most indispensable concept underlying the energies of modern writing is that of 'the enemy'" (76). This friend/foe system creates what Fussell calls "the modern *versus* habit," which results in a "rhetoric of binary deadlock" (79) that admits no "Hegelian hope of synthesis" (77). Fussell argues that the either/or rhetoric established in the Great War is a foundational trope of modern writing. It is, however, not without aesthetic drawbacks: "Simple antithesis everywhere. That is the atmosphere in which most poems of the Great War take place, and that is the reason for the failure of most of them as durable art" (82). Though this judgment—like Yeats's dismissal of Wilfred Owen ("passive suffering is not a theme for poetry")[46]—rings overly harsh, Fussell's attention to the dualistic legacy of Great War poetry helps explain how MacNeice's poetry of World War II fundamentally departs from the Great War poetry to which it consciously alludes.

Yeats's poetry dealing with the Great War is deliberately ambiguous about the conflict, yet a poem like "An Irish Airman Foresees His Death" is still reliant on a dualistic construction.[47] Yeats's pilot speaker (modeled on Major Robert Gregory), finds that "those that I fight I do not hate / Those that I guard I do not love" (3–4). This Irish airman appears to be a strange oxymoron: a neutral combatant.[48] He fights, but fights without allegiance to England or hatred of Germany.[49] Though the speaker's deliberate ambivalence places him outside the friend/enemy dualism, the poem's rhetorical balance—like an airplane balanced between two wings—relies on its stability. There is no option beyond hate or love, merely the ambivalent negation of each. The poem's closing chiasmus,

> I balanced all, brought all to mind,
> The years to come seemed waste of breath,
> A waste of breath the years behind
> In balance with this life, this death. (13–16)

relies on oppositional constructions such as future/past, life/death, to "balance" the rhetorical and formal designs of the poem.

"The Springboard," the title poem of MacNeice's 1944 volume, is deeply indebted to Yeats's "Irish Airman." But MacNeice's allusive airman, the suicidal subject who will "dive like a bomber," suffers from a more inchoate ambivalence while perched "high above London, naked in the night" (2, 18). MacNeice's diver knows "only too well / That circumstances called for sacrifice," but he knows, too, that his death will not "mend the world" (6–7, 11). While Major Gregory's foreseen death appears a consummation of sprezzatura, a "lonely impulse of delight" (11), MacNeice's suicide is fearful, uncertain, shivering over his decision. The poems' formal designs enhance this difference: "Irish Airman's" four symmetrical quatrains rhyming *abab* present a formal balance, compared with "The Springboard's" four five-line stanzas, whose rhyme scheme *abcbc* leaves each stanza's first line to hang untethered, uncertain as the diver himself. Yeats's airman may be ambivalent, but the voice is ever certain, the confident voice of the master poet (or at least, in Gregory's case, the master of an estate). MacNeice takes Yeats's "lonely impulse of delight" and recasts it into a poem whose messy subject's "blood began to haggle over the price / History would pay if he were to throw himself down" (9–10).

Even "The Springboard's" Crucifixion imagery—a common motif in poetry of both wars—is off-kilter. Both poems invoke it; Yeats's use of the chiasmus alludes to the shape of a cross, which itself recalls the design of an early airplane. But whereas Yeats's airman denies any sacrificial meaning to his death, MacNeice's suicide "diver" (whose nakedness implies an ununiformed, perhaps civilian, position; he is certainly not acting under orders, as an airman would) struggles with death as a sort of unmeaning sacrifice. It is "more than fright / That kept him crucified among the budding stars," the speaker explains, "it was unbelief" (4–6). Only if his death "would mend the world," the would-be diver thinks, would it "be worth while" (11) to jump. But like Yeats's airman, MacNeice's diver knows his death cannot heal the broken world:

> But he, quite rightly, long had ceased to believe
> In any Utopia or Peace-upon-Earth;
> His friends would find in his death neither ransom nor reprieve
> But only a grain of faith—for what it was worth.[50] (12–15)

Neither Yeats's airman nor MacNeice's diver has illusions about the impact of his death, but the sense of perfect balance in Yeats's lines,

> My country is Kiltartan Cross,
> My countrymen Kiltartan's poor,
> No likely end could bring them loss
> Or leave them happier than before. (5–8)

is absent from MacNeice's poem, in which the subject's friends will find "neither ransom nor reprieve." Kiltartan's poor appear to be equally short of happiness and at risk of loss, but MacNeice's Londoners are in certain need of rescue. There is no such balance in MacNeice's poem; the sense of a carefully constructed binary is askew. Though Yeats's "Irish Airman" "foresees" his death, the actual poem keeps his balanced plane aloft. While the liminal zone between opposite forces is always a productive space for Yeats, in MacNeice's poem, such balance cannot be sustained: the figurative plane must crash in the final stanza.

Unlike Yeats's poetry, its dialectical motion generally kept in check by the poet's vatic voice, "The Springboard" shifts its voice and point of view from the watchful "I" of the first stanza to third-person narration in the second and third, then to a speculative "we" in the fourth. MacNeice's poem does not witness the diver's suicide but visualizes it in the first-person plural, makes it speculative and shared:

> And yet we know he knows what he must do.
> There above London where the gargoyles grin
> He will dive like a bomber past the broken steeple,
> One man wiping out his own original sin
> And, like ten million others, dying for the people. (16–20)

The logic is far from dialectical. By an act of singularity—"One man wiping out his own original sin"—the diver will, Christ-like in his doubter's crucifixion, share his guilt, die for the people. There is something subversive in this death. First, by likening him to a bomber over London, MacNeice hints at a figurative treason: Luftwaffe bombers over London are there to destroy the city, not themselves. The Luftwaffe pilot represents the epitome of the enemy other in most Battle of Britain literature, but MacNeice's diver internalizes the friend/enemy dualism, wiping out distinctions. Second, if the suicide dies "like ten million others . . . for the people," his death is truly antipropagandistic: it ironizes the war's vaunted casualties, civilian and combatant, by making suicide equivalent to death by war action—not to mention that any chance of salvation, peace, or Utopia is precanceled by the third stanza. This poem, astonishing in its visual imagery, refuses an opposition between sin and salvation or self and other. The final stanza's conflation of "I" into "we" and the death of this singular suicide into "ten million others" confounds the expected uses of words like "crucified" and "sacrifice" by eliminating their figurative exchange of death for life. In this vision, a soul can neither "mend the world" through prayer, like one of Kavanagh's or Devlin's supplicants, nor can he sacrifice himself to save the city, RAF-style. Instead, MacNeice presents an ironic antihero "wiping out his own original sin." MacNeice is not, in this admittedly strange poem, conflating the two sides of the war, but he attacks the notion of a righteous individual sacrifice. While the poem deliberately recalls imagery from the First World War, it presents a new type of war casualty that renders the friend/enemy dualism down to one unit: the complicit, destructive self.

The sense of complicity that underlies MacNeice's World War II poetry is the result of a new kind of war, a war that to MacNeice was both inevitable and undesirable, albeit necessary. Like many leftist thinkers in his coterie, MacNeice was troubled by the idea that civilians were complicit in a "war machine" that destroyed individual agency. As the "Prayer Before Birth" begs, "I am not yet born; O fill me / With strength against those who would freeze my / humanity, would dragoon me into a lethal automaton / would make me a cog in a machine" (28–31). As a leftist, he was critical of the political establishment and skeptical of the notion that the "good guys" (Tories masterminding the war effort) were of unalloyed good, no matter how evil the forces they opposed. Where Kavanagh's and Devlin's pilgrims ask forgiveness for their own personal sins, MacNeice's prenatal petition begs forgiveness for "my treason engendered by traitors beyond me, / my life when they murder by means of my / hands" (15–17). In this poem, original sin is not just inescapable, it is imposed by powers outside the self, which is complicit in crimes of murder or treason, regardless of personal intention.

MacNeice's use of George Herbert's line, "Even poisons praise thee" as an epigraph for "Prayer Before Birth" offers a link between the discourses of original sin in that poem, which opens the collection, and the title poem, "The Springboard." Here one sees MacNeice the bishop's son reaching back to a very English form of religious poetry; "Prayer Before Birth" has a formatting reminiscent of Herbert's "Easter Wings" but without the symmetry. As with "The Springboard," this "Prayer" relies on the stability of earlier forms (here, Herbert's metaphysical Christianity) in order to reveal their modern destabilization. The epigraph for MacNeice's poem comes from a stanza near the end of Herbert's "Providence" (1633):

> Ev'n poysons praise thee. Should a thing be lost?
> Should creatures want for want of heed their due?
> Since where are poysons, antidots are most:
> The help stands close, and keeps the fear in view.[51]

Counterpointing Herbert's extolling list of God's creations, MacNeice's poem opens, "I am not yet born; O hear me. / Let not the bloodsucking bat or the rat or the stoat or the / club-footed ghoul come near me" (1–3). Herbert counterpoises poison with antidote, suggesting that the former points us to the surplus of the latter; MacNeice, on the other hand, sees the "fear in view" while suggesting no earthly "help stands close." Herbert's speaker offers the poem itself as salvific, explaining, "Man is the worlds high Priest: he doth present / The sacrifice for all" (13–14), and so, "most sacred Spirit, here I present / For me and all my fellows praise to thee" (25–26). It is "just," the speaker explains, "that I should pay the rent / Because the benefit accrues to me" (27–28). MacNeice's wartime poems find his speakers in a world where antidotes are absent, sacrifice is meaningless, and certainly no benefit "accrues" to those who give themselves to the war or the machine. In referencing Herbert, MacNeice offers another bent repetition, a contortion of his bishop father's Anglican theology in which the sacrificial lamb can only wipe out his own sin and the antidote seems complicit with the poison.

MacNeice's worry about complicity is upheld by the fact that the Second World War involved civilians in ways and numbers never before seen. Civilian mortality in the Great War accounted for 6.5 million (or 43 percent) of the 15 million total deaths, while civilian deaths in World War II are generally counted as 60 percent, or 30 million, of the 50 million total combat-related deaths (not including the mass killings of civilians conducted by Hitler's, Stalin's, and other regimes).[52] Aerial civilian bombardment changed the meaning of the home front in Britain, making combatants of nearly everyone. War had taken the metaphor out of the "home front," and the line between civilian and soldier poets blurred. As a civilian poet, MacNeice wrote about air raids, bombings, and casualties of war as an eye witness. The sense of complicity in his poems belies firm divisions between home and front, peace and war, even the belligerence of his London and the neutrality of his native Ireland. This is achieved formally through MacNeice's use of various forms of repetition, like refrain and reflexive imagery, with which he generates both contrast and correspondence, alluding to the established system of oppositional thinking but, often as not, collapsing it by the end of the poem. Instead of creating a dialectic that moves toward resolution, MacNeice's war poems demonstrate a process of formal and tropological conflation.

"Bad War Poetry": Duplicitous Doubles in *Springboard*

The language of war is a language of doubleness, of duplicity—not a language of external oppositions, rights and wrongs (this is the language of propaganda), but a language of multiple overlapping and sometimes conflicting meanings and intentions. In "Conversation," for example, MacNeice explores the impact of wartime life on human interaction:

> Ordinary people are peculiar too:
> Watch the vagrant in their eyes
> Who sneaks away while they are talking with you
> Into some black wood behind the skull (1–4)

The man in "Conversation" is doubled: himself and the vagrant in his eyes. This vagrant may or may not be the threatening other, engaged in duplicity (as in Bowen's *The Heat of the Day*). Or it may be the vagrant desire of the escapist, represented for MacNeice by neutrality and a Yeatsian dreamscape of the West of Ireland. In "Conversation," man's second nature is given its own agency, a sort of runaway reflexive metaphor, in which the vagrant "sneaks" off with the rest of the poem. It concludes,

> Vagrancy however is forbidden; ordinary men
> Soon come back to normal, look you straight
> In the eyes as if to say 'It will not happen again',
> Put up a barrage of common sense to baulk
> Intimacy but by mistake interpolate
> Swear-words like roses in their talk. (13–18)

By "mistake," the poem insists, we "interpolate" more than we ought; swear words to balk closeness become—like the strange intimacy of the murderer and victim in "Dublin"—gestures of intimacy, like roses, in our talk. The presence of roses may remind readers of MacNeice of "Snow," in which roses point to the strange surplus of a world perceived through the two sides of the glass. The desire for vagrancy, like the desire for simultaneity in "Snow," is for MacNeice an entrenched part of human nature. In "Conversation," language itself creates a framework for escape, a process of incessant interpolation, forever adding something to that space "between the snow and the huge roses" ("Snow," 12). The interpolated language in "Conversation" reminds one of the vagrant language of wartime, in which codes, secrets, and foreign tongues proliferate meanings.

This view of war language as duplicitous mirrors the poet's view of war itself. For MacNeice, war "was a choice of evils and . . . it was clear which was the lesser. But it is hard to risk your life for a Lesser Evil on the off-chance of some entirely problematical betterment for most likely a mere minority in a dubious and dirty future."[53] Particularly from the vantage point of his return to London in 1940, a sense of dubious doubleness reigned in MacNeice's poetic subject matter and rhetoric. In *Plant and Phantom* and *Springboard*, the duplicity of that choice of evils—the bad and the worse—is carried into the duplicity of human nature itself. The volumes are full of strange doubles, like the "vagrant" in "Conversation" and the subject of "The Gardener," a man whose being "not quite all there" (6) implies a mysterious sense of surplus, of being "here" and "elsewhere" at once, not unlike Yeats's Crazy Jane. The poems are not straightforward manifestations of the self-enemy external dualism but of doubles existing simultaneously (and dangerously) within the subject. As with Bowen's use of the wartime "saving hallucination,"[54] MacNeice's poems witness to the desire to exempt oneself from the war (to be "not all there") that yet lurks beneath a cagey willingness to commit or be committed.

Springboard has a nervousness to it, a conglomeration of all its doubled refrains and petitions, and of the interspersing of poems with very short lines, like the nervous chatter in the refrain of "The Libertine," "leave me easy, leave me alone" (5). Like "Conversation," the poems in *Springboard* are worried about communication, the ability of words to get from one place to another, making sense. In "Babel," the eponymous tower itself has "nerves," and the double refrain, repeating on lines 2 and 4 of each of the four quatrains, worries over the ability to communicate: "Can't we ever, my love, speak in the same language?" "Have we no aims in common?" The poem hints that the tower's fall might be prevented if, by mastering language, humankind found some "aims in common." This hope, of course, was the idea behind the League of Nations, which failed to prevent a second "war to end all wars." Instead, the speaker finds that "exiles all as we are in a foreign city"; instead of being in league, everyone is now an outsider (9). The awkwardness of the syntax, when "we are all exiles" would do, foregrounds the loneliness of the exile and speaks to the difficulty of language for the exilic self. Terence Brown says of MacNeice that "he was the true exile . . . exile from Ireland left him, finally, a stranger everywhere."[55] As in *Autumn Journal*, in "Babel" MacNeice conflates Europe's "family drama" with a pair of lovers' failure to communicate. The poem's babble of refrain evokes the babel of European radio airspace in wartime, with each belligerent nation broadcasting propaganda to the other. The penultimate line's "shall we go, still quarrelling over words, to the wall?" (15) recalls Field Marshal Haig's famous "backs to the wall" order of World War I, which was often recycled by Churchill in radio broadcasts.[56] Words in the tower, words in the air—the poem destabilizes Churchill's development of an imagined community of Britain at war by imagining that community as part of the doomed Tower of Babel.

In *The Poetry of W. B. Yeats* (and in his other public responses to the Auden emigration controversy), MacNeice writes about the different roles of propaganda and poetry. After the Spanish Civil War, MacNeice was the more convinced that these two realms should remain separate.[57] In early 1939, MacNeice was concerned that the armchair route of going to work for the "Ministry of Propaganda," as he termed it in a letter to Eleanor Clark, would force him to sacrifice his values as a writer. "If one's going to be defiled," he said, "one may as well keep one's mind out of it."[58] By November, his stance (and his relationship with Clark) had shifted a bit; if he were to join the war effort, which he felt he ultimately must do, MacNeice wanted no special treatment. He wrote to E. R. Dodds, "If it is my war, I feel I ought to get involved in it in one of the more unpleasant ways. Ignoring the argument that writers are more use writing" (367). This would mean, he continued, "allowing myself to be . . . conscripted. Joining up, I think, would be over-doing it" (367). In no hurry to "over-do" things, MacNeice may have seen conscription as both the path of least resistance and the option that least compromised his intellectual faculties.

In "Louis MacNeice's War," Peter McDonald writes, "MacNeice's darker poetry of the Home Front looks harder and more searchingly at issues of complicity and guilt than much of the writing of its time."[59] This echoes the fact that the choice to turn propagandist was not completely his own. Rejected by the Royal Navy, MacNeice returned to London in December 1940 as an "ex-expatriate" and took up a post in the (broadly propagandist) Features Department of the BBC.[60] Having defended Auden's emigration, MacNeice carefully constructed the public version of his own return, remarking in *Penguin New Writing* that he was returning to London "not because I thought I could be more *useful* in England than in America, but because I wanted to see these things for myself . . . I thought that if I stayed another year out of England I should have to stay out for good, having missed so much history, lost touch."[61] (It didn't hurt that the relationship with Clark seemed to be in a permanent holding pattern.) As Eliot and Pound did during the Great War, MacNeice made his dangerous way to a wartime London because, as a writer, he didn't want to miss history.[62] In the same essay, MacNeice goes on to say, "I have never really thought of myself as British; if there is one country I feel at home in, it is Éire . . . but I am glad to be back in England and, in particular, London" (82). It is from the point of view of an outsider that MacNeice went to London to write the war, and this may help explain why one can see in his poetry—what John Stallworthy calls "the work of the right hand"—a more complex consciousness at work than in his propaganda, "the work of the left" (227).

An essay called "The Morning after the Blitz" in the May 1941 *Picture Post* gives a sense of MacNeice's propaganda writing. MacNeice discusses wandering London the morning after a giant air raid. He sees, "All these shattered shops and blazing stores, this cataract of broken glass, this holocaust of hall-marked and dog's-eared property—there was a voice inside me which (ignoring all the suffering and wastage involved) kept saying, as I watched a building burning or demolished: 'Let her go up!' or 'Let her come down. Let them all go. Write them all off. Stone walls do not a city make.'"[63] This sentiment is in keeping with the propaganda message, "London can take it." The essay goes on to mention wisecracking survivors and upbeat booksellers with shops full of broken glass. But MacNeice uses this same material quite differently when he turns it into poetry. In "Brother Fire," the cry to "Let her go up!" is transmuted to the more violent call, "Destroy! Destroy!" in which the fire-watching speaker "echoes" the fire's "thoughts" in his own (18). To the speaker of the poem, the fire raid's "gluttony" is but "Lenten fare," and there's no disguising the dark catharsis of pure destruction (7).

Contemporary critics noticed the difference between these two modes, and *Springboard* came out to mixed reviews, several of them hostile. As Peter McDonald puts it, the volume "seemed to be bad war poetry (as, in the propagandist sense, it is)."[64] The American critic Coleman Rosenberger, reviewing both Louis MacNeice and French Resistance poet Louis Aragon, writes, "A comparison of MacNeice's translation of Aragon's *Richard Coeur-de-Lion* with any of MacNeice's own poems written during the same period suggests why the French poet became the leader of the popular Resistance movement while the English remained a lonely commentator talking to himself. [MacNeice's] are not poems to rally resistance but are poems of shared guilt. MacNeice cannot see the beam in his enemy's eye for the mote in his own."[65] What makes *Springboard* "bad war poetry" for Rosenberger is MacNeice's refusal to play into the oppositional system of us and them. McDonald remarks on the volume's awareness that "war involved even the individual who is not in active service in a degree of (perceived or actual) guilt," as "Prayer Before Birth" clearly demonstrates.[66] MacNeice's awareness of guilt extended, furthermore, to citizens of neutral Ireland. In Éire, the impact (and even, from some vantages, the sights and sounds) of Europe's war could not be ignored. Individuals who remained intellectually or emotionally neutral made, as MacNeice's poetry reveals, a moral choice of their own. In the poems of *Springboard*, the ramifications of war guilt—for the soldier, the noncombatant, and the neutral—are not merely expressed at the level of content but are also deeply woven into the poems' formal designs through repetition and reflexive imagery. Wartime complicity (that is, the belligerent's in the "war machine" and the neutral's in escapism or passive collusion with the fascist threat) was not just a matter of ethics for this nonneutral Irishman but something deeply inwoven into language itself.

Springboard develops the theme of shared and inborn guilt through tropes of suicide, murder, and cannibalism. In this way, MacNeice distills the collective murderousness of war down to something individually digestible. In "Thyestes," digestion itself is the crime. MacNeice retells the story of Sophocles's king, who is tricked, at a banquet, into eating his own children. The speaker asks, "When the King sat down to the feast and the golden lid revealed / The human cutlets . . . / Didn't he know—or did he—what he was eating?" (1–2, 5).[67] The question is doubled back, asked twice in mirror formats; this gives it an air of suspicious doubt as it points to the darkness inherent in the scheme of repetition, which is, after all, a digestion and reincorporation. On another level, the scheme of repetition mimics Thyestes's children's relation to their father ("the same again, but different"). If cannibalism is the ultimate crime of complicity, of incorporating the other into the self, the taboo is heightened when that other is, in fact, genetically part of the cannibal's self, his child. In this sense, Thyestes has cannibalized a part of himself.

The second stanza goes on to remark, "Thus Here and We, neither of which is what / The mind and map admit, in perfidy are linked" (6–7). As in "Babel," in "Thyestes" the inversion of syntax (a technique MacNeice uses seldom enough that it grabs attention when he does) troubles the sentence's flow, forcing the reader to hesitate and reread. "Here and We," "mind and map," recall that the geographical boundaries of war—that demolition of atlases[68]—are also constructs of the human mind. People and place are linked "in perfidy," like the shared guilt of the self and other. Nowhere might this resonate more than in MacNeice's native Ulster, where "mind and map admit" to different versions of "Here and We," depending on who is talking. To recall that Northern Ireland's contested border was also the border between war and neutrality is not too much of a reach for this poem's geography. The stanza finishes, "This green foam frets away our sense of duty / While we, who watch it blossom and bulge, are not / Spectators in our hearts but murderers of beauty" (8–10). An echo of the failed pastoral longings in "The Closing Album" is audible, as the famously (snot-)green Irish sea seems to be the Lethe envisioned here. To watch it rise and recede (full of drowned sailors, but we'll get to that) is not to be merely escapist but murderous.

"Thyestes" concludes with yet another upending of Crucifixion imagery, claiming that "we" are not just murderers of beauty but "messmates in the eucharist of crime / And heirs to two of those three black crosses on the hill" (14). The word "messmates" indicates that this is a martial, rather than an ecclesiastical, sort of eucharist, while the context of cannibalism is a reminder of the gruesomeness inherent in the concept of Eucharist: eating Christ's body and drinking Christ's blood. If this martial eucharist is a metaphor for the sacrifice demanded in fighting a "good war," for the necessity to die to combat fascism, it is a metaphor that indicates what darker crimes underlie the idea of sacrifice. For in a world where men "garnish to pollute and breed to kill" (13), the breeding of cannon fodder is akin to Thyestes's cannibalism of his children. Meanwhile, the "we" of the poem are perfidiously linked to the map, no matter which side of the green sea they stand on. Equally, the poem's "we" are to inherit the two thieves' crosses at Golgotha, only one of which will be saved. But which?

"Brother Fire," a parable poem about the morning after an air raid, opens with another cannibalistic image of kinship between the forces of life and of destruction. Here the routine of putting out fires caused by incendiary bombs—generally vaunted in Blitz mythology as the collective, heroic work of Londoners who "can take it"—is transmuted into a "shared guilt" rather than a shared virtue:

> When our brother Fire was having his dog's day
> Jumping the London streets with millions of tin cans
> Clanking at his tail, we heard some shadow say

> 'Give the dog a bone'—and so we gave him ours;
> Night after night we watched him slaver and crunch away
> The beams of human life, the tops of topless towers. (1–6)

MacNeice himself notes the dangerous doubleness of fire in the 1942 essay "Broken Windows," where he writes, "All fire destroys but we use it on our hearths & in our furnaces."[69] It is this duplicitous nature, the intimacy we share with our murderers, that he plays upon in calling fire "brother," referencing again that genetic repetition of kinship: sameness in difference. But what is really striking about "Brother Fire" is the pair of reflexive metaphors that motivate the poem. In *The Force of Poetry*, Christopher Ricks writes that the "reflexive" image is "that which goes beyond saying of something that it *finds* its own resemblance, and says instead, more wittily and mysteriously, that something *is* its own resemblance. [It is indicative of] balance and yet conflict; inclusion and yet exclusion; withdrawal and yet emergence; microcosm and yet macrocosm; self and yet all else."[70] As in any trope of repetition, words and subjects in reflexive images become the same again, but different. In the case of "Brother Fire," the Fire's "dog's day" transmutes it into a dog itself, allowing it, through the next cliché, "'Give the dog a bone'—and so we gave him ours," to literally run away with the poem. The easy collusion between the dog and the speaker (the people) is indicated by the offhand nature of the clichéd remark, "Give the dog a bone" and how easily this throwaway language becomes a complied-with request, "throwaway" language figuratively throwing away the whole city. The pluralized speaker, embodying the voice of London, then gives the fire-dog "our" bone—"our" autonomy—acting out the unholy complicity inherent in this brotherhood with fire and with "man's best friend."

In the third stanza, the voice of the city addresses its "brother," calling, "O delicate walker, babbler, dialectician Fire, / O enemy and image of ourselves" (13–14), and asking,

> Did we not on those mornings after the All Clear,
> When you were looting shops in elemental joy
> And singing as you swarmed up city block and spire,
> Echo your thoughts in ours? 'Destroy! Destroy!' (15–18)

Having acknowledged in the second stanza that the dog's "gluttony" was but "Lenten fare" to the people, the complicity between the voice and its semblable, Fire, is intensified.[71] The firebombs' destruction of the city is only bread and water compared with the people's unacknowledgeable lust for catharsis. "Brother Fire" echoes the cannibalistic imagery of "Thyestes," this time speculating on a type of king who certainly knew what he was eating. The voice of the city, after all, has willingly given its own bones for the fire-dog to munch.

Not merely the imagery in this poem but also the rhetoric is reflexive. The speaker echoes his own metaphor in the shout of "Destroy! Destroy!" Edna Longley notes that in this poem "the manipulation of language" is associated with "the destructive urge" (88). Indeed, the very manipulation of language that creates the rhyme between "joy" and "Destroy" conflates the joy in poetry's musical elements with the destruction inherent in this poem's matter (as the assonance of "you" "looting shops" loosens the line like music, at the same time drawing dark connections). The almost baroque intensity of MacNeice's style, his layering of sound and rhyme, creates an atmosphere of decadent destruction. The alliteration of "singing," "swarmed," "city," and "spire" in the penultimate line, for example, connects the joy of song with a sonic reminder of the relation of the "dog" to the spiraling Luftwaffe bombers. The poem's creative language of destruction indicates the dangerousness inherent in language, that which creates and also destroys. In its particular description of "Fire" as a "dialectician," the poem reminds us of the poet's own dialectical practices, which in *Springboard* so often end (as here) in destruction rather than constructive resolution. Echoes and reflexive images underwrite this multiplied speaker's relationship with war; it is a relationship of doubled urges: at once to create—to write, to sing—and to destroy.

"Brother Fire," a poem about duplicitous doubling—the speaker's multiple selves and their "enemy and image"—presents MacNeice as a poet whose ideas about war are far from cut-and-dried, propagandistically approved. The poem centers on how a person in wartime can be her own destroyer, can give the dog of fire her own bones. The speaker of "Brother Fire" is far from patriotic, far, even, from neutral; like a double agent, he is both loyalist and traitor to himself. MacNeice's other highly canonized war poem, "Neutrality," also concerns questions of loyalty and kinship in wartime, but this time in a context apparently removed from the siege of

London: neutral Ireland's western coast. "Neutrality," too, is a poem of duplicitous doubles; in this case the doubles are Ireland, "The neutral island facing the Atlantic," and the human heart, "The neutral island in the heart of man" (1–2). Instead of pairing the human element with an easily identifiable "enemy" of itself, as in "Brother Fire," "Neutrality" pairs it with a concept that in the Emergency signed itself as benign, pacifist, and, in de Valera's rendering, morally correct. In "Neutrality," MacNeice draws out the "vagrant" desires in the *Springboard* volume, playing further on the reflexive imagery of cannibalism and kinship in "Thyestes" and "Brother Fire" to uncover the dark complicity within the concept of neutrality—but also in the ordinary human heart.

Terence Brown noted in 1999 that "Neutrality" is often read "too literally."[72] In 1975, Brown found the poem "a savage indictment" of Ireland's "callous self-absorption," and this has been the standard reading since the poem was published.[73] It has been called "bitter invective"[74] by Richard Danson Brown and "a political and hostile view of [Irish] policy" by Edna Longley.[75] Declan Kiberd writes that in the poem MacNeice's "deep contempt for Ireland's policy" is "crude[ly]" evident.[76] The general critical line calls the poem "angry" and "bitter" and finds in it "a clear sense of moral priority," evident of what Heather Clark calls the poet's "certainty of action."[77] But, as in most of MacNeice's best work, there is more to "Neutrality" than meets the eye. When Clair Wills suggests that in "Neutrality" "Louis MacNeice lambasted the country as a whole,"[78] she is acknowledging only half the poem's intent.

"Neutrality" opens by visually and syntactically stacking two "neutral islands" on top of each other, as mirror images:

> The neutral island facing the Atlantic,
> The neutral island in the heart of man,
> Are bitterly soft reminders of the beginnings
> That ended before the end began. (1–4)

MacNeice's opening repetition posits the two "islands" as twins, complicit with each other. The comma separating them indicates that the second line can be read as a clause describing the first; they are parallel concepts. If the poem is going to be a "savage indictment," it is an indictment of two "neutral" concepts at the same time—the Irish government's foreign policy and the war-tested chambers of the human heart. Peter McDonald's remark that "certainly, there is a level of anger here; just as certainly, there is also a level of complexity" is an important corrective.[79] The opening stanza signals a typically MacNeicean interest in complexity: the contradictory rendering "bitterly soft" and the chiasmus "the beginnings / That ended before the end began" are in keeping with MacNeice's paradoxical modes throughout *Springboard*. McDonald contends that to "debunk MacNeice's poem as a piece of crude rhetoric or propaganda would be a risky misreading" (395). Indeed, it would have to ignore the "vagrant" desires embedded throughout the volume.

Wills has written of the Irish experience of the war as something far more complicated than what the word "neutrality" connotes, something that was not "in the least like peace" (59). I believe that is a closer estimate of what MacNeice is doing in the four stanzas of "Neutrality." The subsequent three stanzas all begin by demanding a closer look—a look into the reader's own heart. In so doing, the second and third stanzas make clear references to Yeats: "Look into your heart, you will find a County Sligo" (5), the second stanza instructs. At the center there is, "A Knocknarea with for navel a cairn of stones," where "You will find the shadow and sheen of a moleskin mountain / And a litter of chronicles and bones" (6–8). Critics have not missed the Yeatsian connections here. Michael Moir suggests that by reducing "history . . . to debris" in "a Yeatsian West," in "Neutrality" MacNeice makes an "attempt to inoculate himself against the attractive fantasy the West offers."[80] In this stanza, Yeats country and the mythical past of the West of Ireland are reduced to "litter," to a bone heap, though readers of Yeats must know of the generative powers in that "rag and bone shop of the heart" of which MacNeice's speaker is demanding inspection.[81]

In the third stanza, the speaker again urges, "Look into your heart," where, this time, "you will find fermenting rivers, / Intricacies of gloom and glint" (9–10). Here, Yeatsian imagery flirts with MacNeice's own penchant for dazzle, though the archaic diction he uses to describe the escapist heart's contents, "ducats of dream and great doubloons of ceremony" (11), is roundly pejorative. These dreams are bankrupt in wartime, currencies that "nobody to-day would mint" (12). Terence Brown reads this "Yeatsian romanticism, its aristocratic celebration of ceremony," in the poem as "complicit with a kind of escapism which must be resisted . . .

a recognition that there is something deathly about such solipsistic imaginative self-regard in the face of the war."[82] Certainly, MacNeice's diction here contributes to the standard reading of the poem's bitter decisiveness. However, that same diction, so suffused with Yeats, suggests that the escapism that enthralls the heart is as alluring as it is vain. If MacNeice here makes an attempt to "enumerate old themes" from Yeats country, his heart-consciousness recalls Yeats's late masterpiece, "The Circus Animals' Desertion," and Yeats's own entanglement of "enchanted islands, allegorical dreams" with "themes of the embittered heart," themes he himself condemns as "vain."[83] And yet the heart, Yeats's poem concludes, is the very refuse pile where poetry gets its "start."

The fourth and final stanza of "Neutrality" shifts the focus from the reader's heart to the outside world:

> But then look eastward from your heart, there bulks
> A continent, close, dark, as archetypal sin,
> While to the west off your own shores the mackerel
> Are fat—on the flesh of your kin. (13–16)

The bitterness in MacNeice's diction here *is* palpable. That final flesh-eating image is particularly damning when regarded in the light of the many bodies of Allied sailors and civilians that washed up on the west coast of Ireland during the Battle of the Atlantic.[84] Because Ireland refused to lease its Atlantic ports back to the British navy, popular sentiment in the United Kingdom indicted Ireland for "murdering" those sailors sunk by U-boats, a hangover from the years of colonial rule that made Britons feel entitled to the ports of Cobh and Berehaven. In 1942, when this poem was written, its damning final stanza would have been a readily apparent allusion to this, MacNeice's analysis, according to Wills, of "the human cost of Ireland's decision" (128). But it is not as straightforward an allusion as many who cite this poem as "evidence" of MacNeice's opinion may think.[85] MacNeice himself wrote perceptively about the port situation in a "London Letter" to *Common Sense* in May 1941, admonishing that "those who propose the application of a strong hand to Éire [in taking the ports by force] are forgetting their history."[86] Ireland's decisions, he says, must be her own. If "Neutrality" is "evidence" of anything, its reception has been evidence of readers' desire for the poem to take sides, to make a statement about politics (just as MacNeice criticism has been so long bogged down in the attempt to assign him an "English" or "Irish" side). Instead, the poem makes a statement about the complicated complicity of the human heart.

"Neutrality" cannot be merely an "indictment" of Ireland's decisions, for that "neutral island" the speaker indicts is also located "in the heart of man." The repeated imperative, "Look into your heart," indicates complicity not just between the speaker and the "neutral island" but between the speaker and the reader, too. Such a second-person address is as unusual in MacNeice as the plural speaker of "Brother Fire." As the other poems in *Springboard* and *Plant and Phantom* demonstrate, the communalizing impulses of wartime prevent the speaker—and the self—from remaining singular and intact. If mankind in wartime is "not quite himself," then, "Neutrality" and "Brother Fire" suggest, he might be you as well. Just as Kavanagh's and Devlin's shifting pronouns indicate a slippage between speaker, pilgrim, and reader, MacNeice's "Neutrality" claims that in every heart is the desire to escape to a County Sligo, a Knocknarea and its mythical past, just as every heart is close to the "archetypal sin" of its own dark urges. As "Dublin" reminds us, we are all "close, as close . . . As the killer is close one moment / To the man he kills" (32, 35–6). McDonald claims that in pairing the rhyme of "sin" with "kin" in "Neutrality," MacNeice "does not shy away from [what it is to be] kin—whether deliberately or not, and whether knowingly or not, with the 'archetypal sin' of an evil world."[87] Indeed, the troping of kinship throughout *Springboard* is always brutal: a king who cannibalizes his children, a "brother" fire who devours the city, and, in "Neutrality," a heart that looks away while its kindred drown.

The corpse-eating mackerel in "Neutrality" are linked to "Thyestes" and "Brother Fire" as part of a sustained use of cannibalistic imagery in *Springboard*. These mackerel are, after all, food for the people of that "neutral island": the assumption is implicit that another round of incorporation will take place, when the "you" of the poem eats the mackerel that have fattened on "the flesh of your kin." The "sin"-ful bonds of kinship in these poems take the incorporation scheme a step farther: cannibalism, in these poems, is not just the consumption of human flesh but the consumption of one's *own* flesh. In utilizing both schemes and tropes of repetition, "Neutrality" proves that both the "neutral island facing the

Atlantic" and "the neutral island in the heart of man" are complicit in the sins of war. Those mackerel in "Neutrality," however, are no sui generis Atlantic carnivores. They are clearly related to those in the "salmon-falls, the mackerel-crowded seas" of Yeats's "Sailing to Byzantium" (4). Here at last, then, MacNeice employs Yeatsian poetics—repetition, direct address, myth-suffused images of Ireland, and distinctly Yeatsian diction—to rebut a particular Yeatsian worldview. But to reject this Yeatsian romanticism, MacNeice must also acknowledge its power. To refute Yeats, MacNeice must incorporate him.

Noting the imagery of "circularity and self-enclosedness" in "Neutrality," Wills offers a reading of the poem as an indictment of neutral Ireland for escapism and "narcissism" (128). She reads the poem, with its "bankrupt coupling of ceremony and dream," as "a macabre parody of [Ireland's "neutral"] self-sufficiency" (128). According to Wills's reading, MacNeice would believe that "the Irish imagine themselves secure on their cut-off island, but if they would only raise their eyes for a moment, they would find themselves at the centre of a momentous battle" (128). But the poem's demand for introspection tells us something more complicated than this. Read in context with the rest of *Springboard*, it is clear that the "you" addressed in the poem is not Eamon de Valera but every reader, every eater of mackerel or human "cutlets." If MacNeice suggests in his wartime writing that "it is too late / To save your soul with bunting," this is because the soul, like the heart, is already compromised. We are all culpable, MacNeice's reflexive poetry suggests, neutral and pledged alike: if we want to remove the mote from our enemy's eye, we will find it in our own. The real indictment in "Neutrality" is against the vagrant that lurks in every heart, seeking the "neither one thing nor another" of neutrality. And yet this is also a generative space; the compromised heart is the epitome, perhaps, of Yeats's "foul rag and bone shop" where poetry begins. The space of emergency becomes a space of emergence.

CHAPTER 4

Careful Talk

Elizabeth Bowen and Language at War

Just as Louis MacNeice's reflexive poetry is full of troubling doubles, paradoxes, and repetitions, Elizabeth Bowen's prose is riddled with inversions, ellipses, subjunctives, and double, even triple, negatives; her writing has been accused of everything from mannerism to willful opacity.[1] Heather Bryant has suggested that "Bowen's style may be partly responsible for the difficulty in writing about her work. At times, her sentences are convoluted in extremes of syntax . . . her writing—as well as the experience of reading it—can be off-putting."[2] Even at the climax of Bowen's novel of World War II, *The Heat of the Day*, the language is contorted almost to the point of unintelligibility. Stella, the novel's protagonist, has just learned that Robert, her lover of two years, is a Nazi spy: "She could not believe they had not, in those two years, drawn on the virtue of what was round them, *the* virtue peculiar to where they were—nor had this been less to be felt when she was without him, was where he was not, had not been ever, might never be: a perpetual possible illumination for her, because of him, of everything to be seen or be heard by joy."[3] This is willfully tortuous syntax on Bowen's part; it took her ten years to finish the novel. Addressing the comments of her reader at Jonathan Cape that the novel often "abused" style to the "reader's discomfort,"[4] Bowen explained, "I'd rather keep the jars, 'jingles' and awkwardnesses—e.g. 'seemed unseemly', 'felt to falter'. They do to my mind express something. In some cases I want the rhythm to jerk or jar—to an extent, even, which may displease the reader."[5] These "jerks," "jars," and "jingles" are part of Bowen's project to create an experience of reading that is "eventful," as she calls it in *Afterthought.*[6] In fact, the experience of reading *The Heat of the Day* is rather more eventful than the novel itself, in which the melodramatic action of the spy-thriller plot is subordinated to the conversations surrounding it. (Bowen says in her 1945 "Notes on Writing a Novel," "Speech is what characters *do to each other.*")[7] Much of the novel's physical activity is taken up by actions of looking and listening; as the narrator says of Stella, "There came to be something dynamic . . . about her refusal to move at all" (23). The words on the page, and the words that the character-spies are constantly trying to read and interpret for clues, constitute the novel's true eventfulness.

The convolution of Stella's free indirect discourse when she realizes the truth about Robert dramatizes rather than describes her psychic state, and the reader is forced to work alongside Stella as she begins to reinterpret two years of her life. Robert tells her, "You'll have to reread me backwards, figure me out—you will have years to do that in, if you want to" (304), and Bowen's syntax forces the novel's reader, as well, to reread not just the plot for missing clues but the sentences themselves for meaning. When Bowen writes, "She could not believe they had not," the hobbled double negative is important: Stella thinks in double negatives because she has discovered, but is not ready to admit, the truth.

Daniel George, Bowen's reader at Cape, remarked on how, in the manuscript as he read it, "Generally I notice the phrase 'could but' is overworked and so is the trick of double negatives."[8] Bowen's discomforting commitment to the (un)grammatical "trick" of double negatives (as well as triple negatives and even quadruples) binds the novel in a pattern of negative diction.[9] Syntactically, by invoking the double negative, Bowen cultivates ambiguity: while two negatives may mathematically resolve to a positive, this is not always so in colloquial speech. The double negative may denote litotes ("she was not disobliging" the narrator says of the promiscuous Louie), but it may also denote emphasis (like Stella's declaration, "I am not a woman who does not know where to go"), or it may simply denote an unwillingness to speak straight in a crooked world (19, 41). Cast as a difficult or diffident realism by her contemporary critics, Bowen's prose is now read, as James Purdon has put it, as a form of "modernist reflexivity,"[10] a late modernist answer to the "difficulty" of modernist prose, and kindred, I suggest, to MacNeice's poetic reflexivity and Kavanagh's and Devlin's intentional equivocality. In each case, syntactical contortions disclose ethical quandaries. And nowhere is Bowen's strange syntax under more pressure than in her 1948 novel *The Heat of the Day*.

The novel, set primarily in London during World War II, is the story of Stella Rodney, divorcée and civil servant, who is told that her lover, Robert, is a suspected Nazi spy. Harrison, a counterspy who approaches Stella, offers her Robert's immunity in exchange for his place in her bed. For her part, Stella does not refuse Harrison's offer but delays it, becoming a spy on her own lover as she tries to decode the truth. Stella's response to Harrison comes as slowly and circuitously as her sentences do, and, as Robert puts it, none of the novel's characters "seem to have shown any very great patriotic fervour" (214). This is a novel about war and espionage, in which speaking the truth may, depending on the listener, amount to treason. Bowen, therefore, creates a language of war by encoding distrust into the syntax of the novel. Her use of the double negative is intentionally ambivalent; it holds resolution in suspense, just as the narrator suspends resolution in key aspects of plot, like Robert's "fall or leap" from the roof (327). The structure of the double negative governs *The Heat of the Day*, underpins the novel's logic, because it is a space of suspense, of nonknowingness. Such negative grammar is symbolic of the novel's espionage-based epistemology: it is the grammar of Stella's refusal to believe Harrison's story and refusal to disbelieve it, too.

Like her characters, Elizabeth Bowen spent the war engaged in intelligence gathering. From 1940 to 1945, she worked for the British Ministry of Information (MOI), secretly reporting to the Dominions Office about neutral Ireland's attitudes on the war.[11] Her own sense of allegiance (which Sean O'Faolain described as "heart-cloven and split-minded")[12], and her sense of what allegiance to a country could mean, were tested and shaped by espionage. Though *The Heat of the Day* includes two chapters set in County Cork, at the fictional big house Mount Morris, it is rarely read as an Irish novel. It holds a deserved position as a "Blitz novel" in the canon of British Second World War fiction, but its relationship to Irish literary history has generally been relegated to glosses of Mount Morris's place in the big house tradition. Adam Piette, in *Imagination at War*, attempts to map Irish neutrality in the novel by suggesting that "*The Heat of the Day* fictionalizes the England-Éire relationship by transposing the secret story of Bowen's spying on her country into Stella's spying on her lover."[13] Piette writes insightfully about Bowen's novel in its English context, but his reading of Stella as Ireland is an oversimplification. The novel's depiction of allegiance is more complicated than Piette makes it seem, for he makes the mistake of seeking equivalents: "Éire's neutral position is defended by turning Ireland into a kind of Stella figure," Piette first contends (172). He moves on to claim that Stella's "'hybrid' Anglo-Irish self is capable of a double allegiance, to country and to that country's 'enemy' . . . In the end, Stella and Robert form a secret union, an Anglo-Irish union" (172).[14] The flaw in Piette's argument is that being neutral and being Anglo-Irish are not the same thing, as Bowen herself knew. As an Anglo-Irishwoman, she was indeed a hybrid, joking that she felt most at home "in mid-Irish Sea."[15] Bowen was capable of serving as an Air Raid Precautions (ARP) warden in Marylebone and writing a defense of Ireland's neutrality in the *New Statesman*. She included herself in a British "we" in letters to Virginia Woolf, yet made the definitive statement, "I regard myself as an Irish novelist" (not an English or an Anglo-Irish one) in *The Bell*.[16] But hybridity and neutrality are nonequivalents; in a sense they are even opposites, since neutrality demands loyalty to no belligerent parties and hybridity could mean loyalty to more than one. Piette's formula falters in its insistence that this "Anglo-Irish self" would be capable of allegiance to both "country and to that country's 'enemy'" (172); inverted commas or not, neutral Ireland was not England's enemy, even if it could be imagined as flirting with it.[17]

A better metaphor for neutrality in the novel would be Bowen's language itself, her resolutely negative syntax. For one could argue that in declaring neutrality, Ireland, by removing itself from the map of a global war, made what Bowen termed "Éire's first free self-assertion" by mapping itself in a double-negative fashion. In a November 1940 report to the Dominions Office, Bowen wrote, "It may be felt in England that Éire is making a fetish of her neutrality. But this assertion of her neutrality is Éire's first free self-assertion: As such alone it would mean a great deal to her. Éire (and I think rightly) sees her neutrality as positive, not merely negative. She has invested her self-respect in it."[18] Publicly, in the *New Statesman* that year, Bowen argued that declaring neutrality "was Éire's first major independent act. As such it had, and keeps, a symbolic as well as a moral significance—a significance that identifies, for the people, Éire's neutrality with her integrity."[19] Bowen's understanding of the policy was keen; she appears to have understood intuitively how, as the architect of the neutrality policy, de Valera sought to remove his country from the map of war in order to put his country, metaphorically, "on the map"—a diplomatic double negative. If the double negative is the theoretical grammar of Irish neutrality, then in *The Heat of the Day*, Bowen enacts neutrality not by making *Stella* neutral (she is, after all, English) but by encoding it into the language of the novel itself, by riddling its logic and bending back its momentum with negatives.

In an essay on modernist form and propaganda, Megan Faragher compellingly investigates the connection between this novel and Bowen's letters to the MOI, which were both being composed at the same time.[20] Faragher argues that Bowen employed propagandist techniques such as high spotting and reflexiveness to "covertly asser[t] the importance and validity" of Ireland's neutrality when she wrote to the Dominions Office about the Treaty Ports situation in 1940 and went on to "translat[e] the rhetorical strategies of her letters into the narrative structure" (51) of the novel. According to Faragher, "The rhetoric inherent in Bowen's wartime letters for the MOI, not just the big house tradition of equivocation and ambiguity through which her fiction is so frequently interpreted, produces the modernist rhetorical form of *The Heat of the Day*" (52). But in the case of this novel, the big house tradition cannot, in fact, be separated from Bowen's own espionage work: the writing of *Bowen's Court* (1942) was Elizabeth Bowen's pretense for traveling between England and Ireland during the early years of the war. On the one hand, Bowen's information gathering for her family history underwrote her intelligence gathering for the MOI, and, on the other, it was her work for the MOI that granted Bowen the travel permit necessary to write *Bowen's Court*. The reflexive and evasive discourse of espionage and propaganda cannot be disentangled from the prose of either the 1942 family history or the 1948 novel. This chapter shows that, as Faragher argues about the MOI letters, rhetorical strategies from *Bowen's Court* are also embedded in *The Heat of the Day*, a further implication that the modernist rhetoric of Bowen's "Blitz novel" is also part of the rhetoric of Irish neutrality.

If Bowen's rhetoric is a response to both British propaganda and Irish neutrality, so are the reading strategies enacted in the novel. Purdon's argument that the suspicious reading strategies Bowen's characters employ in *The Heat of the Day*—for example, Connie's assiduous "reading between the lines" (153) of the newspapers—align them "with a wide audience of wartime readers whose method"[21] was to read skeptically. According to Purdon, "Confronted with a constant stream of wartime propaganda, [Britons] took to 'reading between the lines' as a common practice" (179). This depiction mirrors the Irish mode of reading advocated by Frank Aiken as a response to wartime information politics. Bowen herself remarks in a 1940 letter to the MOI that "little about recent events in Ireland is to be learned from the papers: one must rely on *carefully-sifted* talk."[22] While the war separated Ireland from Britain more deeply than the Irish Sea, it nonetheless contributed to a parallel skepticism of language on both sides of the divide. Bowen's novel, relying on modes of interpretation that mirror both British and Irish practice, demonstrates the effects of carefully sifting talk.

Bowen's World War II novel embeds the drama of neutrality, treachery, and allegiance in a drama of language itself—a medium that is as confounding and friable as war proved the built environment to be. In the novel, as in the rest of Bowen's wartime writing, the ability to be entirely partial or to cordon oneself off as neutral is called into question by war's incessant breaching of barriers and blitzing of walls. This is enacted formally by the fiction's shuttling between settings in Ireland and England, as well as stylistically in the prose's self-negating syntax. The syntax itself reveals an important embedded trace in the novel: the presence of Bowen's own past, of her family history as a source for her peculiar language of war. Reading *The Heat of the Day* alongside *Bowen's Court* (and a key story, "The Happy Autumn Fields," set simultaneously in Blitzed London and Victorian County Cork) one sees Bowen rending the barrier between the two books as between the two places. As Arthur says in another of Bowen's wartime stories, "Mysterious Kôr," the reader begins to feel that "we're there now, that here's there, that now's then."[23] For Bowen, neutral Ireland and wartime London were imaginatively linked, but they were also rhetorically linked by her work in espionage. *The Heat of the Day* transposes the anxieties of neutrality into a love story, in which the principal characters must read each other as they do propaganda, working through evasive sentences like Frank Aiken's imagined Irish listener sifting through Europe's wireless dispatches, searching for the true story.

Stories: The Creative Force of Propaganda and Metafiction

The Heat of the Day occupies a key place in a late modernist turn toward metafiction as it surveys the nature of "story" to expose language as both its foundational ingredient and its most troubling one. In a novel so governed by language as action, it is not surprising that the characters themselves appear to be more governed by their own senses of writtenness than by anything else. All of them are committed tellers and readers of stories, and it is stories that, they feel, make them real.[24] These stories, of course, are likewise built of language, and even the maligned Louie Lewis, who "blurted rather than spoke" with "a mouth incontinent and at the same time artless" (8), realizes this. Louie Lewis, nearly the same name twice: she might be read as a double positive, whose need to fill her empty self with stories makes her all the emptier. Louie, a factory worker whose subplot twice crosses Harrison's and who opens and closes the novel as a sort of proletarian bookend, takes to reading the paper when befriended by the hard-nosed ARP warden, Connie.[25] Inhaling home front propaganda like oxygen, Louie finds that "dark and rare were the days when she failed to find on the inside of her paper an address to or else account of herself. Was she not a worker, a soldier's lonely wife, a war orphan, a pedestrian, a Londoner, a home and animal-lover, a thinking democrat, a movie-goer, a woman of Britain, a letter-writer, a fuel-saver and a housewife? She was only not a mother, a knitter, a gardener, a foot-sufferer or a sweetheart—at least, not rightly. Louie now felt bad only about any part of herself which in any way did not fit into the papers' picture" (169). These fabrications of "the people's war" are vital to Louie's self-understanding. As Patrick Deer notes, "If [citizens] could not represent themselves during wartime, they must learn to be represented by the official war culture."[26] Unhoused, literally, by the bomb that destroyed her parents and their house at Seale-on-Sea, separated by war from a soldier husband she barely knows, Louie uses casual sex and premanufactured stories to fill the void (hence her "not rightly" being a sweetheart).

It is not until she intrudes on Stella's story that Louie begins to imagine stories for herself. Having unwittingly interrupted Stella's capitulation to Harrison, Louie returns home to tell Connie about her evening. Recounting the events with her own and Stella's roles reversed, Louie literally puts Stella's words into her own mouth. In return, Stella puts words into Louie's mouth—an encounter with "refinement" as a sort of birth into language: Lying in bed, imagining herself as Stella, Louie suddenly thinks, "Mrs. Rodney walked like a soul astray. Those three words reached Louie imperatively, as though spoken . . . Now her lips seemed bidden: 'A soul astray,' they repeated with awe, aloud" (279). Louie's fascination with Stella is class based and linguistic, for Stella has a way with words: "She was refined" (274). Upset by Connie's teasing her about the story (not to mention by Connie's sexual jealousy over Louie's attraction to Stella), Louie responds with a torrent of linguistic anxiety: "It's the taking and taking up of me on the part of everyone when I have no words. Often you say the advantage I should be at if I could speak grammar; but it's not only that. Look the trouble there is when I have to only say what I can say, and so cannot ever say what it is really . . . Now she [Stella] tonight, she spoke beautifully . . . If I could put it like she does I might not be stealthy: when you know you only can say what's a bit off, what does it matter how much more off it is?" (275). While many critics find Bowen's treatment of Louie patronizing, it is important to register that in this passage Bowen makes Louie the ("incontinent") spokesperson for linguistics.[27] Simply being able to "speak grammar" is not enough. Louie notes that if she could speak with refinement, she might not have to be stealthy, to beat around the bush with her words, but she hasn't that advantage. Louie knows something more fundamental is holding her back: the inherent disjunction between what she wants to say and her vocabulary's ability to "say" it. On the one hand, Louie's acknowledgment that "when you know you only can say what's a bit off, what does it matter how much more off it is" amounts to a rationalization of deception on the grounds that language is inadequate to the truth; Robert will use a very similar rationalization with Stella when he admits to his Nazi espionage. On the other hand, if Louie should want to express something like the truth, her personal course on general linguistics leads her to a dead end: "From on and on like this not being able to say, I seem to get to be nothing, now there's no one. I would more understand if I was able to make myself understood" (276). Louie directly connects language and ipseity: not being able to express herself, she seems to "be nothing"; language itself becomes a stumbling block to her propagandistic search for identity. Louie can't fit herself into the prearranged home-front narratives because of a double disjunction in writing: one, real people cannot fit neatly into prewritten roles (something Louie is horrified to discover when she reads in the papers that the "refined" Stella turned out to be Robert Kelway's femme fatale), and two, even if they tried, the signs could not match up to what they signified: propaganda, like language, is inexact. Louie cannot "make [her]self understood" because she understands that language itself falls short.[28]

Neil Corcoran writes that "it is through her very attitude to Stella that Louie is saved from the propagandistic version of herself," pinpointing the revelatory moment when the newspaper version of Stella (itself terribly incorrect) reveals that even this "refined" lady doesn't fit the proper role (173). Louie now knows "Stella not to be virtuous. Virtue became less possible now because it was shown impossible by Stella . . . There was nobody to admire" (345–46). This knowledge releases Louie to fashion her own story, even if it, too, is based on a lie about her child's paternity. In this way, through a pair of lies, Louie finds her own sort of truth—a way of being "an orderly mother" (372), though got at by disorderly means—and, as Corcoran writes, the novel ends with "the propagandist narrative . . . deeply undermined" (171) by a thematic double negative.

The story of Stella's iniquity, liberating as it is for Louie, is itself fabricated. Her ability to play the femme fatale in the public story of Robert's "fall or leap" from her roof dates back to the accepted story of Stella's divorce from Roderick's father, Victor, who actually walked out on *her* (327).[29] Stella tells Harrison, "I didn't start the story about my guiltiness, it started itself" (249), but she never fought it, as she would "rather sound a monster than look a fool" (251). "Whoever's the story *had* been," explains Stella, "I let it be mine. I let it ride, and more—it came to be my story, and I stuck to it. Or rather, first I stuck to it, then it went on sticking to me: it took my shape and equally I took its" (251). Stella labors under a sense of writtenness that approaches the metafictional. For instance, of an assignation with her lover, Stella "felt herself to be going to a rendezvous inside the pages of a book. And was, indeed, Robert himself fictitious?" (106). As Corcoran points out, "The sense of being narrated, of being part of a discourse you cannot control, is also congruent with the wartime narratives of propaganda" (171). Stella feels herself written into a narrative, but rather than a war-culture narrative like the ones that haunt Louie, Stella's narrative sensibility is self-consciously fictitious—

from her own backstory with Victor to her interactions with Robert and Harrison. Denied the ability to self-authorize, Stella seems aware of her position as a character not just in a fiction but in *genre* fiction—in her case, a thriller—in which her role as the femme fatale is preascribed.

At several points, Stella attempts to analyze her own life *as* a story. "By the rules of fiction, with which life to be credible must comply," Stella surmises that "[Harrison] was as a character 'impossible'—each time they met, for instance, he showed no shred or trace of having been continuous since they last met . . . 'Appearance,' in the sense used for a ghost or an actor, had, indeed, been each of these times the word. Coming out of that vacuum, the reiterated unrelated story of his desire could but be unmeaning" (155). Bowen's inversion of the reality-realism relationship is telling: in *The Heat of the Day*, life is mimetic of fiction, not the other way around. (Michael North considers "the disconcerting tendency toward instant fictionalization of overwhelming experiences" to be a common theme in Blitz writing.)[30] Harrison's being "impossible," which allies him with the unreal (as a ghost, or an actor in a role), flusters Stella's ability to come to grips with him in the novel's "reality." If reality must comply with the "rules of fiction," but Harrison does not, it is precisely his unfictitiousness that makes him and therefore his "story" about Robert real, believable. To accept Harrison's story as true, Stella must acknowledge that she is not fictitious, must release herself from her prescribed role. So it is that when this unfictitious Harrison finally emerges from the novel's back stage, Bowen's syntax betrays him as distorting. His desire for Stella is "*re*iterated," "*un*related," and "could *but* be *un*meaning" (my emphasis); this is as complicated a sentence as Harrison's spy game is in itself. The double negative "could but be unmeaning" in her free indirect speech allows Stella to distance herself from the truth of the matter: Harrison's desire for Stella actually means a great deal to Robert's safety. Yet Harrison's proposal is also, this same sentence implies, a "story," the truth or reality of which Stella will have to decide for herself.

The information passed between Harrison, Stella, and Robert is consistently couched as "story." When, two months after Harrison first appears in Stella's flat, Stella confronts Robert with what Harrison has told her, she says that someone "came to me with a story about you. They said you were passing information on to the enemy" (210). Hoping to confirm this in the negative, Stella goes on to pose the accusation to Robert in the negative: "But it isn't true, is it?" (211). When Robert gets around to responding—which is a matter of finding the words to speak—he speaks of that story as a living being. "Someone comes to you with a story," he reiterates, "with you, the story takes—seeds itself in some crack that you felt between us" (212). (Later, furthering the story-gestational metaphor, he says, "You're two months gone with this" [213].) As Stella does with the story of her divorce, Robert sees the story of his treachery as a living, growing being—something that can overtake a person. On the other hand, he is prepared to deny Stella's charges by cataloguing the type of story they seem to be: "crazy, brainspun, out of a thriller" (212), which is precisely the type of story Stella has imagined for herself. By altering the type of fiction in which he and Stella find themselves, Robert hopes to alter that fiction's "rules." Something out of a thriller, he implies, cannot possibly be true.

Thrillers: Genre, Espionage, and the Limitations of Language

But the conditions of truth and fiction that Robert relies upon are less steadfast than he tries to argue, especially as Stella has already acknowledged the apparent fictitiousness of their whole affair. Similarly, Graham Greene's Arthur Rowe, inadvertently caught up in a spy ring in *The Ministry of Fear* (1943), remarks on the war's inversion of the rules of life and fiction: "It sounds like a thriller, doesn't it, but the thrillers are like life . . . The world has been remade by William Le Queux."[31] If the thrillers are like life, and if, as North argues, wartime life feels instantly fictionalized, there is a strange play between "truth" and "fiction." For the novelist, this shores up the mimetic claims of the thriller ("the thrillers are like life") just as it questions the nature of the reality that fiction should mimic. The great experimental modernists, like Joyce and Woolf—the latter Bowen's friend and mentor—fractured narrative to achieve a new form of mimetic fiction. *The Heat of the Day* argues for a sort of reversal, in which life itself is fractured into fictional narratives. In this sense, Bowen's late modernist novel takes for granted a modernist sense of narrative while pushing into the metafictional territory often associated with postmodernism.[32]

So when Stella accuses Robert's "reality" of being that of a thriller, he searches for a way to weave a false narrative, knowing that Stella, as he says, already had "acted on the assumption that [Harrison's story about him] was true" (213). Robert must now attempt to lie openly to his lover, to fabricate an alternative "story": "He spoke, when he began to speak, as a man who, in an emergency more fantastic, more beyond the possibilities of experience, than any man should be asked to meet, casts round him for words at random, realizes their futility before uttering them, but does all the same utter them, as the only means of casting them from him, again, rejected" (211–12). Bowen's use of "emergency" here reminds the reader of the "Emergency" that underpinned her real-life spy story and the difficulties it imposed upon her own use of words. In the novel, Robert ultimately connects his inability to find words (those instruments of lies and truth) with an impossibility of Stella's even being able to make her accusation. His immediate answer to Stella's "story" is, "But it can't be true that you're asking me this? . . . What *do* you want me to say? There's nothing *to* say—what does one say in a situation that doesn't make sense?" (212). Robert's reaction is to question the terms of *asking* rather than answer the question itself. By positing the uselessness of words (after all, Bowen says of his family, "The Kelways communicated with one another with difficulty, in the dead language"), Robert evades Stella's accusation (283). No reason to speak when "there's nothing *to* say."[33] In fact, it is the hollowness of official, nationalistic language—its "dead currency"—that propels Robert to spy for Germany in the first place. When he finally opens up to Stella, on their last night together, Robert attempts to explain himself: "What is repulsing you is the idea of 'betrayal,' I suppose, isn't it? In you the hangover from the word? Don't you understand that all language is dead currency? How they keep on playing shop with it all the same: even you do. Words, words like that, yes—what a terrific dust they can still raise in a mind . . . I have needed to immunise myself against them . . . by saying them to myself over and over again till it became absolutely certain they mean nothing" (301). Robert's reaction to Stella is poststructural, *avant la lettre*, in its insistence on language's shortcomings. He attempts to excuse his fascism on the basis of the disconnection between sign and signified. Like Louie, he thinks that if "you only can say what's a bit off, what does it matter how much more off it is?" What does it matter, Robert implies, what you say at all, which secrets you speak, and to whom, if words themselves are meaningless?[34] Knowing his fate is sealed, Robert brings himself back to the idea of fiction, of story, when he at last tells Stella, "You'll have to reread me backwards, figure me out—you will have years to do that in, if you want to" (304). If his life is a book, it's one with an unreliable narrator; to understand him, Robert implies, Stella will have to "reread" their story all over again, to see if the beginning held the germ of the end.

The beginning of their story, as it happens, is unreadable. Stella and Robert's first words to each other are lost, muted by a falling bomb ("direct hit, somewhere else" [104]). The narrator remarks, "What they *had* both been saying, or been on the point of saying, neither of them ever now were to know. Most first words have the nature of being trifling; theirs from having been lost began to have the significance of a lost clue" (104). If theirs is a story to be reread, it's a thriller in which the initial clue is erased. This is bad news for the rereader of such a mystery. For the reader of Bowen's novel, however, Robert's introduction is Harrison's accusation; he enters the story already suspect.[35] Stella's subsequent acts of espionage are also acts of "reading" Robert—their visit to Holme Dene, which she reads as a grotesquerie of the gothic family home, is her key performance of reading.[36]

When Stella asks Robert why he concealed the true story (of his deception), words again take the stage. He says, "In a ring, once any one person begins to talk . . . No, how was I to tell you in so many words?" "You could have told me not in so many words," replies Stella. "He again reflected. 'Sometimes I thought I had'" (304). Espionage poses unique challenges to language and to knowing. If information is passed through "talk," it must be encoded talk. "Careless talk," after all, "costs lives," according to the MOI's slogan. ("Careless Talk" is also the title of a very short story Bowen published in the *New Yorker* in 1941, in which a bombed-out Londoner visiting town from her new country home is schooled in the art of negation and ellipsis over a non-conversation at lunch.) Before being confronted with Stella's suspicions, Robert attempts to make light of Harrison's appearance in her life, suggesting that "perhaps he listens for careless talk" (110). Stella counters, "Why—who's been talking carelessly?" "Everyone, I imagine," says Robert, "You know how I talk" (110). When Stella answers, "Only how you talk to me. I don't count" (111), the scene recalls the famous Fougasse poster from the "Careless Talk Costs Lives" campaign, in which a couple share a romantic table as a cartoon Hitler, crouched beneath it, scribbles down their conversation:

"Of course there's no harm in *your* knowing!"[37] This poster ghosts Stella and Robert's quiet dinner after he first denies her accusation: "They were not alone, nor had they been from the start of love. Their time sat in the third place at their table. They were the creatures of history" (217). Between Stella and Robert, his treason, his fascism, lies beneath the table, emblematic of their time.

But if careless talk costs lives, so, the spy ring makes evident, does care*ful* talk. And if Robert wants to hint to Stella about what he is really doing, he must do it carefully, and "not in so many words." For words, if "dead" or even hollow at the core, are still dangerous. Robert's attempt to tell Stella without the use of dangerous words falls short. His realization of this comes out hobbled, again, with double negatives: "It seemed impossible that being as we were you should not know . . . But I did not know you did not know till you asked me" (304–5). Here, epistemology itself is canted in the negative—a not knowing what another does not know. In *The Heat of the Day*, one cannot know anything until someone asks. The novel's governing epistemology is based on its framework of espionage; nothing can be taken for granted as known. Stella's deliberate decision to *not know* what she suspects about Robert makes her, for a time, complicit with the enemy.

The battle of this novel—and of the novel's perception of World War II—is the battle of what one can *know* through the slippery medium of words. As Stella's enlisted son, Roderick, points out, "Conversations are the leading thing in this war! Even I know that" (67). This is a war, Roderick implies, less about action than about diction: "Everything you and I have to do is the result of something that's been said. How far do you think we'd get without conversations? And can you really suppose that someone where Robert is doesn't have conversations *about* conversations, even if he doesn't have conversations himself?" (67). One might go so far as to say that here, Roderick and his mother are having a conversation about conversations about conversations; the chance of deducing anything from such talk becomes murkier with every remove. Stella—still reeling from Harrison's bombshell, dropped just before Roderick's arrival on the scene—asks her son, "Do *you* believe what you're told?" (67). For her own part, Stella has just been told something staggering, but Roderick reports, "Well, I am not told much. In fact, Fred says, it comes to seem fishy when one *is* told anything. Go by what you find out for yourself, he says" (68). The irony is that Roderick himself seems to go by Fred. Finding out for yourself, in this novel, is always a form of espionage; anything told to you is automatically "fishy."

When Roderick's distant cousin Francis Morris dies, the young soldier is surprised to inherit the Morris estate in Ireland. Eager to do right by his cousin, Roderick scrutinizes Francis's will in order to "find out" what this legacy will mean: ' "*In the hope that he may care in his own way to carry on the old tradition*'—Why must lawyers always take out commas?" "Because," Stella says, "what they write is meant to be clear without them" (95). "Well, in this case it isn't," replies her son: "Which *did* Cousin Francis mean? . . . Does he mean, that I'm free to care in any way I like, so long as it's the tradition I carry on; or, that so long as I care in the same way he did, I'm free to mean by 'tradition' anything I like? . . . What we must make out is, what Cousin Francis meant. That might make all the difference to what I do" (95–96). In this short conversation, Roderick repeats "mean" or "meant" eight times; words, for him, must fundamentally *mean* something, but the trouble is that, in actual use, meaning is often unclear. Words (and punctuation marks) can be misused, misinterpreted, can easily become unclear, cryptic. Roderick's reading of the will enacts the novel's characterization of reader as cryptographer.

In *The Heat of the Day*, epistemology and even ontology are twisted up in espionage, for spying is a game of deciphering and telling the stories that make people "real" or "fictitious," true or false, faithful or unfaithful. Espionage also questions the validity of a "true" language, of a language capable of *saying* or giving meaning, for not only might words be false, a cover-up, but also at heart (as Robert acknowledges) they are only signifiers, which don't technically *say* anything at all. In his study of the genre, Allan Hepburn writes that "the spy novel demands deciphering because it always means something other than itself."[38] "Spy novels," he contends, "promote themselves as codebooks, or at least coded books" (50). So when Robert tells Stella that she'll have to "reread [him] backwards," he is also offering her instructions for code breaking, for a hermeneutics of a life "out of a thriller." "Interpretation [in the thriller] requires vigilant separation of truth from lies," according to Hepburn; this makes them "a hermeneutical exercise" in code breaking and skepticism (xvi). Bowen demands precisely such exercise from both her readers and her characters in *The Heat of the Day*—not just in her use of the generic conventions of the spy novel (which, if read backwards as Robert suggests, would give one all the answers up front, raveling rather than unraveling its tortuous tale) but also in the texture of her language, its syntactical contortions, its unwillingness to speak directly.

When Stella confronts Robert with her suspicion that he's a Nazi spy, and he calls the accusation "crazy, brainspun, out of a thriller" (212), Robert offers a better generic fit for his story than the narrator's "ideal book about nothing" (97). The spy novel, a genre of which Bowen was personally fond, is the appropriate medium for this relationship, with its elusiveness of language, its mandate to speak only in code and trust nothing that you hear.[39] *The Heat of the Day* is Bowen's only real incursion into the spy-thriller genre, and in many ways it does not seem to fit.[40] It is not a quick read, suspense does not seem to propel the plot any faster, and one might fairly accuse it of a real dearth of action.[41] Yet, for its subject matter of espionage, of boundary crossing, of linguistic distrust, there is no better form. *The Heat of the Day* can *only* be a spy novel; its form is inseparable from its themes. What Susan Osborn says of Bowen's short stories—"in many ways the style of these stories is in their substance; their contents are indistinguishable from what contains them" (194)—is perfectly appropriate as a description of Bowen's style in this spy thriller, for the contents of the novel are "indistinguishable" from the circuitous, conniving sentences in which it is written.

In tipping off Stella to Robert's activities, Harrison succeeds, as Stella tells him, "in making a spy of [her]" (152). From that moment on, everything Robert says becomes a potential lie; everything Stella says is constructed to elide what she knows. They are reminiscent of the "happy" couple at the end of *The Ministry of Fear*, the survival of whose relationship rests on Arthur's having to keep from Anna that he knows what she thinks he's forgotten, and on her never letting on about a past that she thinks he doesn't remember. Greene writes, "They had to tread carefully for a lifetime, never speak without thinking twice; they must watch each other like enemies because they loved each other so much. They would never know what it was not to be afraid of being found out" (215). In *The Heat of the Day*, Robert's challenge with Stella is "to know what I knew, to keep my knowing unknown, unknown all the time" (307). Between him and Stella, this nervousness is embedded in the extremely care*ful* talk that destroys (rather than saves) their life together.

Bowen dedicated *The Heat of the Day* to her lover, Charles Ritchie, who writes in his 1973 diary that the World War II novel "is the story of our love, with a flaw in it, or did she feel a flaw in me?"[42] In Ritchie's 1942 diary, the flaw is revealed: "[April 9, 1942] I told her the other evening that I was a crook, which was a guarded way of saying that I had been and would continue to be unfaithful to her. She said my 'being a crook' was the use I made of my surplus cleverness—like her writing . . . [April 20, 1942] I think but am not sure that she knows what is happening and has decided to close her eyes to it—if so I admire her all the more" (30). Ritchie's remark about *The Heat of the Day* reveal a powerful subtext to Robert Kelway's political treachery—personal, sexual unfaithfulness. In fact, one of Robert's first deflections, when Stella mentions Harrison, is to ask, "Has anybody been telling you I'm two-timing?" (111). Bowen's knowing silence about Ritchie's sexual infidelity (Bowen, for her part, had been married to Alan Cameron for nearly twenty years at the time) mirrors Stella's about Robert's political treason. Bowen's connection of Ritchie's "being a crook" with her own writing builds the anxieties of treachery into writing itself. So this novel—in which Robert "realizes [words'] futility before uttering them, but does all the same utter them" (212), in which Louie "only can say what's a bit off" (275) and in which Roderick finds that "everything I try saying must sound . . . no must *be* ridiculous" (336)—reveals language as a *crook*ed medium: all the more impossible to grasp and, ultimately, all the more deadly in what Stella herself sees as "a crooks' war" (34).[43]

Migrations: *Bowen's Court* and the Gothic Language of London

The slippery syntax of *The Heat of the Day* has its formal correspondence in the novel's shuttling between settings in London and Ireland. Bowen herself migrated between two homes in the 1940s—her house in London and her family's estate in County Cork. In addition to enabling her reports for the Dominions Office, Bowen's travel to Ireland allowed the completion of the research and writing of *Bowen's Court* (1942), a history of her family and, by extension, of Anglo-Ireland. Most critics glance at *Bowen's Court* in the course of assessing Bowen's two big house novels, *The Last September* (1929) and *A World of Love* (1954); few consider its importance to *The Heat of the Day*, despite the fact that Bowen was writing the novel and the history at the same time.[44] Perhaps this is because the novel's two chapters set in Ireland concern what might rightly be considered a subplot: Stella's son Roderick has inherited Mount Morris, Francis Morris's County Cork estate. In the middle of the novel, Stella goes there to "take possession" in Roderick's absence while he serves in the army. At the end of the book, Roderick finally has leave to travel and visits the place himself.[45]

Mount Morris's location in Cork and its status as a place outside war allies it with the real Bowen's Court and the novelist's own experiences of neutral Ireland. W. J. McCormack writes that "the very minimalism with which [*The Heat of the Day*] admits its Irish setting" emphasizes its importance to the novel, but what's important to McCormack is "the rigorous pessimism with which the author addresses her diagnosis [of the relationship between Britain and Ireland]" (211). McCormack is in line with other critics who see Bowen's Court, rightly, as the real-life model for Mount Morris but fail to notice the ghostly presences of *Bowen's Court* in the novel.[46] In fact, *Bowen's Court* provides a secret subtext to Bowen's novel of secrecy, in both the novel's structural echoes of Bowen's own wartime travel to and from Ireland and London and, less transparently, its syntactical negativity and contortion. In *The Heat of the Day*'s syntactical features, Bowen directly borrows—even copies—many of the structures of *Bowen's Court*. However, she applies these structures not to the fictional estate Mount Morris but to her depiction of London under the Blitz. Blitzed London, characterized by a diction of absence and ghostliness, is described in a gothic mode that might appear more at home in a big house novel than in a thriller.

As a thriller, *The Heat of the Day* splices the diction of the plantation gothic mode with the contorted linguistics of the spy novel. In her own spying experience, Bowen called this "smoke-screen use of words . . . a trick of the Irish mind," and the sentences in *The Heat of the Day* often set a smoke screen around information they seem almost hesitant to impart.[47] In a passage about the morning after a particularly bad air raid, exemplary of Bowen's style in the novel, the reader must sift through the shape of the sentences to decode the information they present:

> Most of all the dead, from mortuaries, from under cataracts of rubble, made their anonymous presence—not as today's dead

> but as yesterday's living—felt through London. Uncounted, they continued to move in shoals through the city day, pervading everything to be seen or heard or felt with their torn-off senses, drawing on this tomorrow they had expected—for death cannot be so sudden as all that. Absent from the routine which had been life, they stamped upon that routine their absence—not knowing who the dead were, you could not know which might be the staircase somebody for the first time was not mounting this morning. (99)

All those negatives—*anonymous*, *not* as today's dead, *un*counted, torn-*off*, death *cannot* be, *absent*, *absence*, *not* knowing, could *not* know, *not* mounting—add up to a world that is defined by absence rather than presence. London becomes defined by unreality rather than reality.[48] The negatively contorted grammatical logic in that last sentence recalls a similar passage in *Seven Winters*, published by the Cuala Press in 1942 as a companion book to *Bowen's Court*: "When they first made me understand that I had been born in Dublin, I said: 'But how?—my birthdays are always at Bowen's Court.' A house where a child no longer is is virtually rolled up and put away. So by having been born where I had been born in a month in which that house did not exist, I felt that I had intruded on some no-place" (4). What is of concern in the final sentences of both passages is the cryptic presence of absence. In Blitzed London, one cannot know which extant staircases exist only through nonuse. On the other hand, Bowen's Court has the ability to exist as a house that "did not exist," because Elizabeth Bowen was not there. In both cases, space is reconstituted, through negative syntax, as "no-place."[49]

"No-place," this place accessed through cryptic syntax, turns out to be one of Bowen's chief wartime locations. Roderick, who finds in his mother's flat that "the reality of [his] fancy was better than the unreality of the room," discovers a perfect "no-place" in Mount Morris, his unseen new home. For Roderick, "by geographically standing outside war [Mount Morris] appeared also to be standing outside the present. The house, nonhuman, became the hub of his imaginary life, of fancies, fantasies only so to be called because circumstance outlawed them from reality" (52).[50] Similarly, in her history of her own County Cork home, Bowen admits that for her, the "no-place" of Bowen's Court was an important refuge during the war: "I suppose that everyone, fighting or just enduring, carried within him one private image, one peaceful scene. Mine was Bowen's Court. War made me that image out of a house built of anxious history."[51] One might also say that the writer's refuge was *Bowen's Court* the book, which she completed during the war and which gave her access to history, allowed her to live, as Roderick did at his imagined Mount Morris, "outside the present." For in Bowen's writing, text and shelter are conceptually linked. Of her family estate, Bowen writes, "Like Flaubert's ideal book about nothing, it sustains itself on itself by the inner force of its style" (21). This is a peculiar formula for a home: self-sustaining as an artifact, as is a book, yet made of "nothing" but style. Still, it is tempting to posit literature as a safe space in lieu of a home. After all, the fate of Bowen's Court suggests this. In 1959, when Bowen could no longer afford its upkeep, the house was sold and promptly demolished by its new owners. Where "Bowen's Court" once meant a house, it is now the title of a book.[52] The space of Bowen's Court is now preserved within the hermetic space of *Bowen's Court*.

Bowen reuses the Flaubert metaphor in *The Heat of the Day* to describe Stella and Robert's relationship: "What the inheritance came to be for Roderick, Robert was for Stella—a habitat. The lovers had for two years possessed a hermetic world, which, like the ideal book about nothing, stayed itself on itself by its inner force" (97). It is anachronistic to compare the demolition of their relationship to the demolition of Bowen's home, but Bowen—who had seen her neighbors' big houses burned in the Troubles, and who had fictionally torched her own in *The Last September*, who had been bombed out of her London home three times by the end of World War II—knew that style or inner force alone cannot sustain a building or a love affair. The friability of Bowen's Court underwrites the fragility of Stella and Robert's supposedly "hermetic" relationship, which is ultimately destroyed, rather than sustained, from within.

In an early draft of *The Heat of the Day*, Bowen ghosts London with her big house's past. Underlying the city's wartime camaraderie, she writes, "was the emotional unity of a garrison."[53] In the published version, Bowen expands the comparison to ally wartime Londoners even more with the garrison's provisional and colonial aspects. She writes that "the stayers-on in London" were "campers in rooms of draughty dismantled houses, in corners of fled-from flats—it could be established, roughly, that the wicked had stayed and the good had gone. This was the new society of one kind of wealth, resilience, living how it liked—people whom the climate of danger suited . . . There was plenty of everything in London—attention, drink, time, taxis, most of all space. Into that intimate and loose little society of the garrison Stella and Robert had both gravitated" (102–3). Here, wartime London resembles the colonial garrison society in Cromwellian County Cork that Bowen describes in *Bowen's Court*. "In Ireland," she writes, "the Cromwellians were people of the ruins" (87). Their search for more space, for a "new society" based on colonization's promise to the settler of a land with "plenty of everything," where one can live how one likes so long as one is suited to the "climate of danger," recalls the habitations of the wartime denizens of Bowen's London. Bowen writes of her ancestor Henry Bowen, colonel in Cromwell's army, that, after taking possession of his Irish lands, "he took up his quarters in the small, semi-ruinous castle just across the Farahy stream . . . Farahy castle was crabbed, draughty, rough and built on a ridge of limestone; cold exhalations travelled up through its walls. To this cold shelter only, Henry would be driven back by the drenching rains, impatiently fording the stream in spate. Into this dark doorway he turned at the close of long dusks. In these chambers he muttered and walked at nights" (74–75). By correlating the wartime Londoners to the early, roughest members of the Anglo-Irish colonial garrison, Bowen draws telling parallels. Stella and Robert, "the wicked [who] had stayed" in London's "draughty dismantled houses," begin to resemble Ireland's own "wicked" band of dispossessors in their "crabbed, draughty, rough," and ruinous castles. Something in the suspicious vulnerability of the garrison sticks to these colonizers of the demolished metropolis. Later, when Stella feels that "occupied Europe [is] occupying London" (139), the novel reminds the reader again of this colonial parallel.

In a mirror of the anxieties that drive the Anglo-Irish big house novel, Stella and Robert's London garrison is destroyed from within—the suspicion of evil lurking within supposedly safe walls of home and family is not only the thriller's trademark but also a wartime gothic nod to the plantation gothic mode.[54] Bowen's use of parallel language makes London and Bowen's Court equally uncanny, both populated by the sorts of questionable people who mutter and walk at nights. For in fact they are: the novel's London is full of spies, of the sounds of feet shifting on dark pavements, of dark nights and secretive pacts; the ingredients of this spy-thriller London echo the ingredients that make up the gothic garrison. It is as though the ghosts of the many wars in Bowen's Court's neighborhood are reawakened by the new ghosts created by London's position on this new war's civilian "front line."[55] The clear division between Bowen's two homes in Cork and Marylebone begins to recede while, as the narrator of *The Heat of the Day* says, "The wall between the living and the living became less solid as the wall between the living and the dead thinned" (99–100).[56] With Bowen's literary borrowings, the meaning of Ireland's neutrality thins, too.

Readings of *The Heat of the Day* have often worked from the assumption that Ireland—with all its Celtic twilight and seeming apartness from the war—is the haunted, othered space in the novel, not London. After all, an imaginary Ireland is Roderick's "saving hallucination," and upon waking there, Stella finds that "her place in time had been lost" (196).[57] But these Irish dislocations are only a dim mirror of what Stella feels in London, where "no kind of sleep accounted for the distance she felt between herself and yesterday—and, indeed, between herself and today. Nothing she saw or touched gave token of even its own reality: even her wrist watch seemed to belie time; she fancied it had lost hours during the night" (105). Lostness in time is a common denominator in her London flat and at Mount Morris. This is part of the novel's "radical disruption of a classical, linear temporality" that Bennett and Royle call "blitz-riven" (91, 95). The novel's migrations between London and Ireland help to underscore Bowen's "blitz-riven" sense of time and place that works to haunt London as it dispossesses Ireland of its traditional ghosts. In London, Stella becomes part of a company of "shades," whereas at Mount Morris, she "know[s]" herself to be "outside the society of ghosts" (192–93).

Bowen offers Stella as a corrective to assumptions that by diplomatically and geographically lying outside war Ireland was unaffected by it. Her first sensations upon arrival are typical of many travelers' coming across from blacked-out Britain, astonished by the lights on Dublin Bay: "The exciting sensation of being outside war had concentrated itself round those fearless lights . . . around the harbour water, uphill above it, the windows had not only showed and shone but blazed . . . dazzling reflections in damp streets made Dublin seem to be in the throes of a carnival" (186). But arriving at Mount Morris, Stella finds that the absence of electricity, combined with an extreme shortage of oil and candles, makes for its own sort of blackout. Bowen writes, "Stella had assumed there to be no shortages of any kind in Éire. In the end . . . what she had not cared to suspect was in fact true . . . she was burning up light supplies for months ahead. Well on into the winter after Stella's departure the Donovan family went to bed in the dark" (186). This moment of pathos for the Donovans, the Mount Morris caretakers who sacrifice their own comforts in their effort to properly "wait on" their new mistress (herself unaccustomed to the experience), comes across as a heartfelt corrective to English ideas of Ireland's neutrality by the novelist whose MOI reports strive to offer similar context (185).[58]

Just as the Ireland of *The Heat of the Day* is not free from war's privations, neither are its people entirely "neutral-minded," as Aiken's censorship encouraged them to be. Walking in the Mount Morris woods, Stella feels "the peace of the moment," imagining that this might be "the very day in which . . . something might intervene to save her" (197). At just this moment, an ecstatic Donovan calls to her, shouting, "Montgomery's through! . . . It's the war turning" (198). This reference to the Second Battle of El Alamein is the first moment in the novel in which specific historical events enter the narrative, and the comment belongs to the Irishman, Catholic, serving class: "I would give much to have a hat to bare my head with: the day's famous" (198).[59] Donovan goes on to identify ecumenically with the Anglo-Irish Montgomery: "We bred a very fast general. Didn't I say to you he'd be a fast general? Hasn't he got them on the run?" (198). World wars do not, of course, turn so simply as that, and there was a lot of fighting left after Montgomery's Egyptian victory, just as the novel has a long way to go toward its own resolution. If victory in North Africa was only "the end of the beginning," as Churchill put it, it is the beginning of the end for Stella and Robert.[60] Bowen acknowledges the complexity of battle, love, and Irish wartime sentiment by ending the chapter not with a newly decisive Stella but with an image of the placidly beautiful Donovan daughter, Hannah. A perfect neutral, Hannah takes her father's audacious news without a blink of emotion, so that "whenever in the future that Mount Morris mirage of utter victory came back to [Stella], she was to see Hannah standing there in the sunshine, as indifferent as a wand" (199). Peace in Ireland is figured again and again as a mirage, even if, in the novel, this "mirage" of victory really appears to be the war turning. For, if "it's the war turning," as Donavan says, then it's Stella's war turning, too; she will go home to confront her lover as a traitor. And it's news of the conclusion of Montgomery's North African campaign, the capture of Tobruk, that punctuates Robert's death. The first Allied victory in battle marks the death of the traitor, and real time—November 11, 1942—puts the end to Stella and Robert's dream life. Rather than exempting her from the historical time of war, Stella's trip to Ireland inscribes her into it.

The London to which Stella returns is haunted by its war dead—"These unknown dead reproached those left living not by their death, which might any night be shared, but by their unknownness, which could not be mended now"—making Bowen's London as susceptible to ghostly happenings as Mount Morris is not (99). Describing the morning after an air raid in her essay "London, 1940," Bowen writes how survivors "come up out of the ground [to] see what we heard happen throughout the night . . . Standing, as might the risen dead in the doors of tombs, in the mouths of shelters, we have nothing to do but yawn at each other or down the void of streets."[61] These "risen dead" greet Stella on her return from Mount Morris. Arriving at the train station, she finds, "Recognition of anybody by anybody else seemed hopeless—those hoping to be met, hoping to be claimed, thrust hats back and turned up faces drowningly. Arrival of shades in Hades, the new dead scanned dubiously by the older, she thought that she could have thought; but she felt nothing—till her heart missed a beat, her being filled like an empty lock: with a shock of love she saw Robert's tall turning head" (201). This passage on disconnected people manifests in dissociative language: disembarking passengers (made ghostly by their mere arrival in London) exist in a subjunctive limbo, "hoping to be claimed." Disembodied by metonymy and synecdoche without linking pronouns, they become "hats" and "faces" tipping up "drowningly" as they figuratively die into the crowd. Once lost, they are caught hopelessly in the passive voice, "the new dead scanned dubiously by the older," or so Stella "thought that she could have thought." The latter phrase is an act of verbal disassociation so painstaking that it catches the reader's attention, even as it distances Stella from such morbid imaginings. What's more, she feels "nothing;" this phrase marooned, by a dash, from its context (the feeling of Robert's presence is what Stella is missing here) hints that Stella herself may be among the imagined dead—those who feel nothing. Stella is alerted back to life when her heart fails, skips a beat; only through this mimicry of death is it certain she is alive. This little death precipitates Stella's recognition of Robert and hence her confrontation with him in the "haunted" taxi (208).

Curtains: The Blackout and the Breaching of Barriers

In her preface to the American edition of *The Demon Lover and Other Stories* (1945), Bowen plays on the formal splicing of "here" and "there," "now" and "then" in her wartime fiction by describing the splice as the very condition under which she wrote: "Each time I sat down to write a story I opened a door; and the pressure against the other side of that door must have been very great, for things—ideas, images, emotions—came through with force and rapidity, sometimes violence."[62] In the preface, Bowen employs the image of the door, curtain, or wall—the barrier that cannot help but be breached by this war—to conflate the public and private spheres: "It seems to me that during the war the overcharged subconsciousnesses of everybody overflowed and merged . . . Sometimes I hardly knew where I stopped and somebody else began. The violent destruction of solid things, the explosion of the illusion that prestige, power and permanence attach to bulk and weight, left all of us, equally, heady and disembodied. Walls went down; and we felt, if not knew, each other" (95). Here, Bowen reads the blitzing of the physical wall that divides neighbors from one another as the same movement that allows those neighbors' "subconsciousnesses" to "merge." This "violent destruction of solid things" also becomes the destruction of intangible values, so that the physical disruption of the metropolis becomes also the disruption of its politics.[63] In *The Heat of the Day*, the rending of this veil, this curtain, between public and private is formally emphasized by the rending of the curtain of difference between London and Ireland.

In *To Ireland, I*, Paul Muldoon cites Bowen's collapsing of distance between present and past, place and place, in her short stories (particularly the wartime stories of *The Demon Lover*) as an example of her use of the "*féth fíada*, the barrier between being and not-being, between this world and some other, wondrous realm, [which often takes] the form of a woven fabric," a common trope in Irish tales.[64] Muldoon explicitly connects Bowen's use of the *féth fíada* with both MacNeice and Beckett; indeed, Bowen's interest in betweenness is part of a widely shared trope in Emergency writing. It links her work to the ambiguous space of purgatory in the "Lough Derg" poems, to the "mist" separating MacNeice's Wicklow hills from Dublin (and, analogously, killer from victim), to the otherworldly spaces between in Beckett's and O'Brien's purgatorial novels. In each of these treatments, images of the *féth fíada*—like Bowen's blackout curtains—are freighted with their own instability. Clair Wills's essay "The Aesthetics of Irish Neutrality during the Second World War" demonstrates the multidimensionality of this sort of boundary breaking. Wills writes about the dilemma that Ireland's official neutrality created for Irish writers, for whom "the moral politics of neutrality became the occasion for a particularly intense form of self-questioning, often amounting to a kind of fracturing of the self."[65] Wills summarizes the problematic stance: "Ireland should be neutral, but individuals don't need to be, as though public and private aspects of the self can be neatly disentangled" (124). Bowen's conflation of public and private spheres in her *Demon Lover* preface illustrates that such "public and private aspects" cannot be disentangled; in fact, they are further entangled by the Blitz. For Bowen and the other writers Wills examines, "the shifting boundary between the public and the private or intimate sphere [is also] the relation between national and global" (121). In other words, the wall coming down between one London flat and another is also the wall coming down between England (or Ireland) and the surrounding world: both walls are challenged by war. The obvious consequence of such "disruptions," Wills concludes, "is that the private and the personal can no longer function as a place of refuge or exemption" (143).

In *The Heat of the Day*, all of this is figured by the blackout curtain, which is subjected to psychological freight beyond its physical substance.[66] Beyond its function as wartime verisimilitude (Stella attends to her curtains each time she turns on a light at evening), the blackout curtain allows Bowen to reverse the meaning and location of danger, depending on the circumstance. The blackout curtain, protector of London's myriad and separate private, domestic spheres from the threatening sights of the Luftwaffe, ought, by rights, to function as a screen that keeps the dangerous public sphere away from the safe private one. But this is not always the case in *The Heat of the Day*. Early in the novel, when Roderick first arrives for his visit, Stella surveys her blacked-out flat: "The room lacked one more thing: apprehension of time . . . The day had gone from the moment Stella had drawn down the fitted blinds and drawn across them the deadening curtains: now nothing took its place. Every crack was stopped; not a mote of darkness could enter—the room, sealed up in its artificial light, remained exaggerated and cerebral" (59). Here, Bowen reverses the relationship between light and darkness; the curtains, designed to keep indoor light from penetrating outside, instead keep the outdoor darkness from seeping in. The private sphere, while closed off from the "darkness" of the fighting world, is not, however, as cozy and secure as one might expect. Rather, with the curtains drawn, Stella's room becomes "artificial." Instead of the natural, ordinary breath of the closing day, Stella is left with the potentially terrifying "nothing." This reversal is thrown into clearer relief when Harrison visits the flat on Stella's return from Robert's frightful family home. Now the room is fully "haunted," and Stella's only escape is to follow Harrison through the curtains to be "walled away" from it and into a window open on the rainy London night, which seems "as unprecautionary, natural, as that of rocks, woods and hills on which elsewhere rain fell" (153–54). At this moment, the role reversal of the public and private spheres, with regard to their traditional meanings for refuge, is complete. To Stella, the narrator explains, "Tonight, 'outside' meant the harmless world: the mischief was in her own and in other rooms. The grind and scream of battles, mechanized advances excoriating flesh and country, tearing through nerves and tearing up trees, were indoor-plotted; this was a war of dry cerebration inside windowless walls" (157).

To imagine that the novel uses the motif of the curtain to reverse the traditional public-private configuration would, however, be an oversimplification. For as Stella's allegiances change, so does the role of her drapery. At the novel's end, Robert confesses his fascism, and Stella, knowing his hours are numbered, emphasizes her love for him by indulging in an antiblackout fantasy. Aware that Harrison is lying in wait for Robert, Stella understands that opening the curtain will give Robert away. At this moment, Stella thinks "any offence against the black-out seemed to her punishable by death" (311). This notion is both an exaggeration of ARP protocol (which Bowen herself, as an air raid warden, was familiar with enforcing), in which an offense against the blackout could be punished by death from a bomb, and a statement of fact, for giving away treasonous

Robert's position will certainly hasten his death. Space, as mediated by the curtain, here *becomes* a language, a way to communicate between private and public. Stella ultimately tells Robert that she wants to open the curtain, "Want[s] to crash the window open and blaze the lights on. To think of [Harrison] makes me angry—I want to say, 'Yes, we are here, together: what else do you suppose?'" (322). This desired act, a public acting out of her private desire for Robert, would betray the Nazi to the public sphere just as it would betray the lighted private sphere to the Nazis. In this way, Stella's imagined act of complicity in publicly loving Robert would be treasonous to both her country and her lover. There is no simple division between the sides of the curtain. Nor is there a noncommittal or neutral option, since inaction would leave Stella loyal to Robert but disloyal to her Britain, all the while actively compliant with the blackout.

Another passage important to the novel's curtain motif occurs earlier, as Stella's "espionage" over Robert escalates (191). As she begins to envision her lover as an agent for her country's enemy, the fabric of London begins to shift for Stella: "She began to feel it was not the country but occupied Europe that was occupying London—suspicious listening, surreptitious movement and leaden hearts . . . The physical nearness of the Enemy—how few were the miles between the capital and the coast, between coast and coast!—became palpable. Tonight, the safety-curtain between the here and the there had lifted; the breath of danger and sorrow traveled over freely from shore to shore" (139). As the "physical nearness of the Enemy"—not just the Germans in France but her own lover, with his "cold foreign fingers" (306)—becomes palpable to Stella, Britain's island isolation becomes violable. Likewise, through her knowingly loving a spy, as Rau notes, "the ideological threat has infiltrated [Stella's] private sphere" (49), just as the blackout curtain reminds us of the ever-present military threat to the private home. When the "safety-curtain" lifts for Stella, it lifts the divisions between public and private, domestic and foreign, with it.

Reflections: "Bowen's Court at Peace" and the Double Negative of Neutral Space

Bowen's 1945 volume *The Demon Lover* collects a dozen short stories she wrote during the war, each of which challenges the "safety curtains" that purport to separate regions of the mind, of personal relations, of time, and of space. So gothic are its preoccupations that it is nearly a genre book of ghost stories; in the preface, Bowen writes that the stories as collected exhibit "a rising tide of hallucination."[67] These are those "saving hallucinations" that Bowen says are created by "the search for indestructible landmarks in a destructible world," which "produce[s] small worlds-within-worlds of hallucination" (97). As a character in "Mysterious Kôr" explains, "If you can blow whole places out of existence, you can blow whole places into it."[68] And one of the places that consistently blows into this volume of wartime stories is Ireland. One of the collection's longest stories, "The Happy Autumn Fields," first published in 1941, distills many of the volume's energies by being all at once a ghost story, an Irish story, a Blitz story, and a narrative of fractured time. The story epitomizes the shifts between public and private that so trouble Stella in *The Heat of the Day*. "The Happy Autumn Fields" formalizes the splitting of the "safety-curtain between here and there" by taking place at once in both World War II London and Victorian County Cork.[69] Formally, the story's sudden shifts between a rural Victorian mise-en-scène and wartime London are accomplished by the simple insertion of blank lines between the two settings, so that the modernist shuttlecock effect is deliberately jarring. These blanks seem, however, to be enacted *in* the story lines. The story opens in Cork but suddenly breaks off after the line "Oh, the word is lost!" as the character on the London side picks up with an offering of the "lost" name, "*Henrietta* . . ." (675). This is echoed in *The Heat of the Day*, where Stella's and Robert's first words to each other are "lost" (104).

In the London component of the story, Mary, packing her bombed-out city house—a space relegated by the Blitz to those rooms "without windows or doors"—falls through the "safety-curtain" of daily life into a trance or dream of Victorian Cork that renders her "real life" dreamlike (676). Upon coming to to find her lover, Travis, in the house with her, "the unreality of this room and of Travis's presence preyed on her as figments of dreams that one knows to be dreams can do. This environment's being in semi-ruin struck her less than its being some sort of device or trap" (677). Wishing she were back in the "happy autumn" and decidedly previous-century, peacetime fields of her dream, Mary becomes "frantic at being delayed here, when the moment awaited her in the cornfield, she all but afforded a smile at the grotesquerie of being saddled with Mary's body and lover" (677). For Mary has been, for hours, living in the afternoon across the curtain as a young girl called Sarah, who is herself in love with a country squire, Eugene. After the story provides this interlude at Mary's house and returns to County Cork, Sarah herself feels that she has been asleep and dreaming for much of the afternoon—corresponding, of course, to the bewildering time spent as Mary.

An indulgently long excerpt from her father and his siblings' childhood diary (1876) reprinted in *Bowen's Court* reveals Bowen's source text for the family outing in "The Happy Autumn Fields," and Bowen's family tree contains all the fictional family's names.[70] In this way, the relationship between Mary and her presumed ancestors in the short story may be seen to mirror Bowen's with her Cork ancestors as she worked on the history while living through the war in London. If Bowen's Court was the novelist's "saving hallucination" during the Blitz, as Mount Morris is for Roderick, it is safe to assume that we find Mary's corollary in *Bowen's Court* as well. In the Blitzed London of the story, Travis is concerned for the bewildered Mary's safety. After all, he says, "with the lock blown off your front door anyone who likes can get in and out" (677). (In fact, the building appears to be filled with looters in furniture-mover clothing.) What is really going in and out, however, is Mary's consciousness; the blown lock between her private home and the public sphere has also blown the lock on her imagination, blown the lock between the past and the present, the dead and the living. For Mary, in this blitz of time, appears to be both herself and her ancestor, and she is terrified, for just at the point of her waking, it seems that "something terrible may be going to happen" to Eugene in County Cork, rendering there no "to-morrow" for the happy autumn fields (682). Suddenly, a bomb explodes in London: "The one way back to the fields was barred by Mary's surviving the fall of ceiling. Sarah was right in doubting that there would be to-morrow: Eugene, Henrietta were lost in time to the woman weeping there on the bed, no longer reckoning who she was" (683). After Travis does some reading in the family papers, he discovers from a letter that Eugene was thrown from his horse and killed. The letter writer wonders "what made the horse shy in those empty fields" (685). Bowen leaves the reader to infer one answer: it was a German bomb. From the vantage point of the 1940s, the Nazi threat is capable of destroying even the dream of the past, just as, had Hitler's Operation Green been realized, Bowen's own "saving hallucination" of Cork would have shattered.

The rending of the curtain in Bowen's wartime writing collapses difference, collapses her characters' inner and outer worlds, their safe and unsafe spaces, into something else, something blitz-riven: a no-place. This is the key location of war for Bowen, and it straddles the divide between London and Ireland. In a draft of *Bowen's Court* composed early in the war, Elizabeth Bowen writes about the physical and metaphorical space between County Cork and the Battle of Britain:

> Bowen's Court, this December, still stands, in its particular island of timeless quietness, in the south of an island not at war. Only the wireless in the corner of the library conduct's [*sic*] the war's urgency to the place. But the idea of threat and force and danger does not seem so foreign there as it does in England. It is true, there is still the absence of the immediate physical threat. But such threats, to an Irish house, have been felt and felt: in a sense, they have never gone from the air. At the same time, in the house itself, in the country round it, there is the constant image of what peace could be. To be at Bowen's Court is like looking into a mirror at the reflection of something that does not exist.[71]

This is an attempt to reconcile Bowen's Court's sense of timeless separation from war with its garrison role as "an Irish house," an Anglo-Irish ghost house, which had already, by outlasting the burnings of the 1920s, seemed to survive its own death.[72] Bowen collapses distance by contrasting the apparent peace of Ireland's neutrality with the sense that the threat of violence is "never gone" from the Irish air (this recalls MacNeice's West in "The Closing Album"). Bowen's Court, by being at once "timelessly" separate from the current war and never separate from the timeless pressure of conflict, becomes "the reflection of something that does not exist": a mirage, a double negative, a no-place.[73]

In *The Heat of the Day*, the third-person narrator occasionally slips into second and even first person to make totalizing comments on the war experience. One reads, "In these years the idea of war made you see any peaceful scene as it were through glass" (114). Here is that *Bowen's Court* comment rewritten for the novel of wartime experience. Bowen's language of the "no-place" ("to be at Bowen's Court is like looking into a mirror at the reflection of something that does not exist") asks the reader to imagine something at a double divide—a reflection, already a distortion, of something nonexistent—but demands, at the same time, that it be visible. After all, this is an act of "looking," and to look, one must exist, must reflect—if not in the looking-glass sense, in the thinking sense. Bowen's troubled "mirror" is at once reminiscent of *Bowen's Court*'s mirror reflections in her novel of war and of the reflective way Bowen bends language in the novel. A reflection not only mimics but transforms, and these two places in Bowen's work—London at war and Ireland at "peace"—are transformed by and into each other just as the novel questions language's agency and directive to reflect. For if language is a mirror, its transformative work both mimics and distorts what it reflects; a mirror image is like a very fine lie. Like a spy, it seems to be what it is not. And this is both the problem and the mandate for language at war in *The Heat of the Day*.

CHAPTER 5

Unreadable Books, Unspeakable Worlds

Beckett and O'Brien in Purgatory

Non ragioniam di lor, ma guarda e passa.

—DANTE, *Inferno*

In canto 3 of the *Inferno*, just outside the gates of hell, Dante is overwhelmed by a cacophony of cries, "such a commotion of groans and wails of woe . . . outlandish tongues, and accents doloroso," that he weeps "from sheer bewilderment." "Master, what noise is this?" the overwhelmed poet asks.[1] These, Virgil tells him, are the neutral souls, who chose their own good rather than a side when it came to conflict. Their punishment is eternal envy of the decisive ones, eternal babble, and eternal censorship (not to speak of hornet stings). The neutral souls are scorned by both mercy and justice, and though they will cry out interminably, Virgil says, they are not to be spoken of again.

On the train in the beginning of Beckett's novel *Watt*, Mr. Watt finds himself sitting beside a Mr. Spiro, author of *A Spiritual Syringe for the Costive in Devotion*, whose monologue on the problems of the Real Body goes, alas, unheeded. "Watt heard nothing of this," as it happens, "because of other voices, singing, crying, stating, murmuring, things un intelligible, in his ear."[2] "Now these voices," the narrator begins to enumerate, "sometimes they sang only, and sometimes they cried only, and sometimes they murmured only, and sometimes they sang and cried, and sometimes they sang and stated," on and on through each possible combination, "to mention only these four kinds of voices, for there were others" (29). Like Dante in canto 3, among the "howls, shrieks, grunts, gasps, bawls" (*Inferno* 3.27), Watt is assailed by voices he cannot understand, but it is Beckett's reader who may be tempted to weep from bewilderment. Beckett's long intertextual engagement with *The Divine Comedy* suggests that Watt's relationship to Dante in canto 3 is intentional.[3] Both bewildered figures are positioned just outside the gates of hell—Dante literally and Watt figuratively as he is en route to the home of Mr. Knott, the service of whom will prove Watt's mental undoing. But while Dante reports his bewilderment within the neat strictures of terza rima, *Watt* enacts it, forces it upon the reader through seemingly interminable lists, conjectures, and repetitions. In other words, the book is very nearly unreadable in format alone. To read *Watt* is to be aware of reading as particularly difficult work, a sort of purgatorial quest that must be suffered through in order to come out the other side, at the end of the book. While Beckett hints at Watt's position among the neutral souls at the gates of hell, the novel itself suggests Watt's world is purgatorial—only, Watt is trapped in a purgatory he cannot understand or escape.

Chapter 2 of this book focuses on Patrick Kavanagh's and Denis Devlin's poetic explorations of neutral Ireland as the place that Sean O'Faolain called "a purgatory for the artist, and a place or state of punishment where some [artistic] souls suffer for a time before they push on somewhere else."[4] This chapter completes the Dantean circuit to examine what may be the two most powerful treatments of language to emerge from that place, *Watt* and Flann O'Brien's *The Third Policeman*. If Devlin's and Kavanagh's "Lough Derg" poems are distressingly ambivalent, *Watt* and *The Third Policeman* are just plain distressing. T. M. Ragg of Routledge, for example, read Beckett's manuscript with "considerable bewilderment" and found it "too wild and unintelligible" to publish.[5] While *Watt* enacts reading as a purgatorial quest, Flann O'Brien's *The Third Policeman*, written in 1939–40, torments its reader with any number of hair-pulling absurdities (for example, the strange physical properties of its world, in which people can turn into their bicycles and vice versa), only to start all over again in the last chapter, which repeats the beginning almost verbatim. "Unreadable," in the sense that one can never finish reading it, O'Brien's novel suffered a publishing purgatory similar to Beckett's. *Watt*, for all its "immense . . . vitality," lingered on publishers' desks (and in Denis Devlin's suitcase in Washington, D.C.) until Olympia Press published it in 1953, following on the success of the *Trilogy*.[6] *The Third Policeman* was published posthumously in 1967, after O'Brien's wife dug it out of a drawer. Publishers' serial rejections of the novel left O'Brien wounded, and for years he claimed that the manuscript had been lost—poured out into the wind from the boot of a car, according to one story.[7] If Bowen meant for her syntax to "displease" and discomfort her readers,[8] the language in Beckett's and O'Brien's novels is meant to terrify them. Bowen's wartime novel is interested in what we can learn by the difficult practice of reading between the lines, in what can be said without being spoken. Beckett's and O'Brien's wartime novels enact purgatorial worlds where nothing is rationally comprehensible *at all*. Considered "unreadable" and unpublishable, despite or because of their acrobatic language, both novels lingered in manuscript purgatory for so long that when they came to light, critics were slow to connect them with the concerns of their wartime context.

In this chapter, I offer a new approach to these two "unreadable" novels, arguing that their unreadability is an intentional hallmark of their status as traumatic texts. We can approach (but never completely access) the trauma these novels attempt to articulate through their design as purgatorial. *Watt* and *The Third Policeman* are both, however, *failed* purgatories, because their characters' persistent failures to read and communicate their worlds prevent them from acquiring the knowledge necessary for purgation or the language necessary for healing. Where their protagonists fail, these novels fail also, in the sense that neither provides a satisfactory novelistic experience: traditional elements of plot and character development are denied. What both novels offer instead are parodies of rational thinking that result in infinite wrong answers, brought about by the protagonists' false belief that their world makes sense. In their peculiarly late modernist and Hibernian demotics, these novels savage the Irish government's twinned assumptions about a rational "neutral language"—that is, Frank Aiken's and Eamon de Valera's conception that language can be neutered by refusing to name the war and that it can function as a neutral medium by offering unbiased descriptors of a belligerent world. The "gross and net result," as O'Brien's Policeman MacCruiskeen would say, is the thoroughly peculiar language of *The Third Policeman* and *Watt*—

the apotheosis of the failure of the Irish government's "neutral language" and an enactment of the epistemological crisis that the Emergency created.[9] Read in their oft-ignored historical contexts, Beckett's and O'Brien's purgatorial antinovels offer an Irish view of World War II as a traumatic event, one that was both officially and theoretically "unspeakable."

Neutral Ireland and Purgatory as Misprision: Yeats, Beckett, O'Brien, and Ó Cadhain

Samuel Beckett attended the premiere of W. B. Yeats's last play, *Purgatory*, at the Abbey Theatre on August 10, 1938.[10] The action of the play takes place before "a ruined house and a bare tree in the background," a house in which "great people lived and died . . . Magistrates, colonels, members of Parliament."[11] According to the Old Man who was born there, ruination befell this big house when his Ascendancy mother married below her class, to a stable hand who "squandered everything she had" and "burned down the house when drunk" (227–28). For this "capital offense," the Old Man tells his son, the mother is cast into the purgatory that the play depicts in dumb show in the ruined house: "But there's a problem: she must live / Through everything in exact detail, / Driven to it by remorse," until she regrets and thus expurgates her "crime" of sexual gratification and blood "pollution" (229, 231). Standing before this eerie scene, the Old Man confesses to his son that he killed his father in a rage while the house was burning down. Now the audience witnesses the Old Man's killing of the Boy: "My father and my son on the same jack-knife!" (231). Having wiped his blade clean, the Old Man waits in anticipation of his mother's release, saying,

> Dear mother, the window is dark again
> But you are in the light because
> I finished all that consequence.
> I killed that lad because had he grown up
> He would have struck a woman's fancy,
> Begot, and passed pollution on. (231)

But the Old Man sees instead the moonlit scene of his conception played over, a failed purgation: "Twice a murderer," he cries, "and all for nothing, / And she must animate that dead night / Not once but many times!" (232). For the Old Man, the failed purgation is his mother's, but for the audience, a different sin may be at stake: the Old Man's unrepented murders of his father and son. Perhaps, Yeats's play indicates, this is not the purgatory it appears to be—that of the mother—but that of her violent son. Though such a reading of the play contradicts the disturbing eugenicism that unites it with *On the Boiler*, it is just as certainly an indicator of the play's time.[12] The Old Man fails to repent his patricide and murders his son into the bargain: metaphorically, he maps onto that generation of Europeans whose fathers died in the Great War and whose sons would die in World War II. Writing *Purgatory* in 1938, Yeats knew, like everyone else, that the shadow of renewed and catastrophic violence had been cast over Europe. The years between the wars had failed to provide any form of purgation: the great houses of an old Europe were in ruins, and the cycle of violence would continue. Watching the play just more than a month before the Munich Agreement, Yeats's audience, and certainly Beckett, would have been aware that none of these purgatories could end in purgation.

Yeats's Abbey audience was also aware of something else: that when this violence finally erupted, it would happen just across the sea, a war to be fought nearly in view of Ireland but also just out of sight. For as early as 1938, there was already widespread acknowledgment (cemented by de Valera himself) that if war were to happen, Ireland would declare its neutrality in it. In 1939, when *Purgatory* became available to readers, war was just as much a foregone conclusion for Europe as neutrality was for Ireland. Yeats's play became the first of many literary portrayals of purgatory to be drawn by Irish writers as they waited for the Emergency to come to an end.

Yeats's play establishes a precedent of figuring purgatory as misprision. The Old Man fails to properly read his purgatorial situation, and the play ends with the repetition of the dumb show he is forced to watch: the regrettable night of his conception. He is thus trapped in a cycle, unable to unconceive his own life and unwilling to repent his sins. If Devlin's and Kavanagh's penitent poems of Saint Patrick's Purgatory represent ambitious failures, in which the meaning of the pilgrimage is difficult to ascertain, Yeats's *Purgatory* demonstrates the dangers of misprisions that leave one stuck. Three terrifying novels written during the Emergency extend this theme: *Watt*, *The Third Policeman*, and Máirtín

Ó Cadhain's *Cré na Cille* (*Churchyard Clay*), often cited as the greatest modern novel in Irish. All three appear to be set in a purgatory that is simultaneously a depiction of rural Ireland; all are written in intentionally difficult language. (*Cré na Cille*, long considered "untranslatable," was not published in English until 2015.)[13] These novels' concerns with misreading and failing to repent suggest an ethical uncertainty at the heart of Ireland's neutral purgatory, but they also suggest that this space of perdition is linguistically fervid. If, as Beckett argued in 1929, "Hell is the static lifelessness of unrelieved viciousness" and "Paradise is the static lifelessness of unrelieved immaculation," then Emergency Ireland would be somewhere in between: "Purgatory a flood of movement and vitality released by the conjunction of these two elements."[14]

Máirtín Ó Cadhain spent the Emergency incarcerated without trial in the Curragh internment camp, where, as an IRA member, he was imprisoned for the war's duration, along with other belligerents downed in Irish territory.[15] In the Curragh camp, he began *Cré na Cille*, a plotless novel in dialogue set among the dead in a Connemara graveyard. His characters are *interred*, a close proximate to *interned*, and the novel presents World War II as seen from a completely neutral zone: belowground, where the second "War of the Two Foreigners" appears as stale news inevitably censored by the newly dead who report it.[16] Opinions about the war range from a dead republican's "Hitler's my darling. He's the boy for them" to "If England is beaten, the country will be in a bad way," but these remarks are only a fraction of the chorus, and graveyard support for Hitler and Churchill is more often couched in the language of sport ("Up Hitler!" "Up Churchill!") and certainly of less interest to the characters than the ongoing property feud between the dead Catriona and her living sister Nell (6, 240). The principal voice of the war is a downed French airman, whom at first nobody in the graveyard can understand ("Every time he mentions Hitler he starts spluttering away in a torrent of talk" [34]). Over the course of the novel, the pilot acquires passing Irish, but his early remark, "Qu'est-ce que vous dites? Quelle drôle de langue!" (33) serves as a fitting introduction to the text; it is difficult to understand what people are saying, but their language is strange and amusing indeed.[17]

The entirety of *Cré na Cille* is voiced by the dead; interred and trapped, they find, however, that they cannot shut up. Their physical immobility is supplanted by volubility, and as they continue to rehash aboveground grievances, even as graves are piled into graves (many of the corpses are buried directly on top of their neighbors), there seems no release from the bewildering chatter. What is most notable about *Cré na Cille* is the aliveness of its language, which functions to counterpoint the unavoidable stagnation and desiccation of its characters. As a writer, Ó Cadhain was concerned about the possible death of the Irish language, yet his novel rings with its vitality; the characters' speech is consistently witty and lively, bawdy and raunchy and sometimes vile (the dialogue in this book suggests that the Censorship Board did not bother to examine texts in the national language). Ever interrupted, each character vies for attention to his or her words, leaving the reader sometimes lost in a haze of exclamations, interruptions, and trailings off. If language is what survives Ó Cadhain's "dirty dust" (6), it is also terribly difficult to read.

In the graveyard, the newly buried are the only source of information on the outside world, but they tend to enter the text in perplexity: "Christ's cross protect me!—Am I alive or dead? Are the people here alive or dead? They are all rabbiting on exactly the same way as they were above the ground!" (6). Like the narrator of *The Third Policeman*, they seem unaware of their own death. If Kavanagh's farmers in *The Great Hunger* are alive but feel dead, Ó Cadhain's dead are just like the living. "This is much the same as the 'ould country,'" one explains, "except that we only see the grave we are in" (6). The cultural condemnation here is consistent with Kavanagh's, Beckett's, and O'Brien's: life in Ireland is "much the same" as death. In Ó Cadhain's churchyard, there is no peace in the grave. The Frenchman mopes, "On espère tojours trouver la paix dans la mort, mais la tombe ne semble pas encore être la mort" (34), and indeed this sigh for "la paix" suggests that there is no peace aboveground either. As Maggie chides the newly dead Breed, "Peace and quiet, is that what you want, you say? Don't we all want that! Well, then you came to the wrong place looking for peace and quiet" (90). If the interred in the dirty dust are not at peace, the living Irish aren't either; both are in an Emergency they have no power to conclude.

By the time *Cré na Cille* was begun, in the isolation of internment, Samuel Beckett was deep into the notebooks that would become *Watt* and writing from his own position of social and linguistic isolation in a farming village in the South of France.[18] Hiding from the Gestapo in Roussillon after his Resistance cell had been betrayed, Beckett worked on *Watt* as a literary exercise "to keep [his] hand in" while his hands were tied.[19] *Watt* bears strong marks of its writer's state of prolonged suspension as he waited out the war, and, like *The Third Policeman* and *Cré na Cille*, its setting is both obviously Irish and obviously a space of perdition.[20] *Watt* tells the story (narrated by one Sam) of Mr. Watt's service in the mysterious home of Mr. Knott—his arrival, his work belowstairs, and his term as valet to the inscrutable Knott. While *Cré na Cille*'s characters are immobile, Watt's upward progression through Mr. Knott's big house suggests an Anglo-Irish sort of purgatory that recalls the stalemate ending of Yeats's play.

Watt is not Beckett's first venture into purgatorial settings. His 1929 essay "Dante . . . Bruno. Vico . . Joyce" refers to "this earth that is Purgatory,"[21] and the 1933 story "Echo's Bones" is set there. Rejected from the collection *More Pricks Than Kicks* but brought to print in 2014, "Echo's Bones" finds Beckett's Dantean protagonist Belacqua "bent double" on a fence, in mimicry of the indolent lute maker in Dante's Ante-Purgatory, after whom he is named.[22] Everything about the setting is the Irish Pale, except for the fact that Belacqua is metaphorically well beyond it. He finds himself "up and about in the dust of the world, back at his old games in the dim spot [so] that he wondered if his lifeless condition were not all a dream and if on the whole he had not been a great deal deader before than after his formal departure, so to speak, from among the quick" (3). Like his namesake, Beckett's Belacqua exhibits no effort to move from his position, and *Watt* appears to pick up where "Echo's Bones" leaves off, except that, for Watt, the desire for progression is what makes his punishment so traumatic. Gottfried Büttner, who has devoted an entire monograph to *Watt*, believes that "the nightmarish story dwells, not entirely . . . but most intensely, on Watt's *experiences in death* rather than his experiences in life."[23]

Dantean nods in Beckett's novel complement a reading of Mr. Knott's estate as a purgatorial space. For example, Watt's domestic movement winds from belowstairs to above, and there is the false promise of a Virgil-like guide in Erskine: "And now for a little along the way that lies between you and me Erskine will go by your side, to be your guide, and then for the rest you will travel alone, or with only shades to keep you company" (63). Divorced from the outside world, Watt is left to his own devices in Knott's house and grounds, but through this purgatory, he fails to progress. If purgatory itself can be read as an epistemological problem—a space in which one seeks enlightenment and suffers in exchange for expiation—the purgatory of this novel, and of the Irish experience of World War II, is always a failed one. In a chapter titled "The Anglo-Irish Postmortem," Julian Moynahan surveys Yeats's and Beckett's purgatories together, noting the connection to Saint Patrick's Purgatory and to Dante, before concluding that "the scheme of Purgatory in *Watt* . . . turns out to be self-canceling."[24] I argue, further, that the purgatorial aspect of *Watt* is a deliberate failure: a purgatory in which there is simply no chance of purgation.

The concept of purgation fails, too, in O'Brien's *The Third Policeman*. In the novel, the nameless narrator—an admitted murderer and thief—chronicles his quest to find a stolen black cashbox in a hellish "Parish" of rural Ireland and his trials at the hands of three monstrously odd policemen.[25] This rural parish is, it turns out, a *parish* of the *perished*: an afterworld, yet the promise of Virgilian guidance fails here, too. Only after his (unrealized) death does the Narrator discover a voice that "came from deep inside me, from my soul" (25). This guide, who speaks in italics throughout the text (adding yet another metatextual intrusion), "was friendly, was my senior in years, and was solely concerned for my own welfare. For convenience," the Narrator explains, "I called him Joe" (25). But as it turns out, Joe is no less self-aggrandizing than his nameless host and even threatens to "clear out" when the Narrator offends him by calling him "scaly" (25, 118). Maciej Ruczaj reads the Dantean parallels in *The Third Policeman*, suggesting in a note that canto 4 of the *Inferno*, "with its state of confusion, namelessness, and liminality" (103), may be a model for the parish. Ruczaj also points out that, as in Dante, the Narrator's punishments are often tailored to fit his sins. Yet there's a crucial difference at work: while Dante's Mount Purgatory winds in an inevitable ascent, "*The Third Policeman* leaves no space for such an upward continuation; the narrator is not a pilgrim but an inhabitant of the realm, and thus the dawn signals only the deathly repetition of the infernal punishment" (100). "At the end of Dante's pilgrimage, the final union of 'being' and 'knowing' is achieved. Conversely," Ruczaj notes, the Narrator's "revelation consists in . . . 'angry incomprehension' and distortion," and the setting "remains horizontal rather than vertical, it moves in circles, rather than—as the pilgrim-poets do—in the gyre" (100).

Indeed, at the novel's end, when the Narrator returns home from his journeys, he begins them all over again, with no new knowledge to help him: "the re-discovery of the familiar, the re-experience of the already-suffered, the fresh-forgetting of the unremembered" (200). In a letter to William Saroyan, O'Brien explains that "when you get to the end of this book you realize that my hero . . . has been dead throughout the book and that all the queer ghastly things which have been happening to him are happening in a sort of hell which he earned for the killing."[26] As Michael Rubenstein has pointed out, this is not hell but a *sort of hell*, and readings of the novel as an inferno can be reductive.[27] It doesn't help that a paragraph of unused material voiced by Joe (the Narrator's "soul") is included in a "Publisher's Note" on the last page of the novel. The oft-quoted line states, "Hell goes round and round. In shape it is circular and by nature it is interminable, repetitive, and very nearly unbearable" (200). But it is important to note that this material was cut from the novel; the result is a publisher's decision that has shaped interpretations of the book for decades. Recently, Carol Taaffe has described *The Third Policeman* as "a parable of a soul in purgatory," which I think is more apt, although I think that perhaps this interpretation has been stymied by the fact that it is a purgatory with no chance of purgation.[28] If this is a soul in purgatory, it will be there forever.

Arsene's remark to Watt, upon leaving Mr. Knott's house, makes for a fitting comment on the Narrator's journey in *The Third Policeman*, as well: "And if I could begin it all over again, knowing what I know now, the result would be the same. And if I could begin again a third time, knowing what I would know then, the result would be the same. And if I could begin it all over again a hundred times, knowing each time a little more than the time before, the result would always be the same, and the hundredth life as the first, and the hundred lives as one" (47). Much suffered, nothing gained: the servant's experience at Mr. Knott's big house in *Watt* teaches him nothing, gets him nowhere. This is consistent with Michael Robinson's suggestion that Beckett's postwar protagonists are "not in Hell but Purgatory: a Purgatory of waiting on the verge of timelessness. It is a grimmer place than that imagined by Dante [in whose] *Purgatorio* eventual ascent, the toil uphill, was certain for even the most indolent of its inhabitants, but in Beckett there is no certitude . . . no known end and no discernible path."[29] *Watt* shows that Beckett was already using this scheme during the war. Watt, like O'Brien's Narrator, experiences a "non-directional" purgatory akin to the one Beckett describes in Joyce's *Work in Progress*, which "excludes culmination."[30] Here, Beckett writes, "There is a continuous purgatorial process at work [with] neither prize nor penalty; simply a series of stimulants to enable the kitten to catch its tail" (33). *Cré na Cille*, *Watt*, and *The Third Policeman* are terribly funny books—that is, they are funny *and* terrifying; in each, there is a linguistic vitality not unlike the kitten's vitality when chasing its tail. Like the kitten's, the protagonist's quest in each novel is ridiculous, maddening, and irresolvable,[31] yet in the novels' language there is a sense of surplus, and repetitive cycles somehow feel less like a pointless circle than a kitten's play.

The fact that these three novels were written in isolation and not published for years makes their peculiar symbiosis all the more compelling; one cannot argue that they were influenced by one another.[32] *Watt* and *The Third Policeman*, especially when considered alongside *Cré na Cille*, indicate the zeitgeist of Irish neutrality: a literature marked by strong antirealistic tendencies, language that appears to play itself to death, and themes of death-in-life, or life-in-death. In some aspects, they are absolutely kindred to Bowen's realistic *The Heat of the Day*, sharing both metafictional and gothic tropes and intentionally difficult language. Sharing with Bowen, MacNeice, Kavanagh, and Devlin concerns about wartime culpability that manifest in reflexive language, *Watt* and *The Third Policeman* participate, like the Lough Derg poems, in a persistent imagining of Emergency-era Ireland as a purgatory of society and language, albeit one with little chance of escape or redemption. Echoing the concerns of Yeats's *Purgatory*, both *Watt* and *The Third Policeman* can be read as black comedic takes on the death of the foundational Anglo-Irish genre better associated with Bowen, the big house novel. Beckett's and O'Brien's conscious distortion of that generic heritage makes their Emergency novels exemplary participants in the shift from modernism to postmodernism—a shift typically dated to the Second World War but that, given the composition of these novels (*The Third Policeman* was completed in 1940 and *Watt* in 1945), happens during, rather than after, the war. I suggest, following Tyrus Miller's reading of *Watt*, that these are exemplary late modernist novels, works self-consciously composed in a transitional poetics.[33] They utilize modernist language play without affirming any redemptive possibilities for it.

Watt and *The Third Policeman* each concern characters who cannot escape from an isolated, rural Ireland that is both relentlessly illogical and characterized by cyclical movement and linguistic breakdown. In both texts there is the promise of a centrally organized source of knowledge or asylum (represented by Knott and Policeman Fox) that remains inscrutable, unfulfilled. The protagonists' efforts to attain knowledge are characterized by forms of misreading that spill over into the trope of unspeakability. Confronting the moment of his death, Flann O'Brien's nameless protagonist in *The Third Policeman* can say only that "something happened," though he cannot say what that something is; his post-death narrative begins in aphasia: he cannot "convey with known words the feelings which came knocking at my numbed mind" (23, 24). Watt, in Beckett's novel, appears to be a member of the living, though even his humanity is frequently called into doubt. By the novel's temporal conclusion (for his story is related out of sequence), Watt's inability to read what happened at Knott's house has left him unable to articulate himself at all; his "world became unspeakable" (85), and he is left interned in an apparent asylum, almost as the living dead. Like *Cré na Cille*, these novels depict life in Emergency-era Ireland as a place akin to Dante's neutral zone, where no one can be read or understood, only trapped in bewilderment. *Watt* and *The Third Policeman* invoke the idea of purgatory, as the characters seek release from their suspended existences, but in each case they inhabit a purgatory that fails: unable to understand their situations or to let go of earthly sins, they are trapped in an ongoing emergency.[34] In the remainder of this chapter, I show how *Watt* and *The Third Policeman*, far from ignoring the war, frame the Emergency as a central traumatic event in the development of Irish literature and culture during the twentieth century. Their multilevel tropes of "unreadability" comprise a narrative strategy for writing a war so often reduced to the rhetorical figure of the "unspeakable."

Reading Beckett and O'Brien in Context

In spite of the novels' similarities, *Watt* and *The Third Policeman* have never been explored together in depth. This is perhaps because the impossibility of making an argument of influence has short-circuited a comparison that seemed obvious to Brian Cosgrove as long ago as 1976, when he reviewed Anne Clissmann's study of O'Brien, the first monograph on the author's work: "Speaking of *The Third Policeman*, Miss Clissmann fails to mention the surely related world of Beckett's *Watt* (both fictions deal with a pilgrim who, placed in an alien world, strives desperately to relate the absurdities he undergoes to his own limited sense of order and logic); and it is a major shortcoming of the whole critical venture that O'Brien and his contemporary Beckett are never placed in any meaningful juxtaposition."[35] This critical "shortcoming" has, however, persisted, in spite of the many critics who have more recently mentioned the connection without pursuing it.[36] In the conclusion of the revised edition of his *Flann O'Brien: A Portrait of the Artist as a Young Post-Modernist* (2009), Keith Hopper notes *Watt*'s and *The Third Policeman*'s "striking post-modernist parallels . . . shared concepts of relativity and language; similar metaleptic intrusions (particularly the use of mock footnotes); and even a metafictional appearance by the author-god of *Watt*."[37] The implications of this tantalizing comparison are left for the reader to ponder. The most likely reason that what Cosgrove calls this "major shortcoming of the whole critical venture" has gone so long unresolved is that the "critical venture" itself has been interested in creating a Beckett and an O'Brien to suit its theoretical whims. The two wartime novels have scarcely been historicized as Irish novels of the wartime experience, partly because of their delayed publications and partly because critical attention to both Beckett and O'Brien has focused on their roles as foundational postmodern writers, supposedly divorced from historical circumstance and read as cosmopolitan chroniclers of human alienation.

Interpretations of *The Third Policeman* have ranged widely over time, and a clutch of publications surrounding O'Brien's centenary in 2011 offer no real consensus, though a focus on the novel as a Menippean satire has been sustained since Keith Booker's 1995 monograph on O'Brien and Bakhtin.[38] A 2011 special issue of *Review of Contemporary Fiction* devoted to O'Brien offers five different articles on *The Third Policeman*, displaying a dizzying variety of interpretations of the novel through, for example, Parmenides and philosophy of mind, Thomist Catholicism, and 'pataphysics, along with comparisons to Nabokov and, most valuably, to

Dante.[39] In his 2010 book *Public Works*, Michael Rubenstein usefully contextualizes the novel, saying that the setting is "not a Catholic hell but a national hell. The hell of *The Third Policeman* is the landscape of the national imaginary incorporated into the state's modern grid, resulting in sublime horror and comic farce" (106). Rubenstein's use of historical context is savvy, yet what I argue is that *The Third Policeman* is not either a purgatory or a satire but both: purgatory *as* satire. Only by reading it as an Emergency text does this become clear.

Beckett described *Watt* to George Reavey as "an unsatisfactory book . . . but it has its part in the series, as will perhaps appear in time."[40] Beckett's caution that *Watt*'s "place" would "appear in time" has a stronger resonance when one considers that the novel's own historical time is often left unacknowledged by those who attempt to "place" it. Critical studies of *Watt* typically focus on poststructural interpretations that ignore the novel's historical position as a novel of the Second World War and as an Irish novel, in particular. The resulting readings, part of a longstanding critical tendency to universalize the characters and settings of Beckett's late work, are a mismatch with *Watt*, a wartime novel that embodies the transition between Beckett's more "Irish" prewar fiction and his postwar writing in French by insisting on its localized setting (in the end, an addendum jokes, "For all the good that frequent departures out of Ireland had done him, he might just as well have stayed there" [217]).

Jonathan Boulter, for example, offers a compelling reading of *Watt* as a traumatic text, a "doubled testimony of an impossible event," but he universalizes the text nearly to the point that it becomes more, rather than less, perplexing.[41] He writes, "*Watt*, finally, is a deeply melancholic story about the impossibility of knowing the Other and the effects on the self of the recognition that events and people may always exceed one's interpretive grasp" (107). Perhaps because his major focus is Beckett's postwar writing, Boulter reads *Watt* as if historical circumstance could be entirely vacated from its meaning. Certainly, later texts like *The Unnamable* (1958) offer themselves more easily to such interpretations, but *Watt* is insistent on, and even mimetic of, its setting's place and time. Tellingly, Boulter ends his discussion of *Watt* by stating that in the novel "Beckett's true task—to find . . . a 'literature of the unword'—is partially realized" (107), an indication that, like so many readers, Boulter is reading *Watt* just to establish "its place in the series" of Beckett's philosophy. Working in a similar vein, Stan Gontarski claims that *Watt*'s "textual anomalies and signals of incompletion . . . suggest irresolution and negation, textual and aesthetic, and so anticipate the epistemological crises that dominate Beckett's subsequent work."[42] But *Watt* does not *anticipate* epistemological crisis: it *enacts* it. Read in its historical context, *Watt* becomes more than an exercise in the development of the mature Beckett; it is a deliberate attempt to enact the impossibility of wartime epistemology. If it is a "doubled testimony of an impossible event," the impossible event is World War II, and its impossible witnessing maps onto its Irish setting: the country that missed the war.

Set in a recognizable facsimile of south County Dublin, *Watt* at first glance appears unconcerned with the war that raged during its composition, in which Ireland was a declared neutral. But such a presumption is dependent on the false but common notion that, as Edna Longley has put it, the experience of World War II was "alien" to Irish literature, that Ireland's wartime neutrality somehow neutralized war content for Irish writers.[43] Like much of Ireland's literature written between 1939 and 1945, *Watt* is intensely concerned with wartime epistemology, to the point that with its historical position elided, many of its major concerns are rendered illegible. *Watt* is a problematic book—formally and critically—because it is reflective of a problematic notion: the impossibility of witnessing to trauma—from either within or without. The same is true of *The Third Policeman*, and as with *Watt*, when it is read as a purely philosophical text or a logic game, the result is unsatisfying: bits of the novel are illuminated, but the text as a whole remains a puzzle. But read as purgatorial allegories of neutral Ireland, the design of both books becomes clear. Accounting for these novels' historical situation allows us to read them as key texts in the late modernist literature of war.

Keeping in mind Beckett's caution in "Dante . . . Bruno" that "the danger is in the neatness of identifications" (19), I suggest that purgatory offers a paradigm through which *Watt* and *The Third Policeman* can be productively read.[44] If Dante is the poet of trauma, par excellence, a witness, who, though he may weep, produces a legible report of ultimate suffering, Watt and O'Brien's Narrator are left at the gates of hell, lost in cacophony or aphasia. While *Watt* and *The Third Policeman* are distinctly purgatorial, canto 3 of the *Inferno* offers an additional intertext that comments on the novels' historical frame: like the neutral souls, the experience of neutral Ireland appears to be censored out of its own literary report. There are clear traces of the war in these books, yet as novels set in Ireland, the war is also muted, buried, hidden from view—just what the Irish government's policies of neutrality and censorship intended to accomplish. In this way, *Watt* and *The Third Policeman*, rather than ignoring the Second World War, *enact* the Irish experience of it, akin to Virgil's "let's not speak of them; but let us look, and go from hence" (*Inferno* 3.50–51). The intentional failures built into the novels' structural elements and their sabotage of readability work together, enacting the suffering felt by those forced to wait in silence for a war to end while criticizing the policy of transparent "neutral language" held by the Emergency-era Irish state.

Watt, "Resistant" Language, and the Traces of War

Unlike Dante, who progresses down to hell and back up through paradise, emerging to tell the tale, Beckett's unreadable Mr. Watt makes no progress. If the novel's aim is to tell the story of Watt's service in the home of Mr. Knott—his arrival, his work belowstairs, and his term as Knott's upstairs valet—then the telling is most unsatisfactory. What elements of plot that exist are related out of order. The reader, although privy to an endless series of lists and conjectures, is left continually in the dark as to why, for example, Watt is there in the first place, who Knott is, for what duration Watt remains, and where, exactly, he goes upon leaving. As a witness to Mr. Knott's establishment, and indeed his person, Watt is an unsatisfactory guide. Again and again, the reader is told, "Watt did not know what had happened" (74). He cannot interpret Knott or his home, and all the incidents that occur in the book seem to him "incidents that is to say of great formal brilliance and indeterminable purport" (74)—not unlike the novel itself. Instead of a narrative arc, the reader experiences simply that "series of stimulants to enable the kitten to catch its tail" that Beckett associates with purgatory.[45] One of the effects of this purgatorial stimulus is the strange language of *Watt*, always on the chase for meaning without really capturing it. But the language games in *Watt* are more than ludic Cartesianism: they are traces of Beckett's own experience of the war.

Famously preferring "France at war to Ireland at peace," Beckett intended to spend the war in Paris, but through his translation work in the Resistance cell Gloria SMH, he found himself (along with his partner, Suzanne Déchevaux-Dumesnil) on the run from the Nazis when his cell was betrayed.[46] Written, as Beckett told Reavey, "in dribs and drabs, first on the run, then of an evening after the clodhopping, during the occupation," *Watt* is very much a product of war and disjuncture.[47] The resulting manuscript Gontarski has called "the white whale of Beckett studies, a mass of documentation that defies attempts to make sense of it" (xi). The same might be said of the published novel. This intentional disarrangement—or, better, derangement—is a trace of Beckett's war experience. *Watt*'s unreadability and encodedness are, in fact, the languages of post-traumatic stress and the Resistance spy, as well as a language of Irish neutrality.

Two critics have compellingly historicized *Watt*'s "resistant" language as a product of Beckett's engagement with the war. Marjorie Perloff connects Watt's and Sam's bizarre conversations with the code system used by Beckett's cell in the French Resistance: "The furtive meetings between Sam and Watt," Perloff suggests, "recall the meetings . . . where the 'cut-outs' exchanged coded information."[48] Beckett's job in Gloria SMH was to facilitate the transmission of knowledge from spies in France to military intelligence in London. Speaking both perfect French and native English, the Irishman was brought in to translate the scraps and bits of "cut-out" intelligence and transcribe them into English prose for transportation to Britain.[49] Knowing this, it is difficult not to see the connection between the translation work of the Resistance agent "Sam Irlandais" and that of *Watt*'s narrator, Sam, who translates Watt's cryptic and broken-up utterances into the English-language narrative of *Watt*.[50] With its long, often pages-long, sentences, composed of seemingly endless dependent clauses, the syntax of *Watt* appears burdened by a language that seems self-censored, unwilling to speak. James McNaughton also historicizes *Watt* to explore its resistant language, but from a different angle, reading the novel as "a critique of Irish neutrality."[51] While the setting in neutral Ireland "confounds" *Watt*'s meaning as a war book, McNaughton claims the novel contains "traces" (52) of the war encoded into its language, such as the phrase "a day's march" (51), which concludes the novel. According to McNaughton, "Beckett's quirky methods of containing

European war generate what might be called the propaganda of apathy" (51). Reading the novel alongside the diaries and notebooks Beckett made during his time in 1930s Nazi Germany, McNaughton sees *Watt*'s linguistic contortions as evidence of bourgeois man's search for comfort in lieu of truth (50). Beckett, he claims, "devotes his work not to resistance, but to the strategies by which Watt is seduced and to the rationalizations that Watt develops not to resist" (66). Perloff's and McNaughton's connections between *Watt*'s "resistant" language and the war open up a wider and more complex reading than either of them offer singly, for neither of their readings accounts for the resistant language of trauma. *Watt*'s fraught language is certainly a response to the strange pressures war puts on language: war alters language use in fundamental ways that draw our attention to the ways in which propaganda (as Orwell and Adorno argue) is seductive and, like espionage and code, requires special reading skills.[52] But war also alters the people who survive it, and *Watt*'s resistant language—Mr. Watt's search for "semantic succour" (83)—is also a trace or scar of wartime trauma.

Watt's comic encounter with the Galls, father and son (who come, "what is more, all the way from town, to choon the piano" [70]), is one of the more telling traumatic traces in the text. The Galls' visit turns sinister after they depart, having concluded that "the piano is doomed . . . The piano-tuner also . . . The pianist also" (70, 72).[53] For what happens is, like a half-remembered tune, the incident of the Galls, or Watt's memory of it, persists. The incident "was not ended, when it was past, but continued to unfold, in Watt's head, from beginning to end, over and over again" (72). This is no simple matter of remembering an event, for it distresses Watt intensely and, it seems to him, unreasonably:

> What distressed Watt . . . was not so much that he did not know what had happened, for he did not care what had happened, as that nothing had happened, that a thing that was nothing had happened, with the utmost formal distinctness, and that it continued to happen, in his mind [and it] revisited him in such a way that he was forced to submit to it all over again, to hear the same sounds, see the same lights, touch the same surfaces, and so on . . . If he had been able to accept it, then perhaps it would not have revisited him, and this would have been a great saving of vexation, to put it mildly. (76)

The visit of the Galls reads as a traumatic event; their "fugitive penetration" (70) into the Knott estate is something Watt cannot quite grasp. Like any traumatic event, the memory of the occurrence initially escapes Watt, only to make itself present through repetition, "so that he could neither think of [such events], nor speak of them, only suffer them, when they recurred" (79).[54] *Watt*'s encoding of this, merely a visit from the piano tuner, something that really ought to seem like "nothing," is an example of how the novel censors and subverts traumatic experience. But Beckett's customarily sardonic humor, in the tuner's proclamation of general "doom," hints at something much darker beneath the surface. Watt needs to tell the story in order to be "able to accept it" (76), but he finds himself unable to speak; the event, true to its traumatic nature, "simultaneously defies and demands our witness."[55]

For Watt, the piano tuning itself was "nothing," both because of its essential banality and because of the traumatic nature of its insufferable retelling and endless recurring. Likewise, Beckett's time in hiding in Roussillon from 1943 to 1945 was a form of nothing happening, years of nothing happening, but it was a terrifying nothing, scored by hunger, fear of discovery, physical discomfort, and boredom.[56] Watt's experience of the "nothing" of the Galls' visit suggests that even the "nothings" of wartime are traumatic and play on and on in their own terrifying ways. The syntax used in this section of *Watt*, with its perpetual march of dependent clauses, forces clause after clause of near nothingness upon the reader as well: a grammatical near nothing that keeps happening. In the defiant syntax of *Watt* we can see a literalization of what Caruth says is the voice of trauma: "a language that defies, even as it claims, our understanding" (5).

"Nothing" is precisely what appeared to be happening during World War II in neutral Ireland. The government's policy of censoring reports of persecution and cruelty from across occupied Europe "for fear of eliciting unneutral sympathy" meant that the worst atrocities of the war were screened from Irish eyes.[57] In the Irish press, there were no concentration camps, no massacre at Katyn, no Bataan Death March or Burma Railway, no firebombing of Dresden.[58] Experiencing the war through the warped lens of neutrality made Ireland's island isolation very palpable. In *That Neutral Island*, Clair Wills portrays Irish wartime intellectuals as a "static generation, cut off from the real world of the war . . . intensified by the strict censorship of printed news and other media."[59] As in the static Ireland of the Emergency, "nothing," appears to happen in Watt's story, and this nothing happens in a resolutely parochial world—full of gossip, verbal Hibernicisms, and markedly devoid of women, except as occasional sexual objects. Like the settings of *Molloy* and *Godot*, the setting of *Watt* appears both Irish and insistently ahistorical, but traces of World War II persist in *Watt*, as do strong indicators that its purgatorial otherworld is actually a veiled depiction of Ireland in the late 1930s and early 1940s. While Beckett himself did not experience the Emergency firsthand, being in a real emergency of his own, Mr. Watt appears to have done so, and Beckett's years of hiding in Roussillon, spent at agricultural labor with little contact with the outside world, must have borne a resemblance to life in rural Emergency Ireland.

Watt's physical lameness is symptomatic of the general stagnation of his environment, and the novel, particularly its first and final sections, reads as a diagnosis of the decline of Anglo-Irish culture in independent Ireland, in which nearly everyone is afflicted by age or ailment. Beckett utilizes the "terminal morbidity" of Mr. Knott to comment on the apparent demise of the Anglo-Irish big house genre.[60] In *Watt*, Mr. Knott's big house appears appropriately gothic to the eyes of its future servant; his first sighting of the house fills Watt with "confidence and with awe also, for the chimneys of Mr Knott's house were visible at last, in the light, of the moon. The house was in darkness" (36).[61] The isolation of Knott's big house makes it at once characteristic of its kind and a gesture toward Irish isolationism, which de Valera carefully characterized as the right of the small nation not to interfere or be interfered with. Indeed, Watt's compassionate isolationism within Knott's estate (for instance, his decision to stop interacting with the gardener and merely leave his shed key, in a homemade key-sized blanket, under a stone) may be partially responsible for his descent into linguistic chaos. Watt often wishes that he could discuss his linguistic predicament, but at the same time he isolates himself from conversation, preventing the outside dialogue that could productively unite him with the world. This is akin to the torment of the neutrals in *Inferno* canto 3: cast out of both heaven and hell, their isolation, as well as their censorship from the poem itself, is part of their punishment.

Double Negatives: Neutral Language in *The Third Policeman*

The Third Policeman was written mostly in 1939 and completed by February 1940, while O'Brien, under his real name, Brian O'Nolan, continued his work in the Irish civil service. In mid-1940, as his new novel went the rounds of various publishing houses, being serially rejected, O'Brien began channeling his creativity into the pen of Myles na gCopaleen and his *Irish Times* column "Cruiskeen Lawn" (which would run until his death in 1966). Indeed, as I suggest in chapter 1, the column is a more straightforward (though no less playful) indicator of O'Brien's opinions on politics and print culture during the Emergency. But the war is by no means absent from *The Third Policeman*, any more than it is absent from *Watt*, or absent in many ways from Irish letters from 1939 to 1945. In a wry take on censorship and neutrality, the war appears in *The Third Policeman* as an absent presence, most notably in the novel's insistence on "no as a general principle," a system of communication that "leads to peace and contentment" (28, 30). Like Elizabeth Bowen, O'Brien uses negative syntax as a grammatical construct for neutrality, creating for his Narrator the impossible condition of "negative nullity neutralized" (102).

The most telling historical trace in *The Third Policeman* is its relationship to atomic energy and bombs. As R. W. Maslen has written, the novel is "built into its time, entrapped by it, caught up in its interior workings" in its portrayal of atomic energy.[62] The world of the novel exploits new science—particularly the notion of the atom and of atomic half-life—by interpreting it over-literally, to the point of utter ridiculousness. As Sergeant Pluck explains the novel's "Atomic Theory," "Everything is composed of small particles of itself and they are flying around in concentric circles and arcs and segments and innumerable other geometrical figures too numerous to mention collectively, never standing still or resting but spinning away and darting hither and thither and back again, all the time on the go. These diminutive gentlemen are called atoms" (84). And these atoms, the sergeant explains, have the potential to exchange places with one another, as between an anvil and a hammer: "The gross and net result of it is that people who have spent most of their natural lives riding iron bicycles over the rocky roadsteads of this parish get their personalities mixed up with the personalities of their bicycle as a result of the interchanging of the atoms of each of them and you would be surprised at the number of people in these parts who are nearly half people and half bicycles" (85). In addition to governing the scientific properties of the parish in the novel, according to Maslen, "the presence of atomic theory in O'Brien's book, then, links the local crises of the newly fledged Irish nation with the deepening global crisis at the end of the 1930s" (102). The novel continuously plays on the idea of the bomb: the narrator is killed by a bomb, and MacCruiskeen's light-and-sound machine looks just like a bomb, "a black box with coloured wires coming out of it and there was a small ticking sound to be heard as if there was a clock in it" (106). This trope is telling, given that even in neutral Ireland the great fear of the populace was aerial bombardment.[63] It is a particularly black joke, then, when the narrator asks for "a small weapon suitable for the pocket which will exterminate any man or any million men who try at any time to take my life," and Pluck hands him a tool "that will change any man or men into grey powder at once if you point it and press the knob" (138)—an uncanny foreshadowing of what weapons technology would wreak in the 1940s.

Other traces of Emergency life abound in the novel in ways that are prophetic of Irish conditions, if not indicative of them. For instance, Ireland suffered a tremendous fuel shortage throughout the war, rendering a recently motorized country dependent on horse carts and, predominantly, bicycles. If the parish of *The Third Policeman* is rural Ireland in a vacuum, populated, like *The Great Hunger*, almost entirely by aging bachelor farmers, its bicycle-bound, local police-enforced isolation is not terribly different from Ireland during World War II.[64] There are sly nods to Emergency shortages—when he has the chance to acquire anything he wants in Eternity, the narrator requests bananas (the tropical fruit was famously unavailable)—and slyer ones to the Irish government's proposed solutions for them. Policeman MacCruiskeen's insistence on the usefulness of his "patent" inventions, like the "box full of noise" that he and the sergeant plan to convert into "light and heat for our official life in the dark winter" (110), is the predecessor of the Myles na gCopaleen Research Bureau, which spun many a "Cruiskeen Lawn" column parodying de Valera's Emergency Scientific Research Bureau. The quest for self-sufficiency in the barracks and its utilities recalls the Shannon hydroelectric scheme, which was founded in the previous decade with the aim of providing nationwide electricity. But the effect of Emergency shortages and rationing was that rural Ireland was darker than ever. Michael Rubenstein notes the failure of such public works when he reads the uncanny landscape of O'Brien's parish as "an allegory of the nation-state [which] accuses the nation-state of what, according to the novel, would be its epic failure" (117).

According to Rubenstein, it is "the palimpsest of bureaucratic, statist ideology that makes O'Brien's childhood landscape into a kind of hell" (114). Rubenstein reads the novel as a critique of the young state, and indeed the novel's landscape, in which "the tall hills and the fine views of bogland had been arranged by wise hands for the pleasing picture they made when looked at from the road" (37), suggests one that is altered to taste by a higher power. Such "wise hands," having made "the colour of the bogs . . . beautiful and the greenness of the green fields supernal," appear to be those of the government, linking state power to aesthetic autonomy, Fianna Fáil ideology to the arrangement of the landscape, which, in O'Brien's parish, is nevertheless unsettling: "too pleasant, too perfect, too finely made" (39). If the landscape is reminiscent of a perfect, self-sufficient Gaelicism that de Valera "dreamed of," for the Narrator of *The Third Policeman*, the dream becomes a nightmare.

Following the Narrator through the parish, a reader might be inclined to disbelieve that this novel was written before de Valera's famous 1943 speech, in which he imagined Ireland as "a land whose countryside would be bright with cosy homesteads, whose fields and villages would be joyous with the sounds of industry."[65] For here in the parish, according to the Narrator, "The world rang in my ear like a great workshop. Sublime feats of mechanics and chemistry were evident on every side. The earth was agog with invisible industry . . . Men who were notable for the whiteness of their shirts worked diminutively in the distant bog, toiling in the brown turf and heather" (125). At another point, the Narrator notes, "Brown bogs and black bogs were arranged neatly on each side of the road. . . . Sounds came from them to the Sergeant and myself, delivered to our ears without charge by the west wind, sounds of laughing and whistling and bits of verses from the old bog-songs" (86). If these "neatly arranged" fields are "joyous with the sounds of industry," they come at a price to the Narrator's mind, for they unnerve him entirely. At this idyllic vista, he confesses to Joe, "I would not mind being working this minute on a steamer in the middle of the sea . . . coiling ropes and doing the hard manual work. I would like to be far away from here" (86).

Like many of the descriptive passages in the novel, this one relies on a curious version of the pathetic fallacy to attribute industrial qualities to the natural world—the bogs are "arranged," the wind delivers "without charge," a happy "coterie of fowls" is heard "disputating loudly in the unrelenting manufacture of their eggs," and even "a canopy of lazy smoke had been erected over [a cottage] chimney to indicate that people were within engaged on tasks" (86). The landscape itself appears to be a facsimile of statist ideology, deliberately overwrought and mechanically productive, rather than an organic creation. The police barracks itself "looked as if it were painted like an advertisement on a board on the roadside and indeed very poorly painted. It looked completely false and unconvincing" (52). In general, as the Narrator explains, "It was a queer country we were in" (77). It looks not like Ireland but like a bad advertisement of Ireland: "There was a number of blue mountains around us at what you might call a respectful distance with a glint of white water coming down the shoulders of one or two of them and they kept hemming us in and meddling oppressively with our minds" (77–78). Overwrought with a de Valeran aesthetic, the parish is inhumanly perfect; even the landscape is able to meddle with and oppress the inhabitants' minds.

In a parish given up wholly to the machinations of grim bureaucracy, it is no surprise that Emergency press censorship leaves its impact on O'Brien's novel as well. The Narrator's imagination of the policemen's defeat of the Hoppy Men (an unlawful brotherhood of one-legged men, suggestive of the outlawed IRA) as a "miraculous victory with no fighting" (172) is reminiscent of the bloodless Irish press, in which victories were often reported without any details of the fighting.[66] The censor's neutrality edict forbade even the printing of death notices for Irishmen serving in the Allied forces, ensuring, as Carole Taaffe puts it, "that the [*Irish*] *Times*'s obituaries slowly filled with fatalities from 'lead poisoning'" (134). And so, playing a similar game of substitution, *The Third Policeman* uses the Atomic Theory to bicyclify the censorable body: "a slow puncture" (121) does double duty as a fart joke, and in a story devoid of female characters, "bikesexuality" takes the place of sexuality.[67] In one incidence, the sergeant tells the story of "a new lady teacher" who "was not very long here until [a local man] went away into the lonely country on her female bicycle. Can you appreciate the immorality of that?" (89). The sergeant keeps his own feminine bike locked in a cell, a fitting commentary on the constitutional role of women in Ireland, and it is on this "sensuous" and "docile" lady *rothar* that the Narrator makes his escape from the barracks. "How can I convey the perfection of my comfort on the bicycle," he marvels, "the completeness of my union with her, the sweet responses she gave me at every particle of her frame?" (173). Salacious indeed! And yet, even operating (as he presumed) below the censor's radar, O'Brien leaves his Narrator at a loss for words.

Suffering for the Sake of Suffering: The Novels as Critiques of Irish Policy

Both engaged in the postrevival critique of Irish literary pieties, Beckett's and O'Brien's novels take on modern Irish literature's foundational big house genre in order to disassemble it. *The Third Policeman* begins when two small-time Catholic farmers, the Narrator and his hand, Divney, rob and kill the rich Old Mathers outside his big house; Divney even attempts to rationalize the act as "social justice" (15). In *Watt*, Mr. Knott's big house is both a typical Anglo-Irish mansion and a gothic house of horror and secrets. In both novels' cases, entry into the isolated big house equates with entry into purgatory; both Watt and the Narrator will enter their respective big houses to find themselves locked in cycles of terror and failed purgation. Unlike typical gothic heroes or heroines, their searches for the houses' secrets yield no revelations. Though *Watt* and *The Third Policeman* may qualify as appropriately gothic in the big house sense, they fail to qualify properly as traditional *novels*. Because these are *failed* purgatories, their characters exhibit no positive growth or development and their narrators falter at establishing suspense, resolution, and rapport with the reader. Julian Moynahan has written that *Watt* "acknowledges Anglo-Irish tradition by a series of parodic reductions amounting to cancellation" (216). Indeed, both Beckett and O'Brien acknowledge literary tradition—Anglo-Irish as well as Irish Gaelic—only to mortify it. The Emergency's cultural strictures resulted in two of the first great antinovels, late modernist masterpieces that play on conventions of Irish society and genre by desiccating them, crucifying language and tradition in order to remake it.

If Dante's purgatory "implies culmination,"[68] *Watt* and *The Third Policeman* exclude it because the protagonists' failures to witness to their worlds prevent them from acquiring the knowledge necessary for purgation, or release. Watt's and the Narrator's linguistic failures make visible two allied critiques of wartime survival and speech. The (anti)purgatorial structures of the novels themselves, on both thematic and formal levels, serve to critique the idea that through war's suffering some expiation occurs, that the experience of war can lead to a purified world. If the suffering of World War II was suffering in the service of a just war, a war that in Britain was additionally justified by the promise of a more socially equable postwar state, *Watt* and *The Third Policeman* offer no such justification. The novels' settings in Emergency-era Ireland, moreover, point to the ways in which the rationale of war as expiation was empty in Ireland, where the concept of neutrality answered neither the promise of defeating fascism, nor of an improved economy, nor even of a united Ireland. While the state's neutrality, cloaked in the "sacred egoism" that Ernest Boyd coined as the "tenacious selfishness, without which [small nations] must abandon the struggle for life,"[69] was promoted in terms of its outer sacredness—the preferment of prayerful peace—its sort of inner egoism is exactly what Dante punishes his neutrals for. Ireland's Emergency isolationism was essentially conservative, and Emergency-era policies left the nation culturally and economically stagnant for many years. The Emergency scarred the national psyche but left little concrete evidence to redeem it. Beckett's and O'Brien's purgatories without purgation—suffering for the sake of suffering—mock the emptiness of the promise that either a world war or exemption from it can justify its means.

Standing on the scaffold awaiting execution, the Narrator of *The Third Policeman* muses, "Down into the earth where dead men go I would go soon and maybe come out of it again in some healthy way, free and innocent of all human perplexity" (159). The irony here is that he is already dead but decidedly unfree and in a place far more perplexing than the world of the quick. Unaware that his sentence represents justice for the murder he committed while alive, the Narrator yet hopes his hanging will be somehow purgative. But his very position narrating the story shows this to be impossible. The promise of purgation is a mockery.

As O'Brien's Narrator constantly seeks escape or redemption (from farm life, from Divney, from the policemen, from the scaffold), Watt, too, is a perpetual asylum seeker. For him, "Mr Knott was harbour, Mr Knott was haven, calmly entered, freely ridden, gladly left" (135). Or so Watt wants to think: "Not that Watt felt calm and free and glad, for he did not" (135). In both novels, the failure of the purgative structure to leave the protagonists "calm and free and glad" mimes the failure of neutrality to salve the conscience or "pray [Europe] whole again," as Devlin puts it. This failure manifests itself in the novels' weird language, which offers a second critical lens on the Emergency, for as both novels pick apart the idea of a purgative conflict, they also mock their readers' desire for a penetrable text, offering linguistic contortions and distortions that enact an implicit criticism of the Irish government's wartime policy of "neutral language."

As detailed in chapter 1, the "neutral language" policy was the lynchpin of Ireland's wartime neutrality, based on the government's twinned mandates that public language could be neutered by refusing to name the war and that it would function as a neutral medium by offering unbiased descriptors of a belligerent world. The policy was enforced by the notorious Censorship of Publications Board, headed by Frank Aiken under the auspices of de Valera.[70] The professed aim of Ireland's Emergency press censorship, according to Aiken, was to give the Irish people "a better and a clearer opportunity of getting all the news of this war in an unbiased manner."[71] The result, as chapter 1 demonstrates, was a series of thoroughly peculiar language usages in the print culture of the time. *Watt* and *The Third Policeman* offer additional examples of these stylistics of neutrality. One of the traces of the war on *Watt* and *The Third Policeman* is their notoriously weird demotics; both novels appear burdened by a language that seems reluctant to speak. Marjorie Perloff calls Sam's narrative one of "curious formalism, a sort of pseudoarchaic English" (126). Of *The Third Policeman*, Terence Brown writes, "The English language cannot be taken for granted as a medium of communication. [The narrator writes in] an English that reads as if it had already achieved the condition of a dead language like Latin, oddly punctilious and formal."[72] If Watt and the Narrator of *The Third Policeman* exhibit similar difficulties in movement—the Narrator is peg legged and Watt walks stiff kneed, in "a headlong tardigrade . . . a funambulistic stagger" (30–31)—their stories also mirror each other in the stiffness of their language, its difficulty in getting across.[73] Both novels employ idiosyncratic diction, and their general styles give one the impression that the books are borne out of the past, like something existing in afterlife.[74]

In the thoroughly peculiar language of *Watt*, Beckett demonstrates what happens when language's presumed neutrality is followed to a rational dead end. Every attempt to express what he has seen in Mr. Knott's estate brings Watt closer to disintegration; his witnessing offers only a grammar of traumatic repetition. Because he imagines that he can simply interpret a complicated world, Watt's quest for enlightenment actually leaves him "dumb, numb, and blind."[75] Words fail the Narrator spectacularly in the parish, where he must learn to replace ordinary diction with the policemen's bicyclish patois, and he cannot, furthermore, remember his own name. Indeed, he finds that it is difficult "to convey with known words" his experiences in the parish, where it is increasingly impossible for him "to believe what my eyes were looking at" (24, 26). If the narratives of war and neutrality call truth's accessibility into question, *Watt* and *The Third Policeman* go even farther than Bowen to demonstrate how acts of reading can *only* be skeptical. The Narrator's scholarly glosses on the fictitious philosopher of science, de Selby, are ample enough caricatures of the dangers of misprision, but the de Selbian inventor, Policeman MacCruiskeen, crafts things that can leave people "crazy as tuppence-half-penny and cranky as thruppence" (77) just from exposure to them. In Beckett's novel, Watt's attempts to "read" Mr. Knott, like Sam's attempts to understand Watt, are, like the reader's relationship with the novel as a whole, fraught with difficulty and even (for Watt) with danger. The novel's elaborate, disordered structure is part of a critique of wartime language use and reading practices—both of which involve, like Beckett's translation work in the Resistance, decoding, reordering, combing for bias and for truth. Adding to the physical difficulties of wartime were the inevitable epistemological difficulties that readers of propaganda, both neutral and belligerent, had to face.

Unreadability in Beckett and O'Brien

The problem of accessing truth in wartime is compounded by the problem of how to articulate it, and these two novels are overloaded with textual difficulty. O'Brien's extensive use of metafictional devices, such as self-conscious narration and footnotes, leads Keith Hopper to connect *The Third Policeman* with *Watt* as novels that move "away from the optimistic rationalism of the Enlightenment values which underpin the modernist project towards a more pessimistic and sceptical position" (227). Beckett not only utilizes the same devices in his book but also includes, at the end, eight pages of "Addenda," noting, "The following precious and illuminating material should be carefully studied. Only fatigue and disgust prevented its incorporation" (247). The validity of the novels' texts is thereby questionable from the beginning (*The Third Policeman* opens with epigraphs from Shakespeare and the fictional de Selby, deliberately toying with definitions of the "real" text). The very narration of the novels is skeptical. Neither Sam nor the Narrator has a stable position from which to tell his tale. O'Brien's Narrator, after all, has been dead "all the time" (200) and narrates from beyond the grave. The novel's ending makes clear that the Narrator is forever narrating *The Third Policeman*, with the Narrator repeating the beginning of his journey in perfect ignorance. Any notion of narrative authority is thoroughly undermined at the novel's end, throwing everything the reader "knows" into doubt.

The reader is midway through *Watt* before Sam introduces himself as narrator, upsetting the reader's assumption of a more plausible third-person omniscient narrator, and disclaiming, "For all that I know on the subject of Mr Knott, and of all that touched Mr Knott, and on the subject of Watt, and of all that touched Watt, came from Watt, and from Watt alone . . . And this does not mean either that I may not have left out some of the things that Watt told me, or foisted in others that Watt never told me" (125–26). Not only does Sam, here, admit to the inaccuracy of the material provided by Watt—particularly Arsene's twenty-four-page monologue, now retold thirdhand—but Sam's position as narrator is made impossible by the opening and closing pages of the novel itself. There is no way that Watt could have seen and heard Mr. Hackett in the opening scene or the railway employees in the closing one, so Sam's narrative of them is doubly dubious. This is reminiscent of the impossibility, for Irish readers, of accessing the truth of what was happening in the war they were *not* witnessing. The fact that the narrator of *Watt* "both knows too little and too much"[76] is underscored formally by metafictional intrusions, such as the narrator's frequent admissions of ignorance ("But when out walking [Watt's knees] did not bend, for some obscure reason"), including periodic question marks inserted in place of words, and the "Hiatus in MS" frustratingly left at the end of the novel (30, 238). These moments of narrative skepticism are intentionally disconcerting. Holes in the narrative, like the "Hiatus" and the novel's restless lists, like *The Third Policeman*'s intrusive footnotes and disquisitions on de Selby, are placed intentionally at moments of highest suspense, exasperating the reader. Like Watt to Mr. Knott, "weak now of eye, hard of hearing, and with even the more intimate senses greatly below par," the narrator of each text is a "needy witness, an imperfect witness" (202–3). With these uncertain witnesses, the novels' metafictional elements work to undermine narrative authority and break the traditional bond between reader and narrator, frustrating a process previously intuited as a rational one.

Because the ending of *The Third Policeman* rewrites the beginning, it rewrites the narrator's relationship to the narrative. This makes O'Brien's novel "a book to re-read," according to Brown, "for a second reading will be different from the first to a greater degree than is customary in fiction, even of the *policier* and mystery kind" (218). *The Third Policeman* demands its own rereading, but *Watt* enacts it. In part 3, the reader witnesses Sam's difficulty in translating Watt's inverted speech into recognizable English. As the section begins, Sam admits that, in reporting Watt's strange tale of life in Mr. Knott's service, he must struggle with Watt's belabored manner of self-expression: "Watt spoke also with scant regard for grammar, for syntax, for pronunciation, for enunciation, and very likely, if the truth were known, for spelling too, as these are generally received . . . Watt spoke as one speaking to dictation, or reciting, parrot-like, a text, by long repetition become familiar. Of this impetuous murmur much fell in vain on my imperfect hearing and understanding, and much by the rushing wind was carried away" (156). That Watt himself seems to be reciting from a text continues the motif of translation through which the novel is composed: Watt translating his experiences with Knott, Sam translating Watt's disordered story into *Watt*, and the reader translating *Watt* into novelistic sense. This translational impulse is heightened when Watt, relating the time he spent on the first floor, in the direct presence of Mr. Knott, begins to invert his speech. Sam relates,

> The following is an example of Watt's manner, at this period:
>
> *Day of most, night of part, Knott with now. Not till up, little seen so oh, little heard so oh. Night till morning from. Heard I this, saw I this then what. Thing quiet, dim. Ears, eyes, failing now also. Hush in, mist in, moved I so.*
>
> From this it will perhaps be suspected:
>
> that the inversion affected, not the order of the sentences, but that of the words only . . .
>
> that there was perhaps more than a reversal of discourse;
>
> that the thought was perhaps inverted.
>
> . . . But soon I grew used to these sounds, and then I understood as well as before, that is to say a great part of what I heard. (165)

Like Sam, at this point the reader can understand a great part of what Watt says by quickly reversing the words in the clauses. As Watt's thought becomes more garbled and his inversions become more complicated, the reader's skill improves along with Sam's.[77] Phrases like Watt's "geb nodrap" (167) for "beg pardon" soon become as familiar to the reader as real words. But Watt's most complex inversions require more and more complex reading skills. By the end of his story, Watt inverts,

> the letters in the word together with that of the words in the sentence together with that of the sentences in the period. For example:
>
> *Dis yb dis, nem owt. Yad la, tin fo trap. Skin, skin, skin. Od su did ned taw? On. Taw ot klat tonk? On. Tonk ot klat taw? On. Tonk ta kool taw? On. Taw ta kool tonk? Nilb, mun, mud. Tin fo trap, yad la. Nem owt, dis yb dis.* (168)

Most readers (if my own experience is an indication) will find themselves either fighting the desire to skip the text as unreadable or making provisional translations in the margin. For example, my rendering of the above passage reads, "Side by side, two men. All day, part of night. Dumb, numb, blind. Knott look at Watt? No. Watt look at Knott? No. Watt talk to Knott? No. Knott talk to Watt? No. What then did us do? Niks, niks, niks. Part of night, all day. Two men, side by side." Taking into account

Watt's known "scant regard" for grammar, syntax, pronunciation, and spelling, adapting these passages into English requires actual translation rather than mere transliteration. The novel itself—prophetically, perhaps, for English speakers, as this was Beckett's last novel not written in French—is a work in translation.

The Third Policeman, on a second reading, becomes a retranslation. But even on a first reading, themes of translation are apparent. The Narrator quickly realizes that the policemen in the parish speak a strange dialect of English, marked by malapropisms (a first name is rendered a "pronoun," a family name a "cog") and a peculiar idiom (in which a puzzle becomes "nearly an insoluble pancake") (56, 153). In conversation with Policeman MacCruiskeen, the Narrator himself begins to translate: "'That was very competent masterwork,' I said, endeavouring to speak his own language" (71). From this point on, the policemen's diction begins to infect the narration.

A key moment of translation occurs when the Narrator and MacCruiskeen listen to the noises trapped in the policeman's black box:

> The unearthly voice had roared out something very quickly with three or four words compressed into one ragged shout. I could not be sure what it was but several phrases sprang into my head together and each of them could have been the contents of the shout. They bore an eerie resemblance to commonplace shouts I had often heard such as *Change for Tinahely and Shillelagh! Two to one the field! Mind the step! Finish him off!* I knew, however, that the shout could not be so foolish and trivial because it disturbed me in a way that could only be done by something momentous and diabolical. (108)

This is not the first failed translation in the novel. For that shout of "Finish him off!" is an echo of Divney's call to "Finish him with the spade!" (16) when he and the Narrator murder Old Mathers. When Divney delivers the first blow to Mathers, the Narrator notes, "As he collapsed full-length in the mud he did not cry out. Instead I heard him say something softly in a conversational tone—something like 'I do not care for celery' or 'I left my glasses in the scullery'"(16). In this case, a phrase that seems "foolish and trivial" is in fact "momentous and diabolical," but the Narrator, laboring through his purgatory, fails to recognize the connection between the shouts in the box and Old Mathers's last words. These mistranslated shouts divorce sound from meaning at the site of the Narrator's crime. The same thing happens in *Watt* when he begins to narrate his traumatic experience with Knott: sound and meaning lose their grip on each other. This is a loss of language at the site of trauma, and in the space of these novels' translations, something always goes missing.

The Narrator of *The Third Policeman* admits that his "first serious sin" was the theft of a volume by de Selby, "a first edition of *Golden Hours* with the two last pages missing" (9). These missing pages are a telling absence: reading in *The Third Policeman,* as in *Watt,* is a process of bewilderment, and the reader's position parallels the protagonists' as they fail to read the worlds in which they move. J. M. Silverthorne writes that in *The Third Policeman,* the Narrator is "consistently taken in like any good reader," registering but suspending his disbelief in the strange setting of his journey.[78] But the processes of reading described in both *The Third Policeman* and *Watt* are processes of failure. Silverthorne writes that failure is a principle of organization in O'Brien's novel, and I contend that the specific failure operative—in both O'Brien's and Beckett's novels—is a failure to read. In these novels, the protagonists, as well as the narrators, fail to read the world, because they commit the fallacy of believing that the world makes rational sense and that, furthermore, language is capable of expressing it. Beckett's and O'Brien's novels implicitly critique the concept of "neutral language" as based on the fallacious premise that language can be neutral, clear, or transparent. The novels demonstrate these rational fallacies of reading by, as Benjamin Keatinge says of *Watt*, "sabotag[ing] language in a deliberately anti-rational way [thus making] the rational faculties appear as their obverse—insanity."[79] The result is what Hugh Kenner memorably calls *Watt*: "a raid of syntax upon chaos."[80]

In *The Third Policeman*, the Narrator chronicles his lifelong obsession with the work of de Selby in a series of comments and heavy annotations; de Selby's work represents always a crazed conviction that the mainstream conceptions of reality are not as they seem: that the earth is shaped like a sausage, for instance, and that night is merely an unsanitary "accretion of black air" (120).* In an early footnote, the Narrator explains that de Selby's notion that "a journey is an hallucination" is the result of a crucial misreading: "Apparently he had examined [a set of films] patiently picture by picture and imagined that they would be screened in the same way, failing at the time to grasp the principle of the cinematograph" (50n2). Likewise, de Selby's designs for "roofless 'houses' and 'houses' without walls"—"fantastic dwellings" in which "more than one sick person lost his life in an ill-advised quest for health"—are postulated to be the result of the savant's misreading his own "doodling" and his subsequent attempt to explain it (21–22n3).[81] If de Selby's misreadings lead to the deaths of his followers, it is no surprise that the Narrator is among those dead, and less surprising that he does not realize it. "De Selbiana" is a parade of misreadings, a chronicle of forgeries and false names, capped by the infamous "De Selby Codex": "The signal distinction of the manuscript is that not one word of the writing is legible. Attempts made by different commentators to decipher certain passages which look less formidable than others have been characterised by fantastic divergencies" (145n2). Throughout the novel, de Selby's failed interpretations and those of his acolytes function as an allegory for the Narrator's own failure to interpret the parish as an afterlife and, thus, his failure to acquire any purgative knowledge.

* To assume the footnotes of *The Third Policeman* are less important to the story than the body text would be to commit a de Selbian error. As a novel that emphasizes the importance of careful reading, the book is self-policing: In chapters 8, 9, and 11, when the Narrator faces moments of greatest danger, the footnotes threaten to overwhelm the text, demanding the reader's attention elsewhere. The stories told in the footnotes and the body text are not, as might be presumed by their format, parallel but are interlocking. De Selby's concept that "a journey is an hallucination," for example, is treated in chapter 4, the very chapter in which the Narrator's own journey becomes hallucinogenic (as he reaches the barracks); de Selby's study of infinite temporal regression through mirrors counterpoints Policeman MacCruiskeen's infinitely sharp spear and infinitely tiny boxes. The elaborate tale of the de Selby scholar Hatchjaw's arrest for "impersonating himself" functions as a gloss on the Narrator's problematic namelessness (50, 171n1). The result is that the two stories are interpenetrating, in-mixed with each other along the principle of the Atomic Theory. De Selby is not a digression but a cautionary tale in reading, and the Narrator's failure to read de Selby's theories as lunatic is perpetuated in his rational attempts to believe what he sees in the parish.

Similar misreadings characterize *Watt*. By the time Watt replaces Erskine as the first-floor servant, he has failed to acquire any knowledge one might associate with moving up a rung in purgatory:

> Watt was now tired of the ground floor, the ground floor had tired Watt out.
>
> What had he learnt? Nothing.
>
> What did he know of Mr Knott? Nothing.
>
> Of his anxiety to improve, of his anxiety to understand, of his anxiety to get well, what remained? Nothing. (148)

By this point, Watt has read and reread the episode of the Galls in his mind, to no effect but vexation. He has presented "doubly erroneous" (104) miscalculations of the Lynches' ages. He has been brought to tears by his inability to discern whether the painting in Erskine's room depicts "a circle and its centre in search of each other" (129) or any of eight variations on this theme. But just as he cannot interpret the painting, Watt cannot interpret Mr. Knott's world. If Watt is in search of the center of his experience, it remains linguistically inaccessible, and the repetitive language, the obligatory rereadings, the failed translations, all force the reader to experience Watt's trauma from the outside.

The most painful manifestation of misreading in *Watt* is the novel's endless lists, many of which prove, at their completion, to contain completely pointless conjectures. For example, *Watt*'s readers are subjected to eight pages of Mr. Watt's speculations upon the arrangement for how "the dog" (nonresident at the estate) might be summoned to eat Mr. Knott's leftovers; Watt's parade of reasoning even includes a chart listing four possible "solutions" to the dog problem and thirty objections to them (97–98). But none of these solutions are upheld; in fact, Knott's solution was prewritten before Watt's arrival at the estate, making Watt's calculations both needless and meaningless. In spite of all Watt's deductions and calculations, nothing is learned. Reading such lists—and they make up the bulk of the novel's text—is punishing and hysterical, in the sense that it is both very funny and very maddening. Even Sam tires of narrating these lists from time to time, as when he interjects, "(tired of underlining this cursed preposition)" after a long list of repeated "because ofs" (134). For in *Watt*, as John Wall puts it, "language exists in a permanent state of deferral, the meaning of a proposition always only explicable by reference to a second opinion, and so on, to infinity."[82]

Descents into infinity proliferate in *The Third Policeman* as well, where the rhetorical device of *mise en abyme* is augmented by fantastic inventions in regressive science, from de Selby's infinite mirrors to the glass that "magnifies to invisibility" (136) and Policeman MacCruiskeen's spear, on which "the point is . . . so thin that it could go into your hand and out in the other extremity externally and you would not feel a bit of it and you would see nothing and hear nothing. It is so thin that maybe it does not exist at all" (68–69). Roy Hunt writes that in *The Third Policeman*, reality is always displaced by the language of serialism.[83] It operates at every level of the text, from the policemen's inventions, to the catechistical dialogue, to the notion that the Narrator is forever narrating a story that goes on interminably. Like MacCruiskeen's set of infinitely small Chinese boxes, the novel proclaims its ability to go on forever, to be infinitely retold. Any attempt to properly *read* the book, or to open the final Chinese box—fails in the face of infinity.

Mise en abyme in *Watt* is symbolically realized through Watt's awareness that everything at Knott's estate is "a term in the series, like the series of Mr Knott's dogs, or the series of Mr Knott's men, or like the centuries that fall, from the pod of eternity" (131). Rhetorically, the *mise en abyme* of *Watt* is expressed in exhaustive (and exhausting) listings of possibilities: of the steps in Watt's walk, of methods to attract the dog to its food, of the arrangement of Knott's bedroom, of the ever-altering appearance of Knott himself. Formally, the Addenda constitute yet another example of infinite recursiveness. Julian Moynahan reads *Watt*'s rhetoric of infinite deferral as essentially catechistical, in which "the question [is] 'What is it?' and the answer, invariably and relentlessly, is 'It is not that'" (246). (Thus, Beckett's inescapable pun: Watt? Knott.) If this is Beckett's answer to the catechistical Ithaca episode of *Ulysses*, it is an answer that proclaims his difference from the high modernist project. For Beckett, no novel is capable of truly representing reality, and his rhetoric literalizes the impossibility of ever approaching truth. This is particularly heightened during wartime, when trauma, censorship, and propaganda make the subject's search for truth ever more fraught.

Catechistical rhetoric is responsible for *mise en abyme* in O'Brien's novel, too. When the Narrator first encounters Martin Finnucane on the road to the police barracks, Joe suggests that the Narrator find out more about him. "*Ask him his name and occupation,*" Joe insists, and the Narrator begins,

> "I do not desire to be inquisitive, sir," I said, "but would it be true to mention that you are a bird-catcher?"
>
> "Not a bird-catcher," he answered.
>
> "A tinker?"
>
> "Not that."
>
> "A man on a journey?"
>
> "No, not that."
>
> "A fiddler?"
>
> "Not that one."
>
> I smiled at him good-humoredly and said:
>
> "Tricky-looking man, you are hard to place and it is not easy to guess your station." (43–44)

With this approach, the Narrator is in fact *unnecessarily* inquisitive. Nonetheless, he continues guessing: "A man out after rabbits?" "A travelling man with a job of journey-work?" "A water-works inspector?" "With pills for sick horses?" (45). Few of the Narrator's guesses are based on evidence, and it is apparent that the list could go on forever. (Eventually Finnucane announces that he is "a robber with a knife and an arm that's as strong as an article of powerful steam machinery" [45].) As in Moynahan's reading of *Watt*, O'Brien's format is: Is it this? No, it is not. Old Mathers's formula of "No as a general principle," introduced in the novel's second chapter, is an ample hint that any yes-or-no question posed in the parish will never be answered. This is why the policemen's incessant question, "Is it about a bicycle?" is both very maddening, for the Narrator, and very funny, for the reader.

When the Narrator realizes, upon being asked by Old Mathers, that he does not know his own name, he responds, "I can always get a name . . . Doyle or Spaldman is a good name and so is O'Sweeny and Hardiman and O'Gara. I can take my choice. I am not tied down for life to one word like most people" (31). But, although Joe delights in riffing on the possibilities of his Narrator's name and identity ("*Signor Bari, the eminent tenor. Five hundred thousand people crowded the great piazza when the great artist appeared on the balcony of St. Peter's Rome*" [31]), in his dealings with the police the Narrator does need a name. As the police present possible names (including nicknames), the Narrator realizes the necessity of being tied down to one word, the necessity for finding the "right name," for, "If you have no name you possess nothing and you do not exist and even your trousers are not on you although they look as if they were from where I am sitting" (61–62). So on goes the suggestion and rejection of names, "an amazing piece of denial and denunciation . . . An astonishing parade of nullity" (101). Michael Mooney's analysis of *Watt*'s rhetoric is appropriate for *The Third Policeman* here: "The stylistic function of this enumeration is to admit all possibilities, in true sceptical fashion, so that no one meaning is possible. And to this play with language must be linked the destruction of language itself as a vehicle for signification."[84] For the search for the "right name," or for the exact meaning of Erskine's painting, is forever inconclusive, to the point that words themselves begin to shed their meaning.

Beckett and O'Brien demonstrate Mooney's principle both thematically and rhetorically. The endless lists in both novels formally function to delay the narrative and frustrate the reader, leading to the destruction of the traditional novelistic pact between narrator and reader, as evidence of the destroyed value of language for signification. In *Watt*, the lists have explicitly maddening consequences for the reader, and implicitly maddening consequences for Watt, whose lost grip on language is manifested in the inversions of part 3. "In the end," Stephen Connor suggests of the lists' effect, "such extreme consciousness of the shape and sound of language leads to the . . . draining of meaning from the words, so that they do indeed become simply inert noises or shapes."[85] As meaning drains from words for Watt, *Watt* drains words' meanings for its reader. In *The Third Policeman*, the Narrator suffers the consequences of a literal loss of language: unable to provide his name and prove his identity, he is sentenced to hang for a murder that he did not commit.[86] His inability to claim a name from the novel's proliferate lists is a form of failed reading that leads to his doom.

"Semantic Succour," Aphasia, and the Unspeakable

Without the ability to read and understand the world of the novel, the Narrator, like Watt, will never achieve purgation or release. The search for the right words, or what Watt calls "semantic succour" (83), is akin to the "working through" of trauma, in which a witness begins to attempt to "speak the unspeakable" in the course of the "ongoing cognitive/affective process [that may lead] to the reintegration of the traumatic event."[87] But it is clear that, in these two novels the protagonists will be eternally "working through" events for which they can find no semantic relief. Toward the end of his long monologue, Arsene says to Watt, "What we know partakes in no small measure of what has so happily been called the unutterable or ineffable, so that any attempt to utter or eff it is doomed to fail, doomed, doomed to fail" (62).[88] In this remark, Arsene foreshadows the next forty years of Beckett's philosophy of writing, in which silence would become preferable to words, but words would still march across pages in the attempt to "fail better."[89] He also foreshadows what will happen to Watt in the purgatory of Knott's house as words begin to be purged of their meaning. The more Watt thinks about the words he utters, the more they are doomed to fail him. The episode of Watt's encounter with the pot is a painfully funny example:

> For Watt now found himself in the midst of things which, if they consented to be named, did so as it were with reluctance . . . Looking at a pot, for example, or thinking of a pot, at one of Mr Knott's pots, of one of Mr Knott's pots, it was in vain that Watt said, Pot, pot. Well, perhaps not quite in vain, but very nearly. For it was not a pot, the more he looked, the more he reflected, the more he felt sure of that, that it was not a pot at all. It resembled a pot, it was almost a pot, but it was not a pot of which one could say, Pot, pot, and be comforted . . . For he could always hope, of a thing of which he had never known the name, that he would learn the name, some day, and so be tranquilized. (81–82)

Watt undergoes a process in which the "true names" (82) of all things cease to exist. Their essence cannot be grasped in language in a world where language itself has become skeptical. For Watt, this shattering of the imagined bond between signified and signifier is as painful as it is confusing:

> And Watt's need of semantic succour was at times so great that he would set to trying names on things, and on himself, almost as a

> woman hats . . . As for himself, though he could no longer call it a man, as he had used to do, with the intuition that he was perhaps not talking nonsense, yet he could not imagine what else to call it, if not a man . . . So he continued to think of himself as a man . . . But for all the relief that this afforded him, he might just as well have thought of himself as a box, or an urn. (83)

If the premise of the narrative is that Watt tells his story to Sam, then his story is the narrative enactment of his linguistic breakdown in the face of his attempt to find "semantic succour" in explaining himself to another. But testimony, by its nature, is always censored, always doubtful, and Watt's traumatic experiences even led him to doubt his own humanity.[90] His predicament echoes Mr. Hackett's wonderment that Watt is a man rather than a roll of carpet, or a "tarpaulin, wrapped up in dark paper and tied about the middle with a cord" (16)—suggesting that Watt's humanity is in doubt from the first time the reader "sees" him and perhaps has already been diminished by hard living before his service at Knott's. Watt's ontological problem encodes trauma (he could be a man—or the remains of one: a box, an urn) just as it hints at the semantic problems arising from it. It is, of course, equally possible that the words "box," "urn," "carpet," "tarpaulin" could describe Watt, "man" being as arbitrary a signifier as any. But without the ability to trust that words and their meanings are connected, "Watt's world," Sam explains, becomes "unspeakable" (85).

Predictably, words fail the nameless Narrator of *The Third Policeman* at moments of highest terror. His trip to Eternity is "something that I could tell nobody about, there are no suitable words in the world to tell my meaning" (135). In the world of the parish, things are terrifying because they cannot be named, and they cannot be named because they are so terrifying. This tautology compounds the horror of the Narrator's lost name; without it he does not even know who he is: "I did not know my name, did not remember who I was" (31). Like Old Mathers's unreadable cry and the mysterious shouts in MacCruiskeen's box, the word for the Narrator's name is divorced from its meaning at a traumatic site: the last thing the Narrator says to Divney, before he is killed by the bomb, is, "I don't even know my own name" (20). Upon entering the purgatorial parish, his namelessness shifts from an opportunity for exhilaration to something closer to Watt's predicament—abject terror—when he realizes it will also be his doom.

The Narrator initially finds himself arrested as a sacrifice to rural bureaucracy. The police inspector shows up suddenly, announces a crime, and demands the criminal be brought in. Having spent the afternoon hiding and retrieving local bicycles, the sergeant cannot be exposed as a failure, so he casually announces that the murderer is already captured. The Narrator is conveniently at hand: "It is the way we work in this part of the country" (98), explains the sergeant. Soon, the Narrator attempts to bargain his namelessness into neutrality, contending that if he has no name, and no standing under the law, that he cannot be hanged. Sergeant Pluck responds:

> It is true . . . that you cannot commit a crime and that the right arm of the law cannot lay its finger on you irrespective of the degree of your criminality. Anything you do is a lie and nothing that happens to you is true . . . For that reason alone . . . we can take you and hang the life out of you and you are not hanged at all and there is no entry to be made in the death papers. The particular death you die is not even a death (which is an inferior phenomenon at best)[91] only an insanitary abstraction in the backyard, a piece of negative nullity neutralised and rendered void by asphyxiation and the fracture of the spinal string. (102)

Tied into this legal tangle is not just a commentary on the linguistics of naming but also a clever allusion to Irish wartime policy of "negative nullity neutralised." Ireland's effort at neutrality, O'Brien suggests, is an effort to be blameless with regard to all the atrocities of the war, to censor it into unspeakability in order to avoid complicity.[92] But just because "no entry [would] be made in the death papers" for Irish casualties of the war did not mean that their particular deaths were not deaths. Neutrality, its critics claimed, basically pretended that the war in Europe was merely an "insanitary abstraction" in Ireland's backyard. To be neutral was to fancy, as the sergeant puts it, "that you cannot commit a crime and that the right arm of the law cannot lay its finger on you irrespective of the degree of your criminality"; this shirking of culpability appears an overly easy excuse, a way of papering sacredness over egoism. But O'Brien's diabolical sergeant delivers a reminder that to pretend to be no one means that "anything you do is a lie and nothing that happens to you is true." This is both impossible—logically speaking—and completely possible, linguistically speaking (presuming that the connection between any word and its referent is a technical lie). The Narrator's bargain for neutrality leads not to acquittal but to arraignment for murder and conviction to death. As a linguistic construct, at least, the concept of neutrality fails; it is empty at the center.

A fundamental problem of the *mise en abyme* motif is that it has an unstable center. Forever repeating itself, *mise en abyme* cannot have an "essential inherent interior essence" (113), as Policeman MacCruiskeen would say. In a moment of panic that resembles Watt's fears of serialism, the Narrator begins to interrogate the possibility that he himself is part of an infinite regression. He wonders if Joe, his inner voice, is possessed of "a body with another body inside it in turn, thousands of such bodies within each other like the skins of an onion, receding to some unimaginable ultimum? Was I in turn merely a link in a vast sequence of imponderable beings, the world I knew merely the interior of the being whose inner voice I myself was? Who or what was the core and what monster in what world was the final uncontained colossus? God? Nothing?" (118). In a story that will spin out forever, the Narrator has nailed the problem: the infinite recursions of his own narrative are empty at the core. The protagonists of both *The Third Policeman* and *Watt* are in search of an unknowable center, something to render their words speakable. For Watt, it is Knott, the uninterpretable center of the estate. In *The Third Policeman*, however, a centering element is posited: omnium, the formidable substance that powers Policeman MacCruiskeen's inventions, rules the factory-like Eternity, and that the policeman describes as "the essential inherent interior essence which is hidden inside the root of the kernel of everything" (113). Omnium, as it turns out, is the precious thing inside Old Mathers's black box (the entire object of the Narrator's quest), and as Joseph Voelker points out, "since the narrator died when he touched Old Mathers' black box, omnium may also be dynamite."[93] *The Third Policeman* reveals itself to be an antiepistemological text, according to Booker; knowledge in the book is "booby-trapped."[94]

The Narrator's quest for knowledge, like Watt's, is characterized by misreading and rhetorical regression and is "doomed to fail." In each case, exposure to the unknowable center leads to speechlessness. Mr. Knott fails to organize a central meaning to his mysterious abode, just as he fails to "organis[e] his exterior" (212) in any coherent way. Watt's progressive inversions in part 3 indicate his progressive loss of language as he becomes closer to Knott. The nearer Watt gets to Mr. Knott, the farther he falls from knowledge. The more time he spends with Mr. Knott, the less he knows about him: in this way, the trauma (or knowledge) Knott represents is always something missed. Likewise, each encounter the Narrator has with omnium leaves him with less ability to explain what he has seen. As he touches Old Mathers's black box, all he knows is that "something happened" (23); he fails to comprehend that something as his death. Like his inability to recognize the meaning of Mathers's death cry, the Narrator misses the meaning of his own death. Object of the murder plot, sign of the Narrator's unnameable desires, source of the policemen's terrifying power, and cause of the Narrator's unrealizable death—the black box represents that which is "unspeakable."

"Unspeakable" is, of course, an adjective inextricably associated with descriptions of World War II. Today, the Holocaust, the Katyn Massacre, the bombing of Hiroshima and Nagasaki are often troped as "unspeakable" events: no one can witness her own death, no words can be commensurate with what occurred. On another level, these events were officially "unspeakable" in a neutral Ireland that censored news reports of wartime atrocities, lest they engender "unneutral" thoughts. As an imperfect witness of Mr. Knott, Watt deals in unspeakability, witnessing a household so traumatically baffling that all his attempts at testimony lead to silence. The nameless Narrator of *The Third Policeman* finds himself cycling eternally through a world that contains mysteries like Policeman MacCruiskeen's "unbeholdable and brain-destroying bicycle," which would reduce men to "blinded eyes and crazy heads, chattering to each other poor broken words which nobody understood" (165). "Unbeholdable," the traumatic centers of these novels leave their characters speechless, trapped in purgatory.

This is similar to the nature of Irish neutrality in World War II. While those in Ireland suffered from shortages in food, fuel, and income, they suffered too from an absence of information about the unbeholdable war outside, in which, state censorship mandated, they officially take nothing more than a benign and neutral interest. The terms of the First Amendment of the Constitution meant that Ireland's Emergency legislation was legally dependent on the war it was designed to avoid. The irony of Irish neutrality is that Ireland's independence from the war was dependent on the war itself. In this sense, the experience of the Emergency was also the experience of the unspeakable world war that Ireland missed.[95] As neutrality does, Watt and the Narrator fail to speak the meaning of what they have (not quite) seen. At the end of both Beckett's and O'Brien's novels is a breakdown of meaning. The Narrator finds himself once again with no name and no memory; Watt turns dumb, numb, and blind. *Watt* and *The Third Policeman* serve as reminders that "unspeakability" can lead to dangerous silence.

De Valera's and Aiken's idea for "neutral language" was to create a balanced and readable medium for an "unspeakable" war. Watt's and the Narrator's "Cartesian catastrophe," their flagrant failures at rational reading, lampoon the very concept of such a neutral medium.[96] To read, to speak, for Watt and the Narrator, is only to suffer failure. Moreover, it is a painful failure—in both novels, the reader's position parallels the narrator's in that the reader suffers as the narrator does. *Watt* takes this a step farther: Sam suffers Watt's trials as the reader suffers Sam's. This suffering is both thematic and syntactic: *Watt* and *The Third Policeman* are no easy novels to read. When Watt's or the Narrator's purgatorial suffering is at its highest, when the novels begin to behave like novels and create suspense, at these moments the formats of both novels fight against readerly desire—Beckett spins out lists and O'Brien footnotes—and the reader must suffer the malfunctioning language of his or her guide, only to come out at the end of the book with language less intact than before, with the world rendered more "unspeakable."

The rhetorical trope of the "unspeakable," so often used as a cipher for a traumatic event, is fundamental to these two novels and a chief recourse of their narrators. But the trope simultaneously recalls the censorial notion of unspeakability—that about which we are forbidden or unwilling to speak. Thus, as Naomi Mandel writes, "What is unspeakable evokes the privileges and problems inherent in speech while actively distancing itself from them, performing a rhetorical sleight of hand that simultaneously gestures toward and away from the complex ethical negotiations that representing atrocity entails."[97] "Unspeakable" names a double-edged form of censorship—on the one hand, the psyche's self-censoring of traumatic experience, and, on the other, an officialized unwillingness to speak. The latter provides a seductive opportunity for the sort of "sacred egoism" that Emergency censorship sought. As Barry Stampfl puts it, "Complicity is evaded when the artist/critic mounts to the moral high ground . . . offered by the unspeakable" (19). In two novels in which "unspeakability" also signals the failure to surmount Mount Purgatory, Beckett's and O'Brien's Irish protagonists become, in Dantean terms, "unspeakable"—the ones even Virgil wishes to ignore. And yet these "unreadable" novels, by their very linguistic fabric, demand that we cannot ignore them.

This echoes the problem both for Watt's and the Narrator's testimonies and for the Irish experience of World War II, a problem represented by something immense, immediate, but inaccessible. Beckett's and O'Brien's insistence on heightening their protagonists' (and readers') discomfort in moments of violence or suspense is an enactment of the uncomfortable waiting that they experienced during the Second World War. Yet Beckett's and O'Brien's Irish purgatories, failed though their purgations may be, are privileged sites for linguistic experiment. They play diabolical tricks with language, just as Knott and the policemen do with rational thought. As they shatter the novel form—and their readers' nerves—*Watt* and *The Third Policeman* shatter the expected niceties of language use into "mirthless laughter."[98] This is what Arsene calls "the laugh of laughs, the *risus purus*, the laugh laughing at the laugh, the beholding, the saluting of the highest joke, in a word the laugh that laughs—silence please—at that which is unhappy" (48). As Arsene repeats "laugh" into meaninglessness, *Watt*'s reader hears the loud, repetitive tic of the witness who struggles to express his trauma in words. It is the black joke that suffering through war, or suffering through wartime neutrality, has a promise of recompense. There is no room for neutral language in these novels, no room for neutrality, no exit from purgatory. The reader is left, like Dante's neutrals, chasing the whirling banners of words, a kitten that cannot catch its tail.

EPILOGUE

The Emergency's *Improbable Frequency*

> Compromising Ireland's neutrality! Neutrality is an ethos poor Mr de Valera has worked so hard to uphold. But giving help to the Nazis, yes, that's definitely bad too, when you think about it.
>
> —ARTHUR RIORDAN, *Improbable Frequency*

The Rhetoric of Neutrality and the Plain People of Ireland

Announcing the passage of the Republic of Ireland's Defence Forces Second World War Amnesty and Immunity Bill on the floor of the Dáil, Defence Minister Alan Shatter remarked, "It is a tribute to how far we have come as a society that a Bill on such a sensitive issue could receive practically unanimous support from all sides in both Houses of the Oireachtas."[1] The "sensitive issue" at hand was the granting of amnesty to men who had deserted the Irish Defence Forces to serve in the British armed forces during World War II and returned home to find themselves court-martialed, imprisoned, blacklisted from public-sector employment, and denied the dole—a combination nicknamed "starvation orders"—because of the Emergency Powers (No. 362) Order of 1945. The date of Shatter's speech: May 7, 2013. Only a handful of the grantees were alive to receive their amnesty. After taking time to acknowledge the forty thousand men and women who served in Ireland's neutral Defence Forces during the Emergency, Shatter paid tribute to the subjects of the 2013 legislation:

> These individuals contributed in no small part to the Allied victory against tyranny and totalitarianism. That contribution was made not just by the approximately 5,000 who deserted from the Defence Forces but the extraordinary number—over 60,000—of citizens of the then Free State who joined the British forces . . . In total, 100,000 or more from the island of Ireland joined in the fight and it is right that we acknowledge what they did and their courage. Their efforts, in an indirect way, also contributed to the safety of their home country.[2]

Shatter's statement entered into Ireland's official public record an acknowledgment that Ireland's wartime neutrality was buffered by the protection of the very nation from which the neutrality declaration had aimed to separate. As Shatter concluded his remarks, he acknowledged the complexity of the period, a complexity long shielded from investigation: "I hope the Bill provides a statutory foundation to ensure [Irish citizens who fought for the Allies] will never again be ignored or forgotten in narratives covering the history of Ireland from 1939 to 1945. It is important that we acknowledge the realities and complexities of our history."[3]

More striking than the fact that this legislation was enacted sixty-eight years after the end of World War II is Shatter's emphatic gratitude to his colleagues for passing the bill and his acknowledgment that this was still "such a sensitive issue." For what Joe Lee describes as "Irish touchiness about neutrality" in the 1940s has increased rather than dissipated in the past seven decades.[4] The reason for this is that rather than fading into the historical dust, "neutrality" has become a major shibboleth of Irish identity: in an increasingly globalized political system and an increasingly multicultural and secular Ireland, neutrality is something that sets Ireland apart as different from its European counterparts and draws its citizens together as a universalizing manifestation of Irishness.[5] And because the idea of neutrality—incorrectly believed by many Irish people to be "constitutionally" enshrined—dates back to a particular moment in history, the Emergency remains a flashpoint in the Irish cultural imagination.[6] A peculiar moment, to be sure, but one that has, by its adoption as part of a national identity, had a long-term impact on Ireland's role on the international stage.

Irish "touchiness" about neutrality was responsible for the derailments of the European Union's (EU) fundamental Nice and Lisbon treaties in 2001 and 2008. EU treaties must be passed in Ireland by referendum and constitutional amendment, and in both cases, antitreaty campaigners equated neutrality with sovereignty to mobilize the "No" vote.[7] In the events of both Nice and Lisbon, the referendum was amended and put to the people twice; the results were eventually two "Yes" votes, ratifying the treaties with the inclusion in each of a clause that reads, "The State shall not adopt a decision taken by the European Council to establish a common defence . . . where that common defence would include the State."[8] These are the Twenty-Sixth and Twenty-Eighth Amendments to the Republic's constitution. Notably, the Twenty-Seventh Amendment (2004) was enacted to deny Irish citizenship to children born in Ireland of foreign parents; in all three amendments, the definition of Irishness is at stake.[9] As Emma O'Dwyer and her coauthors note in a 2016 study of Irish neutrality, migration now "is the implicit driver of the reconfiguration of the Irish national ingroup," but neutrality is a key symbol for how the ingroup interprets Irishness.[10] Ireland's long history within and without the British Empire drives the equation of neutrality with sovereignty, and thus neutrality with Irishness, but contemporary views of Irish neutrality as constitutional and of Ireland as a "peace-keeping nation" date to the Emergency.[11] Organizations like Shannonwatch, which opposes U.S. military use of Shannon Airport, and the Irish Peace and Neutrality Alliance (PANA), one of the chief supporters of the "No" campaigns for the Nice and Lisbon treaties, rely on a rhetoric that conflates "neutrality" with the moral high ground of "peace."[12] This is a direct legacy of the Emergency's framing of sacred egoism. De Valera's legacy is that Irish national identity is still invested in the "moral authority" of neutrality; his rhetoric has persuaded even the post-Catholic Irish soul.

"We must all be brothers in one holy cause, and no voice of dissension should be heard amongst us," de Valera told the Dáil in 1940, continuing, "We are a small people, but if we are true to ourselves, and courageously defend our rights, with God's help we shall survive the present dangers as we and our fathers survived no less grievous ones in the past."[13] Indeed, there was no voice of dissent as the leaders of all the parties formed a Defence Council that day. Speaking for the Labour Party, TD William Norton added, "As a small nation we have no territorial ambitions; we

PANA poster, 2015.

seek no domination over other lands or peoples; the military power and mammoth commercial greatness of other lands excite no envy or emulation in us. We seek only the opportunity to live in peace; fortified against want by honest toil and not by spoliation, and to be permitted to contribute our quota to the common pool of human liberty and human happiness throughout the world."[14] Here, the opposition perfectly echoed de Valera's characterization of neutrality as peaceful self-centeredness. But this high-minded rhetoric is also the crux of neutrality's ethical problem. As a recent commentator puts it, Ireland's World War II "neutrality was less about a principled stand as it was about hoping to be eaten last."[15] In an EU facing terrorist threats from ISIS and other groups, Ireland's ambiguous tradition of neutrality is once again under ethical scrutiny. Irish neutrality has always been characterized by "pragmatism and ambiguity," Thomas Hachey argues.[16] During the Emergency, Ireland was neutral for the Allies; during the Cold War, the Republic was neutral for the West; despite the Twenty-Sixth and Twenty-Eighth Amendments, it is now neutral for the EU and implicitly for NATO as well, though not a member (Ireland has, however, participated in NATO's Partnership for Peace missions since 1999). Taoiseach Seán Lemass said in 1962, "We do not wish, in the conflict between free democracies and the communist empires, to be thought of as neutral."[17] But if Ireland has not always wished to be thought of as neutral, it still prefers to think of itself as neutral.

In competing narratives, Ireland's tradition of neutrality can be summarized as "a buffer against increasing European integration and thus as a symbol of sovereignty, or as an ostrich-like and morally dubious predisposition of Irish citizens, almost akin to a character deficit."[18] This dichotomy points toward "the ambivalent and sometimes contradictory position which the policy occupies," according to the O'Dwyer study, which found that "participants *did* seem to have genuine difficulty negotiating the definitional ambiguity, moral complexity, and incompatible actions associated with neutrality" (177). In spite of participants' struggle with the "moral ambivalence" (174) of neutrality, the study concluded that "Irish neutrality and national identity were dynamically related. Social representations of neutrality were functional in that they sustained particular self-definitions which emphasized the continuity, distinctiveness and self-efficacy of the national group" (175). Participants frequently defined Ireland as "as a peace-keeping nation" (171) or a "peace-keeping country" (174), claiming that Ireland "punches above its weight" to "have a voice" in international affairs (171). As one participant put it, "we're heard and listened to in the UN and . . . our neutrality enforces that" (171). The study suggests that how Ireland sees its neutrality is impacted by how Irish people perceive neutrality being seen by outsiders. National identity, then, is tangled up in what we talk about when we talk about neutrality. As Hachey puts it, "few countries have made so heavy an emotional investment in the rhetoric of neutrality as have Irish politicians" (39)—or Irish citizens, for that matter. But the political rhetoric that they hear is an echo of the Emergency.

The legacy of Emergency rhetoric continues to ramify today, in a time when almost every news outlet refers to Ireland's foreign policy of "neutrality" as "a sacred cow."[19] From NATO to the Lisbon Treaty, what continues to echo in Irish voters' ideas about neutrality is the ideology that de Valera and Aiken's manipulation of language made possible: neutrality as a form of sacred egoism. It should come as no surprise, then, that the party responsible for tabling two different neutrality bills in the past two years is the party of "ourselves alone," Sinn Féin. The Thirty-Fifth Amendment of the Constitution (Neutrality) Bill of 2016 was designed to amend Article 28—the same article amended to create the Emergency—to include the provision, "War shall not be declared and the State shall not participate in any war or other armed conflict, nor aid foreign powers in any way in preparation for war or other armed conflict, or conduct of war or other armed conflict, save with the assent of Dáil Éireann."[20] Effectively, this provision would prevent the use of Shannon Airport by the U.S. military, and it could allow challenges of UN peacekeeping maneuvers to enter the courts, but a constitutional amendment would also ensure a nationwide referendum on the subject of neutrality, something both Sinn Féin and Labour began pushing for in the wake of the 2016 Brexit vote and EU calls for a strengthened post-Brexit military alliance.

Sinn Féin's public appeal on behalf of the bill included a Change.org petition whose language reflects long-standing characterizations of the policy. For one, it states, "A referendum would bring clarity to this State's neutrality policy which has become blurred, distorted, and riddled with double speak."[21] The irony here is that "double speak" is enshrined in the constitutional amendment that created Irish neutrality, via the Emergency, in the first place. Conversations about Irish neutrality consistently become conversations about rhetorical double-dealing, the same language that characterizes Emergency writing. The petition letter continues, "Sinn Féin believes that if Ireland followed a policy of Positive Neutrality our State could make a highly significant contribution towards the long-held global objective of international peace with justice."[22] In this, the language equates objectives of "international peace" with the idea of a "Positive Neutrality": outward sacredness, inward egoism. In a 2016 Dáil debate, TD Lisa Chambers spoke for Fianna Fáil, which, along with Fine Gael and Alliance, opposed the bill. Chambers moved immediately to cite her party's long-standing commitment to neutrality, reminding the house that "while neutrality was the given policy of successive Governments prior to the Second World War, it was that conflict that put it to the test."[23] In her speech, she cites de Valera in 1940 ("We have chosen the policy of neutrality . . . because we believed that it was the right policy for our people") to buttress support for the policy in general, but she goes on to cite de Valera in 1946, to argue for the negative implications the bill would have on Irish involvement in the United Nations: "It would be fatal for the small nations . . . who have any hope of collective security, to [forget] that when we enter into an organisation of this sort we are committing ourselves to take collective action with other people."[24] The two sides of the debate used similar operative terms, promoting neutrality as a positive means of ensuring international peace and the sovereignty of small nations. In short, the neutrality debate of 2016 was still mired in its own rhetorical convolution but seeking the same political effect: a badge of sovereignty for a small country, an affirmation of—Frank Aiken's favorite word—"balance." And the strange effect is that, in conversations and comments sections, Dáil debates and letters to the editor, the Emergency comes up with improbable frequency.

The 2004 musical comedy *Improbable Frequency* is the first of a number of recent fictional re-creations of the Emergency. In the past several years, best-selling Irish fiction writers Sebastian Barry, Mary Morrissey, and Dermot Bolger have published portrayals of the period.[25] Barry's *The Temporary Gentleman* (2014) opens as Sligo-born Jack McNulty's British warship is bombed off the Ghana coast and traces a postwar life spent mostly away from Ireland and the woman Jack loved. Morrissey's short story "Emergency" (2015) centers on the reaction of two women to a German paratrooper (and his gorgeous silk parachute) landing in their back garden—only, he turns out to be Irish. Dermot Bolger's *The Lonely Sea and Sky* (2016), based on his father's experiences in the Irish merchant marine, fictionalizes the true story of the MV *Kerlogue*'s 1943 rescue of 168 drowning German sailors as it plied between neutral ports in Portugal and Ireland. Another 2016 novel, Jo Baker's *A Country Road, A Tree*, is a fictionalized account of Samuel Beckett's life during the war—including the composition of *Watt*; and Barry Devlin's 2016 television series *My Mother and Other Strangers* focuses on the recalcitrant reaction of a rural Northern Irish community to the installation of an American air base in 1943.[26] It is clear that in an era of political uncertainty, this period exercises an increasingly strong hold on the Irish imagination, allowing writers to explore complex problems of morality and national belonging.

Improbable Frequency, or How This Book Became a Musical Comedy

Probably "the world's only science-fiction romantic spy comedy with singing," *Improbable Frequency* was commissioned by Dublin's Rough Magic

Theatre Company, with book and lyrics by Arthur Riordan and music by Bell Helicopter.[27] Hitting the stage between the Nice and Lisbon referendums, *Improbable Frequency* captivated audiences at a time of Irish self-definition by pointing to the Emergency as a pivotal moment in national identity formation—and poking fun at it. The guileless English protagonist wonders, "Oh, I know they're independent, and neutral as such; / But really, aren't they British, pretty much?"[28] What the play exposes is everyone else's desires for Ireland not to be neutral—and the complex improbability that it actually was. Reviewer Harvey O'Brien remarked that the play's 2004 debut was "given an added frisson by going for the jugular on the issue of Irish neutrality at the outset of the Iraq War when U.S. military transit through Shannon was a hot button issue."[29] This made it, he said, "a disarming surprise."

In fact, *Improbable Frequency* surprised the theater community by being a hit in a genre previously thought to be a contradiction in terms: an Irish musical. Debuted at the O'Reilly Theatre for the 2004 Dublin Theatre Festival, the play won Best Production and Best Direction (Lynne Parker) in the Irish Times Theatre Awards. It transferred to the Abbey in March 2005, putting its satire of the Emergency on the stage of Ireland's national theater. Rough Magic toured Britain with the 2005 production, where it received high praise at the Edinburgh Fringe, and it has since been performed in New York (2008), Washington, D.C. (2010), and Chicago (2013) and revived by Rough Magic in Dublin's largest and most populist venue, the Gaiety, in 2012. Patrick Lonergan says that "it could be argued that *Improbable Frequency* is the model of a successful independent production for the Dublin Theatre Festival."[30] The play's popularity with audiences—in spite or because of its "exasperating" language games—attests to the popular fascination with its subject matter.[31]

The feel of the play—or at least Rough Magic's original staging of it—mimics the cultural memory of the period: the dimly lit Palace Bar swimming in journalists and spies, Dublin described as "a city all lit up at night / lit up so flagrantly!" (7). Something intoxicating and possibly sinister is in the air—literally, in the play's case: scientifically enhanced radio waves that can alter probability (and even make you drunk). These "improbable frequencies" are responsible for keeping Ireland neutral, and they have the side effect of not predicting but impacting the famously censored weather. The show's hero, Tristram, an English crossword champion turned MI5

Improbable Frequency *at the Gaiety Theatre, Dublin, 2012. Photo reprinted with kind permission of set designer Alan Farquharson.*

code breaker, is sent to Ireland in 1941 to expose a radio broadcaster the British think is sending coded messages to Nazi Germany. Wound up in the story are three real figures from the Emergency: Myles Na gCopaleen, John Betjeman, and Austrian physicist Erwin Schrödinger (head of de Valera's Institute for Advanced Studies). In between allusions to Flann O'Brien's novels and the acting out of half a dozen Myles-esque puns (for instance, "the chips are down" results in a person eating feathers from a greasy newspaper wrapping), *Improbable Frequency* points to the Emergency as a peculiarly Irish moment while exposing the most vivid cultural legacy of the period: the suspicion that Irish neutrality was never truly neutral.

Indeed, it's suspected of being everything but. As the British diplomats sing, "Is it smugness or insurgency / That makes them say 'Emergency'? / I feel it lacks the urgency / Of World War Two" (11). The Brits are sure that the IRA is conspiring with the Nazis through their radio broadcasts, and at one point in the Rough Magic production, great red banners unfurl with shamrocks stylized like swastikas—but as Agent Green sings, it's "not that we're Nazis, we just like the style" (16).

Invested in that style is an age-old republican adage: England's difficulty is Ireland's opportunity. Green sings about "Ireland's opportunity," continuing with,

> Although we're not Nazis,
> We're not bloody patsies
> For Churchill and Roosevelt to tease and to taunt,
> So we'll stick to our guns
> And we'll drink to the Huns (17)

At the end of her drinking song, Green chants another familiar adage—this one the familiar justification for neutrality: "The foreign disputes aren't our affair" (17).[32] Or as Myles puts it later in the same scene, "There's not many folk can pull off the bold stroke / Of ignoring the Second World War" (22). In spite of the legacy of British propaganda that Irish citizens were all Nazi sympathizers, in spite of the actuality of Éire's "friendly" neutrality, the most improbable thing in the play is that Ireland really *is* neutral—but only by a serious manipulation of the public through language.

Schrödinger explains in "An Ingenious Device" that

> I said to de Valera, very early in the war,
> You are neutral, by the book, and to the letter,
> But diplomacy alone is not sufficient any more
> Some sub-atomic physics might be better. (66)

An atomic bomb, the horrified British agents presume! But no: what the Nobel-endowed Austrian creates "is not some silly piece of weaponry, / But a Probability Adjustment Tank," nicknamed PAT (66). It shoots "waves of altered probability" to the General Post Office (GPO) to be broadcast over Meehawl O'Dromedary's radio show, "making his every turn of phrase / a sinister reality" (67). The use of Radio Éireann as the centering element of Ireland's neutrality is apt for three reasons. First, its real-life location in the GPO symbolically centers broadcasting power at the site of the 1916 Dublin Rebellion, a location that underscores ideas of national sovereignty. Second, Riordan's use of radio waves registers the key paradox of the Emergency: Ireland's simultaneous sense of isolation and porousness. Both the spy plot and the radio theme point to Ireland's pose of isolationist self-regard while highlighting its inverse—the strange sense of infiltration that the war engendered in spite of the government's attempts to block it out.[33] Radio, as the only international medium that could evade the censor, became a symbol of this cultural doubleness.[34] The play's insistence on the danger of these radio broadcasts forms the third and most important way in which it reflects the real concerns of Emergency writing. For the maintenance of neutrality is depicted in the play as a function of language, since the Probability Adjustment Tank causes people (and the weather) to act out the words of the radio presenter. Language itself is the active element, dangerous, alive.

What makes *Improbable Frequency* particularly remarkable (and exasperating) is that this spy plot is itself written in coded language. Not only does Tristram demonstrate cryptography onstage, the play's many (usually terrible) puns require the audience to decode them as clues. Philomena has promised to be with Tristram when the chips are down, so when a feather-eating punter appears, the audience knows she'll spring into action. Riordan has said that the idea for the play first came to him through the wartime connection between crosswords and code breaking: "Just the idea of poem codes appealed to me hugely."[35] As did the peculiar coded language required by Emergency censorship. Riordan summarizes, "You could, for instance, report drownings or traffic jams or road accidents that took place, but you couldn't report on the floods that would explain all these things."[36] It was a time that, as Myles says in the play, "engender[ed] strange logomorphic manifestations, / Leaving the plain people banjanxed and bewildered" (75).

And it is in this that *Improbable Frequency* really captures the essence of the Emergency: its obsession with the dangers of language. Belinda McKeon noted in the *Irish Times*, "Riordan's script of poetry and pun, as he pokes questions at the sacred cow of Irish neutrality, seems itself a coded language, secrets laced through its bouncing rhymes."[37] It is twisted, self-referential, and absolutely kin to the language of books like *The Heat of the Day*, *Watt*, and *The Third Policeman* (Riordan's debt to O'Brien is obvious, as PAT reeks of both de Selby and MacCruiskeen). *New York Times* reviewer Charles Isherwood called the play's temporally unstable second act "seriously incomprehensible. Or rather, unseriously incomprehensible."[38] This is a reasonable charge: act 2, scene 7 takes place chronologically after scene 4, and the "spoken sequence" in scene 4, titled "Wahrscheinlichkeitsspirale" (Probability spiral), is a thrice-repeated revision of itself, each time offering a slightly different set of circumstances that "could change probabilities retrospectively and rupture the whole course of history" (81). (The third time, half the scene is spoken in German, a nod to what could have happened in the 1940s, given a different set of probabilities.) Serious incomprehensibility, chronological shuffling, and dangerous language that reorders the text as it writes it: Arthur Riordan plays the same games with language that the writers of the Emergency did. The literature of the Emergency is, like this play, contorted with code, bent with syntactical negotiations, a fun house mirror of Irish political rhetoric, as spun through late modernist literary practice.

Is this play just an echo of Emergency writing? Not precisely; it's far too silly for that, but then, *The Third Policeman* might be accused of the same thing, and its silliness is quite serious in the end. McKeon's review concludes, "Just as Riordan's script seems to be settling for cleverness and hilarity, an unnerving sense of truth, or something like it, invades the stage in a memorable final scene, as the meanings of the world, of identity, go astray. This is true satire: you're as likely to shudder as to laugh."[39] The play's closing song is a chorus reprise of Myles's boozy ballad, "We're All in the Gutter":

> Well, here's what we say to the cynics,
> As the vultures are circling around:
> We're all in the gutter,
> But some of us have an ear to the ground. (89)

In a play that winks at the legacy of modern literature, this song subverts the audience's expectations by twisting Oscar Wilde's familiar "We're all in the gutter, but some of us are looking at the stars."[40] Indeed, the song reverses Lord Darlington's famous line by asserting that the neutral Irish are not idly stargazing but actively listening to the rumble of history, more spies than ostriches. The nature of Irish neutrality is left uncertain in *Improbable Frequency*, or as Philomena has it, "sunder love unfinished . . . ten letters" (84). Philomena is the play's true neutral, and her earlier remark about discovering the radio's impact on the weather comes across as simultaneously silly and serious as it exposes the moral equivalences that de Valera's Emergency rhetoric invited:

> PHILOMENA: I noticed, I suppose, the same thing that MI5 did. That the songs seemed to forecast the weather. This was the most appalling thing I'd ever heard!
>
> TRISTRAM: Giving help to the Nazis.
>
> PHILOMENA: Oh, that too, of course, but compromising Ireland's neutrality! Neutrality is an ethos poor Mr de Valera has worked so hard to uphold. But giving help to the Nazis, yes, that's definitely bad too, when you think about it. (56)

One of the central issues in contemporary debates over Ireland's neutrality concerns whom neutrality does or doesn't help—the inverse, perhaps, of the Emergency saw, "Who are we neutral against?" Key debates in 2015–16 were over the U.S. Air Force's use of Shannon Airport for refueling on the way to the Middle East and whether sending Irish UN Peacekeeping troops to relieve French soldiers in Mali in the wake of the Paris bombings would be a breach of neutrality.[41] Since 2016, Brexit and the Northern Irish border have dominated conversations about the policy.[42] The ethics of what neutrality means and whom neutrality helps are still murky; the answer to Philomena's crossword clue is an anagram: "unresolved." As with so many works written during the Emergency, the resolution of *Improbable Frequency* is an irresolution. Tristram and Philomena sing, "Do we wind up our song on a minor chord? / The lyrics in search of that final word— / Unresolved?" and Myles and Shrödinger echo, "Like particle-wave duality, / And the future of Irish neutrality— / Unresolved" (89). Here again, as the Anglo-Irish "unlikely bedfellows" (89) move toward one another in tentative détente, the self-referential lyrics echo the concerns of Emergency writing, a literature that courts ambiguities, contorts syntax, and exposes the dangerous business of reading and writing in a world (though one dare not speak the word) at war.

NOTES

Introduction

1. Michael Kennedy, *Guarding Neutral Ireland: The Coast Watching Service and Military Intelligence, 1939–1945* (Dublin: Four Courts Press, 2008).

2. Éire became the legal name for the Irish Free State under the 1937 constitution. In this book, I use the terms Éire and Ireland interchangeably, though many contemporaries continued to refer to the "Free State." As a rule, I use the name Ireland to refer to the twenty-six-county southern state (which became the Republic of Ireland in 1948), specifying when I mean to refer to the island of Ireland.

3. Treasa Lynch, *Eire Signs of WWII: The GPS of the Past*, www.eiremarkings.org; Peter Homer, *Malin Head: Ireland's Most Northerly Point*, www.malinhead.net.

4. The Donegal Corridor, or the unofficial air travel zone across Donegal from the Atlantic to Lough Erne in Northern Ireland, has been one of the most enduring and hotly debated myths of the Emergency. In 2007, the Irish government officially acknowledged the 1941–45 use of the Donegal Corridor by erecting plaques in Ballyshannon, County Donegal (in the Republic of Ireland), and Belleek, County Fermanagh (in Northern Ireland), to commemorate the collaboration that enabled the Allied flying boats to cross neutral territory. See Anita Guidera, "Plaques Mark Secret Wartime Air Corridor in Donegal," *Independent*, April 19, 2007, and Joe O'Loughlin, "The Donegal Corridor during the Second World War," *Clogher Record* 18, no. 2 (2004): 341–50.

5. Joe Cleary, introduction to *The Cambridge Companion to Irish Modernism*, ed. Joe Cleary (Cambridge: Cambridge University Press, 2014), 10. Subsequent references to this work appear as parenthetical page numbers in the main text. Please note that this practice is followed generally in the present volume and thus numbers in parentheses in the main text refer to the work cited in a preceding endnote.

6. "Taoiseach" (Irish for "chief" or "leader") refers to the prime minister and head of government in the Republic of Ireland (the title was created in the 1937 Constitution of Ireland, replacing President of the Executive Council).

7. Edna Longley, *Louis MacNeice: A Study* (London: Faber and Faber, 1988), xiii.

8. Mark Rawlinson, *British Writing of the Second World War* (Oxford: Clarendon Press, 2000); Patrick Deer, *Culture in Camouflage: War, Empire, and Modern British Literature* (Oxford: Oxford University Press, 2009).

9. Kristine Miller, *British Literature of the Blitz: Fighting the People's War* (London: Palgrave, 2009); Gill Plain, *Women's Fiction of the Second World War: Gender, Power, Resistance* (Edinburgh: Edinburgh University Press, 1996); Kristine Schneider, *Loving Arms: British Women Writing the Second World War* (Lexington: University of Kentucky Press, 1997); Phyllis Lassner, *British Women Writers of World War II: Battlegrounds of Their Own* (Basingstoke, U.K.: Macmillan, 1998).

10. Damien Keane, *Ireland and the Problem of Information: Irish Writing, Radio, Late Modernist Communication* (University Park: Penn State University Press, 2014), 3.

11. Patrick Kavanagh, "Author's Note," in *Collected Poems*, ed. Antoinette Quinn (London: Penguin, 2005), 292.

12. Patrick Kavanagh, "Epic," in *Collected Poems*, lines 1–3.

13. It is significant that Kavanagh was the first poet promoted by Sean O'Faolain and Frank O'Connor in antirevival's best-known journal, *The Bell*.

14. Éire officially became the Republic of Ireland in 1948.

15. Paul Muldoon, *To Ireland I* (Oxford: Oxford University Press, 2000), 68.

16. Antoinette Quinn has called "Epic" a "tactical triumph" that manipulates the reader into "colluding with" the poet's loss of faith in the parochial, "only to wipe the supercilious grin off his face in the closing line"(*Patrick Kavanagh: A Critical Study* [Syracuse, N.Y.: Syracuse University Press, 1991], 360).

17. The use of "rood" also rings as decidedly Yeatsian.

18. Upon signing the Munich Agreement with Hitler in 1938, an appeasement document that granted Germany's "annex" of Czech territory in return for a promise of no aggression against the United Kingdom, British prime minister Neville Chamberlain announced, "I believe it is peace for our time"; quoted in Angus Calder, *The People's War: Britain 1939–1945* (New York: Random House, 1969), 29.

19. Kate O'Brien, *The Last of Summer* (London: Virago, 1990), 81. For more on this novel, see my essay, "No 'Help to the Imagination': Kate O'Brien and the Emergency," *Irish University Review* 48.1 (May 2018).

20. Tyrus Miller, *Late Modernism: Politics, Fiction, and the Arts between the World Wars* (Berkeley: University of California Press, 1999); Jed Esty, *A Shrinking Island: Modernism and National Culture in England* (Princeton, N.J.: Princeton University Press, 2004); Marina MacKay, *Modernism and World War II* (Cambridge: Cambridge University Press, 2007); Thomas Davis, *The Extinct Scene: Late Modernism and Everyday Life* (New York: Columbia University Press, 2016).

21. James Purdon, *Modernist Informatics: Literature, Information, and the State* (Oxford: Oxford University Press, 2016), 6.

22. Donal Ó Drisceoil, *Censorship in Ireland, 1939–1945: Neutrality, Politics and Society* (Cork: Cork University Press, 1996).

23. First Amendment of the Constitution Act, 1939. Oireachtas Éireann is the bicameral legislature of Ireland. It consists of the president of Ireland (from 1938 to 1945, Douglas Hyde), the Dáil Éireann (lower house and primary lawmaking entity, directly elected by proportional representation), and Seanad Éireann (upper house, appointed and indirectly elected). Teachtaí Dála, members of the Dáil, are referred to by the abbreviation TD, and members of the Seanad are called Senators.

24. W. B. Yeats famously asks of Leda's relationship to Zeus in "Leda and the Swan," "Being so caught up, / So mastered by the brute blood of the air, / Did she put on his knowledge with his power / Before the indifferent beak could let her drop?" See *The Collected Poems of W. B. Yeats*, ed. Richard J. Finneran (New York: Scribner, 1989).

25. Thomas Davis, *The Extinct Scene*, 7.

26. Guy Woodward, *Culture, Northern Ireland, and the Second World War* (Oxford: Oxford University Press, 2015), 18.

27. See Ben Tonra, *Global Citizen and European Republic: Irish Foreign Policy in Transition* (New York: Manchester University Press, 2006); Michael J. O'Sullivan, *Ire-*

land and the Global Question (Syracuse, N.Y.: Syracuse University Press, 2006); Brian Girvin and Geoffrey Roberts, eds., *Ireland and the Second World War: Politics, Society and Remembrance* (Dublin: Four Courts Press, 2000).

28. Brian Girvin, *The Emergency: Neutral Ireland, 1939–45* (London: Macmillan, 2006); Ian Wood, *Britain, Ireland and the Second World War* (Edinburgh: Edinburgh University Press, 2010); Robert Fisk, *In Time of War: Ireland, Ulster and the Price of Neutrality, 1939–45* (Philadelphia: University of Pennsylvania Press, 1983). The first dedicated study of the Emergency was Joseph T. Carroll, *Ireland in the War Years* (New York: Crane, Russak, 1975). See also J. J. Lee, "Experiment: 1932–1945," in *Ireland 1912–1985:Politics and Society*, 175–270 (Cambridge: Cambridge University Press, 1989), and Robert Cole, *Propaganda, Censorship and Irish Neutrality in the Second World War* (Edinburgh University Press, 2006).

29. Clair Wills, *That Neutral Island: A Cultural History of Ireland during the Second World War* (London: Faber and Faber, 2007).

30. Terence Brown, *Ireland: A Social and Cultural History, 1922–2002* (London: Harper Perennial, 2004), 159–98.

31. Dorothea Depner and Guy Woodward, eds., *Irish Culture and Wartime Europe, 1938–1948* (Dublin: Four Courts Press, 2015).

32. Steven Lynn, *Rhetoric and Composition: An Introduction* (Cambridge: Cambridge University Press, 2010), 5.

33. The oft-cited remark about Ireland as Plato's Cave is in F. S. L. Lyons, *Ireland since the Famine* (London: Fontana, 1973), 551.

34. Cited in Lynn, *Rhetoric and Composition*, 576. See Plato's *Phaedrus*, available online at http://classics.mit.edu/Plato/phaedrus.html.

35. Denis Devlin, "Lough Derg," in *Collected Poems of Denis Devlin*, ed. J. C. C. Mays (Dublin: Dedalus Press, 2009), line 8.

36. Samuel Beckett, review of *Intercessions*, by Denis Devlin, *transition* 27 (April–May 1938): 289–94; reprinted in *Disjecta* (London: Calder, 1983), 94.

37. W. B. Yeats, *Per Amica Silentia Lunae* (London: Macmillan, 1918), 30.

Chapter 1

1. As early as June 1935, in an address to the League of Nations, de Valera stated that "the Irish people did not want to be dragged into any European or other war, but the Irish people would be prepared to strain themselves to the utmost to defend their own territory." In the Dáil on June 18, 1936, he stated, "We want to be neutral" in any outside conflagration. See Eamon de Valera, *Speeches and Statements by Eamon de Valera, 1917–73*, ed. Maurice Moynihan (Dublin: Gill and Macmillan, 1980), 416. All further citations of de Valera's speeches are from this volume.

2. De Valera, League of Nations address, July 2, 1936, in *Speeches and Statements*, 416.

3. Michael Tierney, "Ireland in the European Chaos," *Ireland Today* 2, no. 4 (April 1937): 14.

4. Gnathaí Gan Irraidh, *The Sacred Egoism of Sinn Féin* (London: Maunsel, 1918); available online in a Project Gutenberg reproduction at http://www.gutenberg.org/files/34108/34108-8.txt.

5. Churchill's V-E Day speech opens, "My dear friends, this is your hour. This is not victory of a party or of any class. It's a victory of the great British nation as a whole. We were the first, in this ancient island, to draw the sword against tyranny. After a while

we were left all alone against the most tremendous military power that has been seen. We were all alone for a whole year." May 8, 1945, https://www.winstonchurchill.org/resources/speeches/1941-1945-war-leader/to-v-e-crowds.

6. De Valera, "National Thanksgiving," radio address, May 16, 1945, in *Speeches and Statements*, 476.

7. Sean O'Faolain, "Ireland and the Modern World," *The Bell* 5, no. 6 (March 1943): 423.

8. Far from the dictates of *sinn féin*, in fact, the Irish economy was interdependent with Britain's war economy. Not only did fifty thousand Irish citizens volunteer for the British Armed Forces (compared with the forty thousand volunteers who made up the Irish Defence Forces) but also nearly two hundred thousand Irish immigrants worked in British factories during the war. The corresponding fall in the Irish unemployment rate, together with wages sent home from Britain, kept Ireland's economy afloat while simultaneously underwriting the viability of Britain's war industries. See Robert Fisk, *In Time of War: Ireland, Ulster and the Price of Neutrality, 1939–45* (Philadelphia: University of Pennsylvania Press, 1983), and Clair Wills, *That Neutral Island: A Cultural History of Ireland during the Second World War* (London: Faber and Faber, 2007), as well as Steven O'Connor, "Why Did They Fight for Britain? Irish Recruits to the British Forces, 1939–45," *Études Irlandaises* 40, no. 1 (2015): 59–70.

9. The blacklisting and branding as "deserters" of soldiers who left the Irish services to fight for Britain represent one example of the long-term power of this rhetoric. This is discussed at greater length in the epilogue of the present volume.

10. These terms are from de Valera's famous 1943 Saint Patrick's Day address. See *Speeches and Statements*, 466.

11. In other words, to answer Yeats's question in "The Statues," "When Pearse summoned Cuchulain to his side. / What stalked through the Post Office" (25–26) was hardened into the bronze monument that Beckett would use as a kicking post in *Murphy*.

12. Mark Quigley, *Empire's Wake: Postcolonial Irish Writing and the Politics of Modern Literary Form* (New York: Fordham University Press, 2013), 7–8.

13. Ian Wood, *Britain, Ireland and the Second World War* (Edinburgh: Edinburgh University Press, 2010), 1. See also Wills, *That Neutral Island*, and Fisk, *In Time of War*.

14. Irish weather forecasts played an important part in the timing of the D-Day landings, although the actual timing of the offensive was carefully guarded from the Irish. The extent of the state's collaboration with the Allies was not revealed until Robert Fisk gained access to previously closed British and Irish government archives for his book *In Time of War*. Much of the true history of the war will never be known: Irish authorities destroyed seventy tons of secret documents in 1945, and many British government archives remain closed (Fisk, ix).

15. At the end of his 1942 novel *Put Out More Flags* (Boston: Back Bay Books, 2002), Evelyn Waugh punishes the misfit London aesthete Ambrose Silk by having him falsely accused of fascism and packing him off (in a fake Roman collar, no less) to sit out the war in western Ireland. This was as much Waugh's commentary on Ireland as on aesthetes like Silk.

16. Quoted in Adam Piette, *Imagination at War: British Fiction and Poetry, 1939–1945* (London: Papermac, 1995), 170–71; see also Elizabeth Bowen, *Notes on Éire*. Ed. Jack Lane and Brendan Clifford (Aubane, Co. Cork: Aubane Historical Society), 2009, 38.

17. The three deepwater ports had long housed British naval installations. They remained under British control under the terms of the 1922 Anglo-Irish Treaty but were returned to Irish jurisdiction after prolonged diplomacy. See Fisk, *In Time of War*; Brian Girvin, *The Emergency: Neutral Ireland, 1939–45* (London: Macmillan, 2006); and Joseph T. Carroll, *Ireland in the War Years* (New York: Crane, Russak, 1975) for a fuller analysis of the ports situation. Most of Elizabeth Bowen's "information gathering" was in relation to public sentiment about the ports. More discussion on this can be found in chapter 4 of the present volume.

18. Louis MacNeice, "London Letter," *Common Sense* 10, no. 5 (May 1941): 142–43.

19. J. J. Lee, "Experiment: 1932–1945," in *Ireland 1912–1985: Politics and Society* (Cambridge: Cambridge University Press, 1989), 245. If Britain had decided to retake the Treaty Ports, it could have been done with relative ease. Lee points out that Ireland's vaunted "self-sufficiency did not extend to [defense] this most basic of all criteria for a sovereign state . . . Ireland pursued, at most, a policy of half-armed neutrality" (235–36).

20. Wartime isolationism meant dramatic shortages of everyday necessities in Ireland, gas and coal in particular, but also key commodities such as fertilizer, soap, sugar, tea, rubber, and batteries. For much of the Emergency, Irish trains relied on turf as a source of fuel, automobile traffic reverted back to bicycle and horse, and electric outages were frequent. Other privations came in the form of transport restrictions and censorship, hence the depiction of Ireland as "Plato's Cave."

21. Constitution of Ireland (Bunreacht na hÉireann), Article 28, No. 3.

22. First Amendment of the Constitution Act, 1939.

23. Legally, the Emergency was not rescinded until 1976, when the Dáil declared, "(a) that the national emergency created by the armed conflict referred to in the Resolutions, pursuant to the said Article, of Dáil Éireann and Seanad Éireann of the 2nd September, 1939, has ceased to exist, and (b) that, arising out of the armed conflict now taking place in Northern Ireland, a national emergency exists affecting the vital interests of the State" (Dáil Debates, National Emergency Motion, September 1, 1976), Essentially, the existing state of emergency was swapped for a new one. The entire proceedings of the Oireachtas, since 1919, are available digitally at http://oireachtasdebates.oireachtas.ie/debates%20authoring/debateswebpack.nsf/startpage?readform. Debates will be cited in this volume by date.

24. Giorgio Agamben, *State of Exception*, trans. Kevin Attell (Chicago: University Chicago Press, 2005), 1.

25. Stephen Morton, *States of Emergency: Colonialism, Literature and Law* (Liverpool: Liverpool University Press, 2013).

26. My thinking about language use in wartime is indebted to Giorgio Agamben, Vincent Sherry, Mark Wollaeger, and Marina MacKay, but particularly to George Orwell, "Politics and the English Language," in *All Art is Propaganda: Critical Essays*, ed. Keith Gessen, 270-286 (New York: Mariner, 2009).

27. Wills, *That Neutral Island*, 277.

28. Elizabeth Bowen, *The Mulberry Tree*, ed. Hermione Lee (London: Harcourt Brace, 1986), 33.

29. Elizabeth Bowen, *The Collected Stories of Elizabeth Bowen* (New York: Anchor, 2006), 590.

30. Censorship of Films Act, 1923. The cultural censorship was only strengthened by Emergency censorship policies, and it continued to plague the Irish literary and

intellectual scene well into the 1970s. See Julia Carlson, *Banned in Ireland: Censorship and the Irish Writer* (Athens: University of Georgia Press, 1990), and Michael Adams, *Censorship: The Irish Experience* (Tuscaloosa: University of Alabama Press, 1968).

31. Constitution of Ireland, Article 40.6.1°, i–ii. Special protection against blasphemy highlights the influence of the Catholic Church on the 1937 constitution, of which de Valera himself was the primary author. The document's language pertaining to Irish women is even more problematically ecclesiastical and has been the subject of long-standing debate.

32. The Emergency Powers Act's censorship provisions were strengthened by Emergency Powers Orders No. 36 (1940) and No. 151 (1942), which, respectively, granted government agents the power to seize banned publications and extended authority to all printed matter. See Damien Keane, *Ireland and the Problem of Information: Irish Writing, Radio, Late Modernist Communication* (University Park: Penn State University Press, 2014) for more on shortwave broadcasting in World War II.

33. Donal Ó Drisceoil, *Censorship in Ireland, 1939–1945: Neutrality, Politics and Society* (Cork: Cork University Press, 1996), 101.

34. In Henry Green's *Loving*, set in an Irish big house during the war, the English servants are in a state of constant suspicion of Nazis among the "natives" (*Living; Loving; Party Going* [London: Penguin Classics, 1993]).

35. Bryce Evans, *Frank Aiken: Nationalist and Internationalist* (Dublin: Irish Academic Press, 2014), 140. According to Evans, the trip was a public-relations disaster, but Aiken secured two ships and half a million dollars' worth of food and coal.

36. Cited in Ó Drisceoil, 120.

37. Ó Drisceoil, 117.

38. Ó Drisceoil's summary of this from sources in the Irish National Archives is backed up by the private memoranda in the Aiken Archive (UCDA P104), which was opened four years after the publication of Ó Drisceoil's book.

39. Seanad Debates, January 27, 1944.

40. Ó Drisceoil, 121. Aiken's January 1940 censor's report even notes his concern about publishing reports of Irish-born refugees arriving from blitzed Britain, because it might appear "unneutral" to receive only Allied refugees (Frank Aiken Papers. University College Dublin Archives, UCDA P104/3466). Muting the return of Irish citizens is a nearly baffling commitment to evenhandedness.

41. Ó Drisceoil, 125.

42. Wills, 54.

43. Mark Wollaeger, *Modernism, Media, and Propaganda: British Narrative from 1900 to 1945* (Princeton: Princeton University Press, 2006), 11.

44. Aiken, Memorandum on Press Censorship, 1939 (UCDA P104/3431).

45. By the end of the first month of the war, the members of the Dáil were already skeptical. TD John O'Sullivan asked the minister, "Do I understand that the Minister refuses to give to Deputies the instructions issued to the Press, so that the country and the Deputies are quite unaware as to what amount of censorship is being exercised on the Press?," reminding Aiken that "the Minister said that Deputies have a responsibility to the country to see that the Government does not exceed its powers or use them improperly but he deprives Deputies of the opportunity to discharge that responsibility." Aiken's response was tart: "Deputies have another responsibility and that is to see that the country does not suffer by inquisitiveness on their part" (Dáil Debates, Questions—Oral Answers: Censorship, September 27, 1939).

46. Seanad Debates, December 4, 1940. This tactic would be workable only until a battery shortage silenced many rural radios.

47. Seanad Debates, December 4, 1940. It is telling, given Aiken's summary, that in "Summer Night," Bowen's Aunt Fran complains, "No one speaks the truth to me but the man on the wireless" (Bowen, *Collected Stories*, 597), though he is incapable of commenting on the family affairs she desires information about.

48. Bowen, "Éire," reprinted in *The Mulberry Tree*, 32–33.

49. See Lee, "Experiment," and Wills, *That Neutral Island*, for more on this refusal.

50. Aiken, Memorandum on Censorship, 1939 (UCDA P104/3429).

51. Aiken, Memorandum on Censorship, 1939 (UCDA P104/3429).

52. This "unneutral commentary" (UCDA P104/3465) seems to have amounted chiefly to a joke about new bunkers on English courses.

53. Aiken, Memorandum on Censorship, 1939 (UCDA P104/3429).

54. See Caleb Richardson, "'They Are Not Worthy of Themselves': The *Tailor and Ansty* Debates of 1942," *Éire-Ireland* 42, nos. 3, 4 (2007): 148–72, for an excellent assessment of the debates in the Seanad. The main Seanad debates on censorship occurred December 4, 1940, December 9–11, 1942, and December 6, 1944.

55. Seanad Debates, December 9, 1942.

56. Although there was a general election June 23, 1943, the Emergency Powers Act did not lapse until September 2, 1946, meaning that the new Dáil did not have real powers of legislation until that time. De Valera remained in power until the general election of 1948.

57. Seanad Debates, December 4, 1940.

58. See Keane's astute reading of the speech in *The Problem of Information*, 2–5.

59. Helena Wulff, *Dancing at the Crossroads: Memory and Mobility in Ireland* (New York: Berghahn Books, 2007), 12.

60. Censorship of Publications Act, 1929.

61. In Kate O'Brien's novel *The Last of Summer* (London: Virago, 1990), set in September 1939, the progressive Martin chides a pious relation, "You know perfectly well, Dotey, that your solicitous Dev. [de Valera] doesn't let an immoral rag within three hundred miles of you. This country is Heaven's ante-room, whether we like the idea or not" (50).

62. Seanad Debates, December 9, 1942.

63. Eric Cross, *The Tailor and Ansty* (1942; repr., Cork: Mercier Press, 1999).

64. Excerpts from *The Tailor and Ansty* were published in *The Bell* 1, no. 5 (February 1941); no. 6 (March 1941); and 2, no. 1 (April 1941). For more on *The Midnight Court*, see Brian Merriman, *The Midnight Court / Cúirt an Mheán Oíche: A Critical Edition*, trans. David Marcus, ed. Brian Ó Conchubhair (Syracuse, N.Y.: Syracuse University Press, 2011), and Ciaran Carson's introduction to *The Midnight Court: A New Translation of Cúirt An Mhéan Oíche by Brian Merriman* (Dublin: Gallery, 2005). The banned edition was Brian Merriman, *Cúirt an Mheán Oíche (The Midnight Court)*, trans. Frank O'Connor (Dublin: Fridberg, 1945).

65. In Kate O'Brien's *Pray for the Wanderer* (New York. Doubleday, 1938), published on the heels of the banning of her 1936 *Mary Lavelle*, the narrator, Matt (a banned Irish novelist), remarks, "Oh, green and trim Free State! Smug, obstinate and pertinacious little island, your sins and ignorances are thick upon your face, and thickening under the authority of your 'sea-green incorruptible'!" (306–7). Here, de Valera acquires Thomas Carlyle's famous

nickname for Robespierre, aligning his censorship with a reign of terror. The borrowed epithet is apt, as de Valera also seemed to hope his islanders would be morally incorruptible.

66. Seanad Debates, November 18, 1942.

67. Samuel Beckett, "Censorship in the Saorstat" (1935), reprinted in *Disjecta* (London: Calder, 1983), 87.

68. In a 1941 editorial, "Dare We Suppress That Irish Voice?" *The Bell* 3, no. 3 (December): 169–76, O'Faolain airs his fears: "Now for the first time in this century we have to face the problem of supporting our own writers . . . The war has marked our literature 'Return to Sender'" (171).

69. Seanad Debates, November 18, 1942.

70. Myles Na gCopaleen, "The Cruiskeen Lawn," *Irish Times*, November 11, 1942. Brian O'Nolan used multiple pen names, but as Flann O'Brien is the best known, I follow the precedent set by other critics and refer to him by that name throughout.

71. Anthony Cronin, in *No Laughing Matter: The Life and Times of Flann O'Brien* (London: Grafton Books, 1989), claims that it may have been the last novel Joyce read.

72. The next novel he wrote was *The Third Policeman*, published posthumously in 1967.

73. Flann O'Brien, *The Poor Mouth*, trans. Patrick Power, in *Flann O'Brien: The Complete Novels*, 407–96 (New York: Knopf, 2007).

74. Brian Ó Conchubhair, "*An Béal Bocht* and *An tOileánach*: Writing on the Margin—Gaelic Glosses or Postmodern Marginalia," *Review of Contemporary Fiction: Flann O'Brien; Centenary Essays* 31, no. 3 (Fall 2011): 191–204.

75. Rónán McDonald, "The Irish Revival and Modernism," in *The Cambridge Companion to Irish Modernism*, ed. Joe Cleary (Cambridge: Cambridge University Press, 2014), 54.

76. See Sean O'Faolain, *Vive-Moi!* (London: Sinclair-Stevenson, 1993), and George Hughes, "Scandalous Matters: Sean O'Faolain, Elizabeth Bowen and the Art of the Modern Short Story," *The Harp* 12 (1997): 113–21.

77. Elizabeth Bowen, *Collected Sories*, 587.

78. Quigley, *Empire's Wake*, 83.

79. See Kelly Matthews, *The Bell Magazine and the Representation of Irish Identity: Opening Windows* (Dublin: Four Courts Press, 2012), for a comprehensive history and analysis of the periodical.

80. Gulliver, "The Open Window," *The Bell* 5, no. 4 (January 1943): 321.

81. The Kavanagh piece in question was "The Old Peasant," an extract from *The Great Hunger*. The Irish issue of *Horizon* was actually compiled at the suggestion of John Betjeman, British poet and cultural attaché to Dublin (and sometime patron of Kavanagh). Copies of the issue were reportedly seized at the docks, but whether its banning was actually content driven or driven by suspicions that Betjeman was involved (he reported to the Ministry of Information) is hard to say. See Wills, *That Neutral Island*, as well as John Betjeman, *Letters, Volume 1:1926–51*, ed. Candida Lycett-Green (London: Methuen, 2006).

82. Sean O'Faolain, "Attitudes," *The Bell* 2, no. 1 (September 1941): 11.

83. Sean O'Faolain, "This Is Your Magazine," *The Bell* 1, no. 1 (September 1940): 5.

84. Virginia Woolf, "Modern Fiction," in *The Essays of Virginia Woolf, Volume 4: 1925 to 1928*, ed. Andrew McNeillie (London: Hogarth Press, 1984), 160.

85. Sean O'Faolain, "Answer to a Criticism," *The Bell* 1, no. 3 (December 1940): 6.

86. Leventhal's article was written for a wartime series on religion in Ireland and was withheld until its publication in *The Bell* (10, no. 3) in June 1945.

87. "Mise Éire," *The Bell* 2, no. 1 (April 1941): 45.

88. Quoted in Evans, *Frank Aiken*, 134.

89. Nichevo (R. M. Smyllie), "Irishman's Diary," *Irish Times*, February 11, 1941. The samurai "San Tiok Eli" was Sean T. O'Kelly, Ireland's minster for finance (and future president); the Latin is from the *Aeneid*: "What region of the earth is not full of our calamities?" (Virgil, *Aeneid* 1:460).

90. Evans, *Frank Aiken*, 148. This is a surprisingly good joke on neutral censorship, really. The official notice is printed in English: "French wit permitted, German daggers forbidden."

91. Flann O'Brien, *At War*, ed. Jonathan Wyse Jackson (Chicago: Dalkey Archive Press, 2003), 8.

92. Jonathan Wyse Jackson, "Editor's Note," *At War*, 9.

93. "Cruiskeen Lawn" continued until O'Nolan's death in 1966. Many of the columns are collected in O'Brien, *At War*; Flann O'Brien, *The Best of Myles: A Selection from "Cruiskeen Lawn,"* ed. Kevin O'Nolan (London: MacGibbon and Kee, 1968); and Flann O'Brien, *Further Cuttings from "Cruiskeen Lawn,"* ed. Kevin O'Nolan (London: Hart-Davis, MacGibbon, 1976). See also Carol Taaffe, *Ireland through the Looking-Glass: Flann O'Brien, Myles na gCopaleen and Irish Cultural Debate* (Cork: Cork University Press, 2008).

94. Flore Coulouma, "Tall Tales and Short Stories: Cruiskeen Lawn and the Dialogic Imagination," *Review of Contemporary Fiction: Flann O'Brien; Centenary Essays* 31, no. 3 (Fall 2011): 162–77.

95. Myles Na gCopaleen, "Cruiskeen Lawn," *Irish Times*, February 15, 1943.

Chapter 2

1. Patrick Kavanagh, "Europe Is at War: Remembering Its Pastoral Peace," *Irish Times*, October 25, 1939, reprinted in *A Poet's Country: Selected Prose*, ed. Antoinette Quinn (Dublin: Lilliput Press, 2003), 8–10. See also Eamonn Wall's essay, "'It is midnight in Dublin and Europe is at war': Patrick Kavanagh's Poems of 'The Emergency.'" *Colby Quarterly* 31.4 (Dec. 1995): 233–41.

2. Kavanagh later repudiated *The Green Fool* as "a dreadful sort of stage-Irish autobiography" (*A Poet's Country*, 288).

3. John Betjeman, *Letters, Volume 1:1926–51*, ed. Candida Lycett-Green (London: Methuen, 2006), 267–68.

4. Other neutral countries (that practiced neutrality in varying degrees of "friendliness") included Belgium, the Netherlands, Luxembourg, Denmark, Norway, Sweden, Finland, Hungary, Yugoslavia, Romania, Bulgaria, Portugal, Switzerland, and Spain. The presence and persistence of the German legation in Dublin, headed by Eduard Hempel, was the subject of two of the biggest controversies of the Emergency: the "American Note" of 1944, in which U.S. Ambassador David Gray officially requested the closure of the German legation, and de Valera's famously controversial (and puzzling) "condolence visit" to Hempel upon Hitler's death.

5. The editorial was probably written by Smyllie himself.

6. Clair Wills, *That Neutral Island: A Cultural History of Ireland during the Second World War* (London: Faber and Faber, 2007), 8.

7. Elizabeth Bowen, *The Collected Stories of Elizabeth Bowen* (New York: Anchor, 2006), 587.

8. A number of new translations of Dante were published in Britain during World War II. The best known are Laurence Binyon's (1938) and John Sinclair's (1939) renditions of the *Purgatorio*, and Dorothy Sayers's 1949 translation of the *Divine Comedy*, which she worked on throughout the war. For more, see Sebastian Knowles, *A Purgatorial Flame: Seven British Writers in the Second World War* (Philadelphia: University of Pennsylvania Press, 1990), 17.

9. Knowles, *A Purgatorial Flame*, 16, 20.

10. Sean O'Faolain, "The Pleasures and Pains of Ireland." *The Bell* 8, no. 5 (August 1944): 369.

11. Patrick Kavanagh, "The Great Hunger," in *Collected Poems*, ed. Antoinette Quinn (London: Penguin, 2005), 88.

12. The literature on Lough Derg is voluminous. A good starting place is Shane Leslie, *Saint Patrick's Purgatory: A Record from History and Literature* (London: Burns, Oates and Washbourne, 1932) and Joseph McGuinness, *Saint Patrick's Purgatory: Lough Derg* (Dublin: Columba Press, 2000).

13. Pilgrims also need sufficient funding; the cost of the pilgrimage in 2017 was €70 (https://www.loughderg.org).

14. See J. C. C. Mays's notes on "Lough Derg" in Devlin's *Collected Poems of Denis Devlin*, ed. J. C. C. Mays (Dublin: Dedalus Press, 2009), 341.

15. Antoinette Quinn, *Patrick Kavanagh: A Biography* (Dublin: Gill and Macmillan, 2001), 198–99.

16. Patrick Kavanagh, "When You Go to Lough Derg," in *A Poet's Country*, 119.

17. Peggy O'Brien, *Writing Lough Derg: From William Carleton to Seamus Heaney* (Syracuse, N.Y.: Syracuse University Press, 2006), xix.

18. Eileen Gardiner, ed., *Visions of Heaven and Hell before Dante* (New York: Italica Press, 1989).

19. Book-length studies of the modern literature of Lough Derg include Terence Dewsnap, *Island of Daemons: The Lough Derg Pilgrimage and the Poets Patrick Kavanagh, Denis Devlin, and Seamus Heaney* (Newark: University of Delaware Press, 2008), and Peggy O'Brien, *Writing Lough Derg*. For pilgrim statistics kept by the diocese of Clogher, see http://www.loughderg.org/.

20. Quoted in Antoinette Quinn, *Patrick Kavanagh: A Critical Study* (Syracuse, N.Y.: Syracuse University Press, 1991), 174.

21. Robert Easting, "The Date and Dedication of the *Tractatus de Purgatorio Sancti Patricii*," *Speculum* 53, no. 4 (October 1978): 778–83.

22. Quinn, *Patrick Kavanagh: A Critical Study*, 174, 177.

23. The phrase is from Thomas Moore's Lough Derg song "I Wish That I Was by That Dim Lake," from his *Irish Melodies* (London: Longman, 1853). The year 1942 was also when T. S. Eliot published his English pilgrimage poem "Little Gidding," the final of the *Four Quartets*. Quinn usefully contextualizes "Lough Derg" with Eliot's poem in *Patrick Kavanagh: A Critical Study*.

24. Kavanagh's business aim was to be Dublin's best-known "ploughman poet," explaining the Irish to themselves, and Devlin's actual business, as a diplomat, was explaining the Irish to the rest of the world. Both of their "Lough Derg" poems, however, are not theodicies but attempts to explain themselves to themselves.

25. Sean O'Faolain, "This Is Your Magazine," *The Bell* 1, no. 1 (October 1940): 7.

26. Tate and Penn Warren edited Devlin's posthumous *Selected Poems* (New York: Holt, 1963), and Coffey edited *The Complete Poems* of Denis Devlin for Dublin's *University Review* in 1963, reprinted as *Collected Poems* (Dublin: Dolmen Press, 1964). The standard scholarly edition is *Collected Poems of Denis Devlin*, ed. J. C. C. Mays (Dublin: Dedalus Press, 2009).

27. Quinn, *Patrick Kavanagh: A Critical Study*, 177–79, and Declan Kiberd, "Underdeveloped Comedy: Patrick Kavanagh," in *Irish Classics*, 590–601 (Cambridge, Mass.: Harvard University Press, 2002).

28. The O'Faolain quote is cited in Quinn, *Patrick Kavanagh: A Biography*, 154. According to Quinn, Kavanagh sent a typescript of the poem to Frank O'Connor but never made further changes to the poem; O'Connor's cryptic marks on the typescript remain, but his covering letter does not.

29. Dillon Johnston, *Irish Poetry after Joyce* (Syracuse, N.Y.: Syracuse University Press, 1997), 167. In his notes to "Lough Derg," J. C. C. Mays says that "details of the phrasing and punctuation of nearly every stanza were revised when it was collected" (*Collected Poems*, 341).

30. Randall Jarrell, *Poetry and the Age* (New York: Ecco Press, 1953), 224–25.

31. The phrase is used repeatedly in Sean O'Faolain's 1957 story "Lovers of the Lake"; see *The Finest Stories of Sean O'Faolain* (New York: Bantam, 1959).

32. Patrick Kavanagh, "Lough Derg," in *Collected Poems*, line 349. Subsequent references to Kavanagh's poetry refer, by line number, to Kavanagh's *Collected Poems*, ed. Antoinette Quinn (London: Penguin, 2005).

33. Kavanagh, "Beyond the Headlines," 1–4.

34. Records of Irish volunteers in World War II are notoriously incomplete, because many volunteers gave false names and addresses; many crossed the border and enlisted in Northern Ireland (where there was no World War II conscription, so as not to incite civil unrest). The more than five thousand soldiers who deserted the Irish Army for the British Armed Forces were treated as criminals upon their return home and officially pardoned by the Irish government only in May 2013. See Bernard Kelly, *Returning Home: Irish Ex-Servicemen after the Second World War* (Dublin: Merrion Press, 2012); Yvonne McEwan, *Ireland's Roll of Honour: World War II* (Edinburgh: Edinburgh University Press, 2009); Steven O'Connor, "Why Did They Fight for Britain: Irish Recruits to the British Forces, 1939–45," *Études Irlandaises* 40, no. 1 (2015): 59–70; and Brian Girvin and Geoffrey Roberts, eds., *Ireland and the Second World War: Politics, Society and Remembrance* (Dublin: Four Courts Press, 2000).

35. Kavanagh, "Peace," 4–9.

36. Kavanagh, *Selected Prose*, 307.

37. Quinn, *Biography*, 193.

38. Quoted in Quinn, *A Critical Study*, 172.

39. Denis Devlin, "Lough Derg," in *Collected Poems of Denis Devlin*, ed. J. C. C. Mays (Dublin: Dedalus Press, 2009), lines 7–8. Subsequent references to this poem are by line number.

40. Quoted in Wills, *That Neutral Island*, 359. *The Leader* (1900–71), launched by D. P. Moran, was a prominent vehicle for Irish Ireland ideology. Its coziness with the Catholic Truth Society and its support of censorship made Sean O'Faolain one of its fiercest critics. *The Bell* was, in some ways, directly pitched against *The Leader*; see

Frank Shovlin, *The Irish Literary Periodical, 1923–1958* (Oxford: Oxford University Press, 2003).

41. Quoted in Quinn, *Biography*, 196.

42. Kavanagh, "Lough Derg," 17.

43. Quoted in Quinn, *Biography*, 196.

44. As Dillon Johnston writes, "Difficulties in Devlin's verse are usually fluidities; where we cannot grasp meaning, we must trace it in a motion that has a definable course. Devlin employs a rhetoric that includes substitution, ambiguity, paradox, and perpetual reference to launch the reader into a circular reasoning or an otherwise continuing pursuit of meaning, which, in effect, teases us out of thought" (*Irish Poetry after Joyce*, 169).

45. Jansenism denotes a movement initiated by Cornelius Otto Jansen, bishop of Ypres (d. 1638). Jansen argued that the Reformation had overemphasized the doctrine of grace and that humanity was utterly depraved and could be saved only by perfect contrition. Condemned as heretical by the Roman Catholic Church, Jansenism nonetheless continued to exercise a hold on certain elements of the population. By the twentieth century, the term "Jansenist" was used to denote not actual adherents to the movement but the strain of puritanical moral rigor upheld by Irish clerics, which hewed closely to conservative politics. See Thomas O'Connor, "Jansenism," in *The Oxford Companion to Irish History*, ed. S. J. Connolly, 318–36 (Oxford: Oxford University Press, 2007).

46. For an in-depth discussion of Devlin and Jansenism, see James Matthew Wilson, "Poetic Jansenism: Religious and Political Representation in Denis Devlin's Poetry," *Éire-Ireland* 42, nos. 3, 4 (2007): 35–59.

47. See Clair Wills, "Paying for Neutrality," in *That Neutral Island*, 383–422.

48. Leslie, *Saint Patrick's Purgatory*.

49. Louis MacNeice, "Neutrality," in *Collected Poems*, ed. Peter McDonald (London: Faber and Faber, 2007). This poem is discussed in chapter 3 of the present volume.

50 Quinn, *A Critical Study*, 177.

51 Rupert Brooke, "Safety," *World War One British Poets*, ed. Candace Ward (New York: Dover Thrift, 1997), 2.

52. Patricia Rae, "Double Sorrow: Proleptic Elegy and the End of Arcadianism in 1930s Britain," *Twentieth Century Literature* 49, no. 2 (2003): 246–74.

53. Quinn suggests that the failure of "Lough Derg" precipitated Kavanagh's turn to the personal over the political in "Advent," but the 1951 sonnet "Epic," which subsumes all of World War II into "the year of the Munich bother," has traditionally been read as Kavanagh's final assertion of the value of the "local row" over the global. But, like "Lough Derg," this tighter, more accomplished poem (perhaps Kavanagh's best) retains crucial ambiguity.

54. "Bringing You the Gift of Hope." www.loughderg.org. July 9, 2017.

55. My translation here is indebted to the popular translation by Douglas Hyde. O Dhálaigh's poem and Hyde's translation appear in Douglas Hyde, *A Literary History of Ireland: From Earliest Times to the Present Day* (London: Unwin, 1899), 467.

56. William Carleton, "The Lough Derg Pilgrim," in *The Works of William Carleton*, vol. 3 (1881; repr., Freeport, N.Y.: Books for Libraries Press, 1970), 799.

57. W. B. Yeats, "The Pilgrim," *The Collected Poems of W. B. Yeats*, ed. Richard J.

Finneran (New York: Scribner, 1989), lines 6–10. Subsequent references to this poem are by line number.

58. Robert Welch, "Language as Pilgrimage: Lough Derg Poems of Patrick Kavanagh and Denis Devlin," *Irish University Review* 13, no. 1 (Spring 1983): 56.

59. Sean O'Faolain's 1957 short story "Lovers of the Lake" follows the same general plot as the "Lough Derg" poems of his contemporaries. In it, a woman asks her non-practicing Catholic lover to drive her to Lough Derg. It becomes clear that she is making the pilgrimage out of guilt over their adulterous relationship. Deciding to join her on the island, her half-pilgrim lover seeks to understand her decision (which he thinks at first is "lunacy") and surprises them both by completing the pilgrimage. The ending of the story, however, is ambiguous, as they kiss "passionately" but retire to separate rooms in a hotel (314, 336). So much in the story is suggestive of Kavanagh's poem that it seems distinctly probable that O'Faolain may have read it, as well as Frank O'Connor, then poetry editor of *The Bell*, who gave Kavanagh feedback on an early draft. The story's plot suggests that O'Faolain is following an established format for writing the Lough Derg experience. Likewise, Seamus Heaney's 1984 sequence "Station Island" is his journey seeking clarity during the Troubles. See Sean O'Faolain, *The Finest Stories of Sean O'Faoláin* (New York: Bantam, 1959) and Seamus Heaney, *Opened Ground: Selected Poems 1966–1996* (New York: Farrar, Strauss, 1999).

60. For example, James Wilson concludes that "these final italicized words manifest the theology that controls the poem's extended critique of earthly injustice, [giving way to a] language of pure address" ("Poetic Jansenism," 49). See also Alex Davis's reading of the poem in *A Broken Line: Denis Devlin and Irish Poetic Modernism* (Dublin: University College Dublin Press, 2000), and Mary Salmon, "Modern Pilgrimage: Denis Devlin's *Lough Derg*," *Studies* (Dublin) 62, no. 245 (Spring 1973): 75–83.

61. Gerard Manley Hopkins, "Carrion Comfort." *Gerard Manley Hopkins: The Major Works*. Ed. Catherine Phillips. Oxford University Press, 2009. Ln. 11, 1. Thanks to Seamus O'Malley for tipping me off to this allusion.

62. Quinn describes Kavanagh's first visit to Lough Derg as a dismal failure; not only was the poet unprepared for the rigors of the fast but also he adopted an exaggerated "poetic" pose for which he was made fun of. It is easy to see the punishment of this "poetic" 1940 pilgrim in Kavanagh's treatment of Robert in the 1942 poem; see *Patrick Kavanagh: A Biography*, 174–75.

63. During the summer pilgrimage season in 1942, the German offensive in the Soviet Union's oil regions took Rostov, where the Nazis massacred twenty-seven thousand Russian Jews. Whether or not Kavanagh knew of the "purge" he was setting his "Christendom's purge" against is unknown.

64. Could this be literature's most bizarre foreshadowing of D-Day?

Chapter 3

1. Louis MacNeice, *Autumn Journal*, in *Collected Poems*, ed. Peter McDonald (London: Faber and Faber, 2007), canto 16, lines 31–32. Subsequent references to this poem are by line number. All quotations from MacNeice's poetry are taken from this volume and cited by line number.

2. In "Louis MacNeice: Irony and Responsibility," in *The Cambridge Companion to Contemporary Irish Poetry*, ed. Matthew Campbell (Cambridge: Cambridge University Press, 2003), Peter McDonald usefully puts critical squabbles to rest: "Of course, Louis

MacNeice was an Irish poet, and thought of himself as being an Irish poet, from the beginning to the end of his writing career. Any doubts, quibbles, or equivocations on that point are not MacNeice's, and they can find little ground in the facts of his life and his writing" (59).

3. Heather Clark, "Revising MacNeice," *Cambridge Quarterly* 31, no. 1 (2002): 78.

4. Indeed, MacNeice considered his radio drama (though commissioned for BBC3) as a highly artistic endeavor and an opportunity to experiment with multiple forms, and to expand his lyrics with sound. That he remained with the BBC for the rest of his life attests to this. See MacNeice's introduction to *The Dark Tower and Other Radio Scripts* (London: Faber and Faber, 1947), as well as Barbara Coulton, *Louis MacNeice in the BBC* (London: Faber and Faber, 1980).

5. Tom Walker, *Louis MacNeice and the Irish Poetry of His Time* (Oxford: Oxford University Press, 2015), 46.

6. Terence Brown, "Louis MacNeice and the Second World War," in *Modern Irish Writers and the Wars*, ed. Kathleen Devine, 165–77 (Gerrards Cross, U.K.: Smythe, 1999); Richard Danson Brown, "Neutrality and Commitment: MacNeice, Yeats, Ireland and the Second World War," *Journal of Modern Literature* 28, no. 3 (2005): 109–28; Michael Moir Jr., "Like the Tombs of Nameless Kings: Louis MacNeice's Western Anti-Pastoral," *Études Irlandaises* 38, no. 1 (2013): 187–200.

7. Letter to John Fredrick MacNeice, December 16, 1940, reprinted in *Selected Letters of Louis MacNeice*, ed. Jonathan Allison (London: Faber and Faber, 2010), 417. For more on the concept of cosmopolitanism in an Irish context, see Nels Pearson, *Irish Cosmopolitanism: Location and Dislocation in James Joyce, Elizabeth Bowen, and Samuel Beckett* (Gainesville, Fla.: University of Florida Press, 2015).

8. W. B. Yeats, *Per Amica Silentia Lunae* (London: Macmillan, 1918), 30.

9. That MacNeice typically wrote for left-wing periodicals tells us something about his presumed audience and attitude. A leftist, but not a Communist, MacNeice wrote for a readership that detested war as imperialistic and capitalistic but detested fascism more.

10. Peter McDonald, *Louis MacNeice: The Poet in His Contexts* (Oxford: Oxford University Press, 1991), 8.

11. Fran Brearton, *The Great War in Irish Poetry: W. B. Yeats to Michael Longley* (Oxford: Oxford University Press, 2000), 119.

12. Dillon Johnston, *Irish Poetry after Joyce* (Syracuse, N.Y.: Syracuse University Press, 1997), 206.

13. McDonald, *Louis MacNeice*; Edna Longley, *Louis MacNeice: A Study* (London: Faber and Faber, 1988); Terence Brown, *Louis MacNeice: Sceptical Vision* (Dublin: Gill and Macmillan, 1975); Robyn Marsack, *The Cave of Making: The Poetry of Louis MacNeice* (Oxford: Oxford University Press, 1982).

14. For instance, Brearton's chapter on MacNeice in *The Great War in Irish Poetry* is titled "Louis MacNeice: Between Two Wars."

15. Terence Brown, *Louis MacNeice*, 86–87.

16. MacNeice, *Letters of Louis MacNeice*. Ed. Jonathan Allison (London: Faber, 2010), 319.

17. MacNeice, "Dublin," *Collected Poems*, lines 57, 60.

18. MacNeice, *Letters*, 371.

19. MacNeice was also working on the never-finished memoir *The Strings Are False* during this period, but his letters to T. S. Eliot, his publisher at Faber, show that through-

out his career, MacNeice conceived of his poetic output in terms of collections—books rather than just lyrics.

20. William Empson coined the term "self-inwoven simile" in *Seven Types of Ambiguity* (London: Chatto and Windus, 1947). MacNeice's own language alludes to this idea of self-in*woven* rhetoric in "Valediction" (1935): "I can say Ireland is hooey, Ireland is / A gallery of fake tapestries, / But I cannot deny my past to which my self is wed, / The woven figure cannot undo its thread" (41–44).

21. MacNeice, "Carrick Revisited," *Collected Poems*, line 10.

22. In *Shelley's Style* (London: Methuen, 1984), William Keach writes that "reflexive images call unusual attention to the act of mind they presuppose, an act of mind which combines a moment of analysis and division, in which an aspect is separated from the idea to which it belongs, and a moment of synthesis and reunion, in which the separated aspect is put back into relationship with the idea" (54).

23. Coleman Rosenberger, "Two Conspiracies: MacNeice and Aragon," *Poetry* 68, no. 1 (April 1946): 44–49. MacNeice's bishop father might have enjoyed this comment, had he lived to read it. The biblical reference is Matthew 7:3–5: "And why beholdest thou the mote that is in thy brother's eye, but considerest not the beam that is in thine own eye? Or how wilt thou say to thy brother, Let me pull out the mote out of thine eye; and, behold, a beam is in thine own eye? Thou hypocrite, first cast out the beam out of thine own eye; and then shalt thou see clearly to cast out the mote out of thy brother's eye" (KJV).

24. W. B. Yeats, "The Road at my Door," *Meditations in Time of Civil War. The Collected Poems of W. B. Yeats*, ed. Richard J. Finneran (New York: Scribner, 1989), 13.

25. MacNeice's earlier critical work, *Modern Poetry: A Personal Essay* (Oxford: Oxford University Press, 1938), outlines his philosophy of poetics circa 1937. *The Poetry of W. B. Yeats* directly revises some of MacNeice's earlier statements.

26. Auden's emigration (alongside Christopher Isherwood) was derided by London-based writers like Stephen Spender, Cecil Day-Lewis, and John Lehmann as the defection of Britain's ablest poet in its time of greatest need; see Mark Rawlinson, *British Writing of the Second World War* (Oxford: Clarendon Press, 2000). The "crisis" excited much print in literary periodicals, as well as a scathing satire by Evelyn Waugh as the defection of "Parsnip and Pimpernell" in *Put Out More Flags* (London: Chapman and Hall, 1942).

27. W. H. Auden, "In Memory of W. B. Yeats," in *The English Auden: Poems, Essays and Dramatic Writings, 1927–1939*, ed. Edward Mendelson (London: Faber and Faber, 1988), lines 33–37.

28. Louis MacNeice, *The Poetry of W. B. Yeats* (London: Faber and Faber, 1967), 31. Subsequent references to this work are by page number.

29. "Time for thought" comes from "Dublin" (57), and "the dazzle on the sea, my darling" is the repeated first and last line of "Leaving Barra."

30. Auden, "The Public v. the Late Mr William Butler Yeats," *Partisan Review* (Spring 1939), reprinted in *The Complete Works of W. H. Auden: Prose, Vol. 2: 1939–1948*, ed. Edward Mendelson (Princeton University Press, 2002), 3–7.

31. In an oft-quoted passage in *Modern Poetry*, MacNeice outlines his theory: "I would have a poet able bodied, fond of talking, a reader of the newspapers, capable of pity and laughter, informed in economics, appreciative of women, involved in personal relationships, actively interested in politics, susceptible to physical impressions." As against the ivory tower, MacNeice believed that "the poet is primarily a spokesman" (1).

32. The effigy of Nelson itself would collapse in 1966 when destroyed by an IRA bomb (his world by then having long since collapsed).

33. Patrick Kavanagh, "Europe Is at War: Remembering Its Pastoral Peace," *Irish Times*, October 25, 1939, reprinted in *A Poet's Country: Selected Prose*, ed. Antoinette Quinn (Dublin: Lilliput Press, 2003), 8–10.

34. In *The Strings Are False* (Oxford: Oxford University Press, 1966), MacNeice writes about the way that the mythical West of Ireland infused his personal mythology. Knowing that war could break out at any minute, MacNeice and Stahl considered canceling their road trip, but MacNeice told himself, "War or no war, you have got to go back to the West. If only for a week. Because you may never again" (210).

35. Neil Corcoran, "The Same Again? Repetition and Refrain in the Poetry of Louis MacNeice," *Cambridge Quarterly* 38, no. 3 (2009): 224.

36. "Carrick Revisited" revisits both the town and the poem "Carrickfergus," which MacNeice published a decade previously.

37. Brearton, *Great War*; and Rawlinson, *British Writing*; Adam Piette, *Imagination at War: British Fiction and Poetry, 1939–1945* (London: Papermac, 1995). In "Desert Flowers," for instance, the English soldier-poet Keith Douglas invokes Isaac Rosenberg's Great War poem "Break of Day in the Trenches": "Rosenberg I only repeat what you were saying."

38. Anthony Thwaite, *Contemporary English Poetry: An Introduction* (London: Heinemann, 1964), 90.

39. Brown, *Louis MacNeice*, 151.

40. The similarities between MacNeice's verse and that of Dylan Thomas, his friend and BBC colleague, who John Stallworthy notes was one of the few people with whom MacNeice would discuss poetry, are apparent in Thomas's own declaration that "I use everything and anything to make my poems work: old tricks, new tricks, puns, portmanteau words, paradox, allusion, paronomasia, paragrams, catachresis, slang, assonantal rhymes, vowel rhymes, sprung rhythm. Every device there is in language is there to be used if you will'" (Quoted in William T. Moynihan, *The Craft and Art of Dylan Thomas* [Ithaca, N.Y.: Cornell University Press, 1966], 62). MacNeice's poems indicate that he shared this philosophy with Thomas. See John Stallworthy, *Louis MacNeice: A Biography* (New York: Norton, 1995).

41. "Neutral." *Oxford English Dictionary*.

42. Paul Fussell, *The Great War and Modern Memory* (Oxford: Oxford University Press, 1975), 231–69.

43. See Patricia Rae, "Double Sorrow: Proleptic Elegy and the End of Arcadianism in 1930s Britain," *Twentieth Century Literature* 49, no. 2 (2003): 246–74, for an analysis of the ways that poets of the late 1930s revised the Arcadian imagery common to Great War poetry in light of the looming new war they imagined.

44. See Terence Brown, *Louis MacNeice*, for further analysis of MacNeice's use of cliché.

45. Fussell, *The Great War and Modern Memory*, 75.

46. W. B. Yeats, introduction to *The Oxford Book of Modern Verse, 1892–1935* (Oxford: Clarendon Press, 1936), xxxiv.

47. For Yeats in the years of World War I, there was more than one war at stake. Marjorie Perloff considers Yeats's ambiguous relationship to the Great War (and the Anglo-Irish War) in "'Easter, 1916': Yeats's First World War Poem," in *The Oxford*

Handbook of British and Irish War Poetry, ed. Tim Kendall (Oxford: Oxford University Press 2007).

48. In World War II, Ireland would provide the reverse oxymoron—combatant neutrals—to fight for (almost entirely) the Allied cause.

49. This was not an uncommon situation for Irish soldiers who volunteered for the Great War, only to find themselves in Flanders while a war for independence began (or perhaps more accurately, began again) at home.

50. If this suicide is a precursor to Roland in MacNeice's 1945 radio play *The Dark Tower*, as he appears to be, then he may be liberating himself from "the bars / Made by his fear" (3–4) by jumping, an exercise in pushing free will to death. In *The Dark Tower*, Roland must fulfill his suicidal quest in order to prove the existence of free will.

51. George Herbert, "Providence," in *The Temple* (London, 1633), lines 88–91.

52. The statistics cited are based on the median casualty counts calculated by Michael White's analysis of dozens of scholarly sources in his "Source List and Detailed Death Tolls for the Primary Megadeaths of the Twentieth Century," in *Historical Atlas of the Twentieth Century*, 2011, accessed February 24, 2017, http://necrometrics.com/20c5m.htm.

53. MacNeice, *Strings Are False*, 21.

54. See chapter 4 in the present volume for more on Elizabeth Bowen's concept of the "saving hallucination," quoted in *The Mulberry Tree*, ed. Hermione Lee (London: Harcourt Brace, 1986), 97.

55. Brown, *Louis MacNeice*, 15.

56. Haig's order to the British troops on the Western Front of April 12, 1918, "With our backs to the wall, and believing in the justice of our cause, each one of us must fight on to the end," while seemingly ironic in its original context, was often reused in British World War II rhetoric. See, for example, Winston Churchill, *Blood, Toil, Tears, and Sweat: The Speeches of Winston Churchill*, ed. David Cannadine (Boston: Houghton Mifflin, 1989).

57. MacNeice, *Poetry of W. B. Yeats*; see also Stallworthy, *Louis MacNeice: A Biography*.

58. MacNeice, *Letters*, 319.

59. Peter McDonald, "Louis MacNeice's War," in *The Oxford Handbook of British and Irish War Poetry*, 385.

60. MacNeice also applied to—and was rejected from—the Royal Navy (on account of his recent life-threatening bout of peritonitis). For more on MacNeice's time in the BBC, see Coulton *MacNeice in the BBC*.

61. MacNeice, *Selected Prose*, 83.

62. For more on Eliot's and Pound's desire to be in London for the Great War, see Vincent Sherry, *The Great War and the Language of Modernism* (Oxford: Oxford University Press, 2003), 78–85.

63. MacNeice, *Selected Prose*,118.

64. Peter McDonald, *Louis MacNeice: The Poet in his Contexts* (Oxford: Oxford University Press, 1991), 128.

65. Rosenberger, "Two Conspiracies," 48. Rosenberger must have been unaware that, in his office at Broadcasting House, MacNeice was far from a lonely commentator talking to himself.

66. Peter McDonald, "Louis MacNeice's War," 401.

67. Longley, *Louis MacNeice*, notes that many of the poems in *Plant and Phantom* (and, I contend, many like this in *Springboard*) are parables (82). MacNeice called parables "double-level writing," which is fitting as a description of these poems. See Louis MacNeice, *Varieties of Parable* (Cambridge: Cambridge University Press, 1965).

68. In part 5 of "The Closing Album," MacNeice asks, "And why, now it has happened, / Should the atlas be full of the maps of countries / We never shall see again?" (9–11).

69. MacNeice, *Selected Prose*, 139.

70. Christopher Ricks, *The Force of Poetry* (Oxford: Clarendon Press, 1984), 34.

71. With its crumbling towers and hypocrite semblables, "Brother Fire" deliberately aligns its London with the "Unreal City" of Eliot's *The Waste Land*.

72. Terence Brown, "Louis MacNeice and the Second World War." *Irish Writers and the Wars*, Ed. Kathleen Devine (Gerrards Cross: Colin Smythe, 1999), 168.

73. Terence Brown, *Louis MacNeice*, 12.

74. Richard Danson Brown, "Neutrality and Commitment: MacNeice, Yeats, Ireland and the Second World War," 122.

75. Longley, *Louis MacNeice*, 25.

76. Declan Kiberd, "Incorrigibly Plural: Louis MacNeice," *Irish Classics* (Cambridge, Mass.: Harvard University Press, 2002), 553.

77. References in this sentence are as follows: "angry" and "bitter" (Clark, "Revising MacNeice," 78); "a clear sense of moral priority" (Danson Brown, "Neutrality and Commitment," 120); "certainty of action" (Clark, 84).

78. Wills, *That Neutral Island*, 127.

79. McDonald, "Louis MacNeice's War," 395.

80. Moir, "Like the Tombs of Nameless Kings," 197.

81. Yeats, "The Circus Animals' Desertion," 40.

82. Terence Brown, "Louis MacNeice and the Second World War," 168–9.

83. Yeats, "The Circus Animals' Desertion," 9, 11, 13, 12, 39.

84. See Fisk, *In Time of War*, for statistics on the Battle of the Atlantic and the recovery of bodies in Ireland.

85. See Clark, "Revising MacNeice"; Richard Brown, "Neutrality and Commitment"; Longley, *Louis MacNeice*; Clair Wills, *That Neutral Island: A Cultural History of Ireland during the Second World War* (London: Faber and Faber, 2007).

86. This comment is strongly reminiscent of Elizabeth Bowen's note in her report to the Dominions Office, "I could wish that the English kept history in mind more, that the Irish kept it in mind less" (Bowen, *Notes on Éire*. Ed. Jack Lane and Brendan Clifford [Aubane, Co. Cork: Aubane Historical Society, 2009], 38.

87. McDonald, "Louis MacNeice's War," 395.

Chapter 4

1. Though nearly every recent monograph on Bowen has mentioned her syntactical acrobatics, Susan Osborn, in a review article on Neil Corcoran's and Maud Ellmann's studies of Bowen, contends that "the most unaccountable absence [in both studies] is any sustained discussion of Bowen's notoriously strange prose style that produces in almost every sentence, either explicitly or subliminally, some disorientation of sense, some unexpected deviation from standard meaning." See Susan Osborn, "Reconsidering Elizabeth Bowen," *Modern Fiction Studies* 52, no. 1 (2006): 192; Neil Corcoran,

Elizabeth Bowen: The Enforced Return (Oxford: Oxford University Press, 2004); Maud Ellmann, *Elizabeth Bowen: The Shadow Across the Page* (Edinburgh: Edinburgh University Press, 2003); Phyllis Lassner, "Out of the Shadows: The Newly Collected Elizabeth Bowen," *Modernism/Modernity* 17, no. 3 (Autumn 2010): 669–76; Anna Teekell, "Elizabeth Bowen's Language at War," *New Hibernia Review* 15, no. 3 (Autumn 2011): 61–79.

2. Heather Bryant, "A Bequest of Her Own: The Reinvention of Elizabeth Bowen," *New Hibernia Review* 12, no. 2 (Summer 2008): 57.

3. Elizabeth Bowen, *The Heat of the Day* (New York: Knopf, 1949), 309. Subsequent references to this work are by page number.

4. The same reader praised the novel for being the first to express the "inexpressible" tenor of life in wartime London. See Michael S. Howard, *Jonathan Cape, Publisher* (London: Cape, 1971), 181–82.

5. Elizabeth Bowen, letter to Jonathan Cape, 1948, quoted in Ellmann, *Elizabeth Bowen*, 166.

6. Elizabeth Bowen, *Seven Winters and Afterthoughts* (New York: Knopf, 1962), viii.

7. Elizabeth Bowen, *The Mulberry Tree*, ed. Hermione Lee (London: Harcourt Brace, 1986), 41. Subsequent references to this work are by page number.

8. Quoted in Howard, 182.

9. W. J. McCormack has noted that "the highly distinctive language of *The Heat of the Day* is required to convey a quality of absence or negativity special to the novel" (*Dissolute Characters: Irish Literary History through Balzac, Yeats and Bowen* [Manchester: Manchester University Press, 1993], 224).

10. James Purdon, *Modernist Informatics: Literature, Information, and the State* (Oxford: Oxford University Press, 2016), 184.

11. Robert Fisk, *In Time of War: Ireland, Ulster and the Price of Neutrality, 1939–45* (Philadelphia: University of Pennsylvania Press, 1983). Bowen's reports to the British Foreign Office are available in the Public Record Office at Kew and are excerpted in Fisk's book. They are also available reprinted in the volume published by the Aubane Historical Society, prefaced with a deeply republican "Review of Irish Neutrality in World War II," by the editors, casting Bowen as a traitor. Bowen, *Notes on Éire*. Ed. Jack Lane and Brendan Clifford (Aubane, Co. Cork: Aubane Historical Society, 2009),

12. Sean O'Faolain, "A Reading and Remembrance of Elizabeth Bowen," *London Review of Books* 4, no. 4 (March 4, 1982): 15–16.

13. Adam Piette, *Imagination at War: British Fiction and Poetry, 1939–1945* (London: Papermac, 1995), 172.

14. Many critics of the novel have claimed Anglo-Irish heritage for Stella, but this is never made clear in the novel itself. Stella's ex-husband, Victor, is certainly affiliated with Anglo-Ireland, as cousin to Francis of Mount Morris, but Stella's own heritage is unmentioned. One of the best diagnoses of Bowen's sketchy treatment of Stella's person and background is Barbara Bellow Watson's assertion that the heroine is "neither flat nor round but translucent." See Barbara Bellow Watson, "Variations on an Enigma: Elizabeth Bowen's War Novel," *Southern Humanities Review* 15 (1981): 131–51. Bowen's narrator suggests that this "translucence" is a condition of wartime living: "It was a characteristic of that life in the moment and for the moment's sake that one knew people well without knowing much about them . . . life-stories were shed as so much superfluous weight" (Bowen, *The Heat of the Day*, 103).

15. R. F. Foster, *Paddy and Mr. Punch: Connections in Irish and English History* (London: Lane, 1993), 107.

16. See letters to Virginia Woolf in *The Mulberry Tree*, 216–17), and The Bellman, "Meet Elizabeth Bowen," *The Bell* 4, no. 6 (September 1942): 424.

17. Ellmann, *Elizabeth Bowen*, noting the influence of Piette's argument, writes of Stella that "she has been practicing neutrality involuntarily" (152). This more succinct formulation is also more accurate.

18. Bowen, *Notes on Éire*, 13.

19. Bowen, *The Mulberry Tree*, 31.

20. Megan Faragher, "The Form of Modernist Propaganda in Elizabeth Bowen's *The Heat of the Day*," *Textual Practice* 27, no. 1 (2013): 49–68.

21. Purdon, 179.

22. Bowen, *Notes on Éire*, 25–26.

23. Bowen, *The Collected Stories of Elizabeth Bowen* (New York: Anchor, 2006), 730.

24. See Corcoran, *Elizabeth Bowen*, for more on the trope of stories in Bowen.

25. Robert Caserio has suggested that Louie is a sort of Septimus Smith to Stella's Mrs. Dalloway ("*The Heat of the Day*: Modernism and Narrative in Paul de Man and Elizabeth Bowen," *Modern Language Quarterly* 54, no. 2 [June 1993]: 263–84). The fact that in Bowen's novel the two figures meet—and in the scene at the direct center of the novel—underscores Bowen's (and the Blitz myth's) idea of the way the war collapsed, or at least temporarily banged together, England's social classes. For insightful readings of women and class in the novel, see Kristine Miller, *British Literature of the Blitz* (London: Palgrave, 2009), and Phyllis Lassner, *British Women Writers in World War II: Battlegrounds of Their Own* (London: Macmillan, 1998).

26. Patrick Deer, *Culture in Camouflage: War, Empire, and Modern British Literature* (Oxford: Oxford University Press, 2009), 7.

27. Hermione Lee argues in *Elizabeth Bowen: An Estimation* (London: Vision Press, 1981) that the clumsy Louie is clumsily written. More recently, critics like Petra Rau and Neil Corcoran have forwarded more sympathetic readings of Louie, arguing for her character's thematic centrality to the novel.

28. In this sense, Louie gains canonical stature as a precursor to Bowen's last heroine, Eva Trout, a character so divorced from language that she finds herself "unable to speak—talk, be understood, converse" (*Eva Trout* [New York: Anchor Books, 2003], 62).

29. For more on the role of the femme fatale in World War II propaganda, see Petra Rau, "The Common Frontier: Fictions of Alterity in Elizabeth Bowen's *The Heat of the Day* and Graham Greene's *The Ministry of Fear*," *Literature and History* 14, no. 1 (2005): 31–55.

30. Michael North, *Henry Green and the Writing of His Generation* (Charlottesville: University of Virginia Press, 1984), 117.

31. Graham Greene, *The Ministry of Fear* (New York: Penguin, 1943), 57–58.

32. See Caserio, "*Heat of the Day*," for an argument placing *The Heat of the Day* on the late modernist (but modernist) edge of Jamesonian postmodern narrative.

33. Heather Bryant and Claire Seiler both write about the quality of the many silences that fill this novel. Purdon sees these silences as the enactment of wartime's information blackout. See James Purdon, "Information Blacked Out," *Modernist Informatics*; Heather Bryant, *How Will the Heart Endure: Elizabeth Bowen and the Land-*

scape of War (Ann Arbor: University of Michigan Press, 1992), 165; Claire Seiler, "At Midcentury: Elizabeth Bowen's *The Heat of the Day*," *Modernism/Modernity* 21, no. 1 (2014): 125–45.

34. In his essay "Politics and the English Language" (*Horizon* 13, no. 76 [April]: 252–65), George Orwell complains about the same essential problem, arguing that having too long carried multiple and irreconcilable political connotations, words like "democracy, socialism, freedom, patriotic, realistic, justice" have been "debased" of their meanings. In his essay, Orwell cites numerous examples of dangerously bad language, one of which is characterized by excessive double negatives (284). Bowen's novel plays upon the instinct behind Orwell's citation of such syntax as dangerously careless by making it dangerously careful instead. See George Orwell, "Politics and the English Language," reprinted in *All Art is Propaganda: Critical Essays*, ed. Keith Gessen, 270-286 (New York: Mariner, 2009).

35. A first potential glance at Robert's photo is even short-circuited ("propped on the chimney-piece . . . were two photographs, not framed yet—the younger of the two men was Roderick") until Harrison picks it up five pages later (Bowen, *The Heat of the Day*, 23).

36. Much has been written about the swastika-shaped Holme Dene, a travesty of the bourgeois home, perpetually for sale, and lurking gothically at the back of a hidden drive. Robert's mother, called Muttikins, runs a fascistic establishment, while Robert's niece and nephew play Hitler in the dilapidated garden. See Corcoran, *Elizabeth Bowen*; Ellmann, *Elizabeth Bowen*; Lassner, *British Women Writers*; Lee, *Elizabeth Bowen*; Watson, "Variations"; and Ashley Maher, "'Swastika Arms of Passage Leading to Nothing': Late Modernism and the 'New' Britain," *ELH* 80, no. 1 (2013): 251–85.

37. Fougasse, "Careless Talk Costs Lives," Imperial War Museum, London, Poster Collection MH 7369.

38. Allan Hepburn, *Intrigue: Espionage and Culture* (New Haven, Conn.: Yale University Press, 2005), 49. This book includes a chapter on *The Heat of the Day*, which Hepburn reads in the context of his focus on the spy's body. He writes, "To my mind, the problem of *The Heat of the Day* centers on complicity by association, the co-opting of Stella into a spy plot by virtue of her affections" (140). I read the novel differently: the role Stella plays in the spy plot is larger than this and is ultimately her own role as a spy on her lover, not as the potentially "contaminated" (149) lover of the spy.

39. Bowen had a lifelong love of thrillers, a genre she took seriously. She counted the popular thriller writer (and diplomat) John Buchan as a close friend and had a long, literary friendship with Graham Greene, with whom she collaborated on a series called "Why Do I Write?" (*The Mulberry Tree*, 221–30). In *Elizabeth Bowen: Portrait of a Writer* (London: Weidenfeld and Nicolson, 1977), Victoria Glendinning writes, "Elizabeth said, every novel is a detective novel" (175).

40. In some important ways, espionage may offer the best possible approach to Bowen's novels, so many of which sit uncomfortably in their classification as drawing-room realism. For espionage—the acme of distrust, ambiguity, of stealthy border crossings—is what underlies the anxieties and interpersonal relations in Bowen's early novels like *The Hotel* (1927), *The Last September* (1929), and *To the North* (1932). Espionage is what links Mme. Fischer in *The House in Paris* (1935) to Anna Quayne in *The Death of the Heart* (1938) and even to the ever-distrustful Eva Trout of Bowen's difficult-to-account-for final novel (1969).

41. John Mepham points out that "Bowen seems to be using the espionage setting precisely to focus on talk in conditions of duplicity, threat and betrayal, but not in order to exploit the entertainment possibilities of the genre" ("Varieties of Modernism, Varieties of Incomprehension: Patrick Hamilton and Elizabeth Bowen," in *British Fiction After Modernism*, ed. Marina MacKay and Lyndsey Stonebridge [New York: Palgrave, 2007], 71).

42. Bowen and Ritchie, a Canadian diplomat, met in 1940 at the home of Susan and John Buchan and were lovers throughout the war. Their relationship lasted until Bowen's death in 1973, despite their separate marriages, homes, and—often—continents. See Elizabeth Bowen and Charles Ritchie, *Love's Civil War: Letters and Diaries, 1941–1973*, ed. Victoria Glendinning (London: Simon and Schuster, 2008). The quotation is from Ritchie's diary of August 18, 1973, p. 473.

43. At the beginning of the novel, when Harrison excuses his blackmail proposal to Stella on account of war's subversion of ordinary morality, she says, "In other words, this is a crooks' war?" Harrison replies by saying that for him "it's a time when I'm not a crook" (Bowen, *The Heat of the Day*, 34). Crookedness, according to Harrison, merely depends on the circumstances in which you deploy it.

44. Corcoran, *Elizabeth Bowen*; Lee, *Elizabeth Bowen*; Ellmann, *Elizabeth Bowen*; Vera Krielkamp, *The Anglo-Irish Novel and the Big House* (Syracuse, N.Y.: Syracuse University Press, 1998); Margot Backus, *The Gothic Family Romance: Heterosexuality, Child Sacrifice, and the Anglo-Irish Colonial Order* (Durham, N.C.: Duke University Press, 1999).

45. However, in Bowen's complex formal vision, Cousin Francis of Mount Morris is wound up in some nebulous war intrigue sponsored by Harrison, who first meets Stella at Francis's funeral. Moreover, Stella's stay at Mount Morris gives her the impetus to confront Robert on her return. In this way, plot cannot be cleanly disentangled from subplot. See Andrew Bennett and Nicholas Royle's discussion of the knottiness of the novel as "sheer kink" in *Elizabeth Bowen and the Dissolution of the Novel: Still Lives* (New York: St. Martin's Press, 1995), 88.

46. See Faragher, "Form of Modernist Propaganda," Piette, *Imagination at War*, Ellmann, *Elizabeth Bowen*, and Krielkamp, *Anglo-Irish Novel*, on *The Heat of the Day*.

47. In a letter of January 5, 1941, Bowen describes her own experiences of espionage to Virginia Woolf: "In Dublin I get engaged in deep rather futile talks; it is hard to remember the drift afterwards, though I remember the words. I suppose that (smoke-screen use of words) is a trick of the Irish mind" (*The Mulberry Tree*, 218). Corcoran warns that in Bowen "acts of writing and reading are themselves constantly offered to readerly inspection and interpretation." In her prose's "negative construction, repetition, inversion, and ellipsis; in a reflexive turning back in upon itself rather than a committed motion forward; in its unyielding refusal of the obvious," Corcoran finds in Bowen "an anxiety that the mere writer herself may not remain in control of the riot" (*Elizabeth Bowen*, 3).

48. A draft version of this passage includes the eerily gothic sentence, "Which homegoing trains and buses, just by so much lightened, bore to their destinations bodiless occupants?" (Elizabeth Bowen, *The Heat of the Day*, hand-corrected TS, 1945–49, Harry Ransom Humanities Research Center, University of Texas at Austin [HRHRC], Bowen archive, box 5, folder 3).

49. See Ellmann, *Elizabeth Bowen*, 1–40, for an intelligent discussion of the concept of "nowhere" in Bowen.

50. Bowen's Court, for Elizabeth Bowen, like Mount Morris for Roderick, is one of many alternative realities that Bowen explores as "hallucinations . . . an unconscious, instinctive, saving resort" for her wartime characters in *The Demon Lover and Other Stories* (*The Mulberry Tree*, 94).

51. Elizabeth Bowen, *Bowen's Court* (New York: Knopf, 1942), 457.

52. On January 5, 1941, Elizabeth Bowen wrote from Bowen's Court to Virginia Woolf, whose London home (like Bowen's) had recently been bombed: "All my life I have said, 'Whatever happens there will always be tables and chairs'—and what a mistake" (*The Mulberry Tree*, 217). Standing outside the Blitz and having survived the Anglo-Irish War, Bowen's Court must have appeared to stand beyond danger. Its eventual demolition seems, in this light, all the more poignant.

53. Bowen, *The Heat of the Day*, TS, HRHRC Bowen, box 5, folder 3.

54. See Jed Esty, "Virgins of Empire: *The Last September* and the Antidevelopmental Plot," *Modern Fiction Studies* 53, no. 2 (2007), for a discussion of Bowen and plantation gothic.

55. MacNeice's poem "Galway" makes a similar gesture.

56. This is clearly an idea that sticks with Bowen. Twenty years later, in *Eva Trout*, Constantine reminds Eva, "The wall's very thin . . . Between dead and living" (90). See Anna Teekell, "Elizabeth Bowen and the Orphan *Eva Trout*," in *Founder to Shore: Cross-Currents in Irish and Scottish Studies*, ed. Shane Alcobia-Murphy, Lindsay Milligan, and Dan Wall (Aberdeen: AHRC Centre for Irish and Scottish Studies, 2011), 177–88.

57. In her preface to *The Demon Lover*, Bowen writes, "The search for indestructible landmarks in a destructible world led many down strange paths. The attachment to those when they had been found produced small worlds-within-worlds of hallucination—in most cases, saving hallucination" (*The Mulberry Tree*, 97).

58. In a 1941 *New Statesman* piece, "Éire," Bowen explains to her British audience, "Materially, neutral Éire in wartime is far from being the home of comfort and ease. Shortage and insecurity are felt everywhere" (*The Mulberry Tree*, 34).

59. The reference is to Montgomery's breaking of Rommel's Egyptian lines in late October 1942.

60. Churchill's remark on Montgomery's eventual victory at Tobruk, the first major Allied victory in the war, was, "This is not the end, it is not even the beginning of the end. But it is, perhaps, the end of the beginning," ("The End of the Beginning," November 10, 1942, Churchill Society, London, http://www.churchill-society-london.org.uk/EndoBegn.html).

61. Bowen, "London, 1940," *The Mulberry Tree*, 22.

62. Bowen, *The Mulberry Tree*, 94.

63. See Kristine A. Miller, "'Even a Shelter's Not Safe': The Blitz on Homes in Elizabeth Bowen's Wartime Writing," *Twentieth Century Literature* 45, no. 2 (1999): 138–58, on how in *The Heat of the Day* "the collapse of physical boundaries between private life and politics represents the breakdown of ideological stereotypes about feminine domestic space and the masculine political arena" (149).

64. Paul Muldoon, *To Ireland, I* (Oxford: Oxford University Press, 2000), 24.

65. Clair Wills, "The Aesthetics of Irish Neutrality during the Second World War," *boundary 2* 31, no. 1 (2004): 124.

66. A hallmark of Bowen's writing is her hyperreal treatment of furniture and furnishings in her work. For example, in *The Last September* (1929), Danielstown house

and its furniture are highly indicative of their inhabitants' states of mind; in *The Death of the Heart* (1938), the furniture often comes across as more human than its owners (as its caretaker, the housekeeper Matchett, is not shy of noticing); and in *Eva Trout* (1969), Eva overfurnishes her home with electronics as a substitute for normal relations with people. In "The Form of Modernist Propaganda," Faragher argues that "blackout curtains literalize the fears" of Britons skeptical of Irish neutrality (63).

67. Bowen, *The Mulberry Tree*, 96; see Thomas Davis, "Elizabeth Bowen's War Gothic," *Textual Practice* 27, no. 1 (2013): 29–47, for more on these themes.

68. Bowen, "Mysterious Kôr," *Collected Stories*, 730.

69. Bowen notes in her preface to *A Day in the Dark* that "the locale of the Victorian family in 'The Happy Autumn Fields' is, though not stated, to me unshakably County Cork" (*A Day in the Dark and Other Stories* [London: Cape, 1965], 9). See also Thomas Davis, "Elizabeth Bowen's War Gothic," and Phyllis Lassner, *Elizabeth Bowen: A Study of the Short Fiction* (New York: Twayne, 1991), for astute readings of this story.

70. Bowen, *Bowen's Court*, 325–42, 453–57.

71. Elizabeth Bowen, *Bowen's Court*, hand-corrected TS, 1945–49, HRHRC Bowen box 1, folder 2.

72. Although *Bowen's Court* is relatively silent on the issue, Corcoran provides a bit of oral history regarding the house's survival of the Anglo-Irish War. He reports that while the Bowen family was absent, the local IRA "took a vote in the house itself about whether to burn it. The vote was, of course, not to do so . . . the implication being that the family had been an exceptionally tolerant one" (*Elizabeth Bowen*, 25n9).

73. The doubling of *Bowen's Court* with Bowen's Court finds an echo in the sonically doubled names of Mount Morris, Roderick Rodney, and Louie Lewis in *The Heat of the Day*. At the end of the novel, Stella discovers that her secret agents double one another: Harrison ("just Harrison") turns out to be another Robert, making these double positives a sort of grammatical doubling just as ambiguous and compelling as the novel's double negatives.

Chapter 5

"The following precious and illuminating material should be carefully studied. Only fatigue and disgust prevented its incorporation." Samuel Beckett, *Watt* (New York: Grove, 1953, 2011), p. 247.

1. *The Inferno of Dante Alighieri*, trans. Ciaran Carson (New York: Granta, 2002), 3.23–25.

2. In his introduction to the 2009 Faber and Faber reissue of *Watt*, editor Chris Ackerley notes several places where he intentionally retained obvious textual errors, illustrating "the extent to which error in *Watt* is deeply rooted" (xvii). As Ackerley notes of the famous "mess" of *Watt's* text, "if no distinction can be drawn between deliberate and inadvertent error then all interpretation is fraught" (xviii). Acknowledging the text's insistence on its own errors, I have chosen to cite from the original 1953 Grove Press edition (Ackerley's parent text), which was reprinted in 2011. Subsequent references to the 1953/2011 Grove edition of *Watt* are cited by page number.

3. Daniela Caselli, *Beckett's Dantes: Intertextuality in the Fiction and Criticism* (Manchester: Manchester University Press, 2006). See also Michael Robinson, *The Long Sonata of the Dead: A Study of Samuel Beckett* (London: Grove Press, 1969).

4. Sean O'Faolain, "The Pleasures and Pains of Ireland," *The Bell* 8, no. 5 (August 1944): 369.

5. T. M. Ragg, letter of June 6, 1945, reprinted in *The Letters of Samuel Beckett, 1941–1956*, ed. George Craig, Martha Dow Fehsenfeld, Dan Gunn, and Lois More Overbeck (Cambridge: Cambridge University Press, 2011), 14n1. When Beckett arrived in England following the liberation of France, his notebooks for *Watt* were seized by customs, and he went through a fair amount of trouble getting them back. It is wonderful to imagine what the customs agents must have made of them!

6. Frederick Warburg wrote, rejecting *Watt* in 1946, "It shows an immense mental vitality, and outrageous metaphysical skill, and a very fine talent for writing," but ultimately, "the book itself is too difficult" (quoted in James Knowlson, *Damned to Fame: The Life of Samuel Beckett* [New York: Simon and Schuster, 1996], 311). Beckett sent the typescript of *Watt* to Washington, D.C., with Denis Devlin in 1946, in the hopes that he might find a publisher. He failed to do so, and Beckett griped about this for a long time. See his letter to George Reavey, June 19, 1946, in *Letters of Samuel Beckett*, 35.

7. See Anthony Cronin, *No Laughing Matter: The Life and Times of Flann O'Brien* (New York: Fromm International, 1998). For the sake of consistency, I follow scholarly convention in this chapter in referring to Brian O'Nolan by his relevant pseudonym, Flann O'Brien.

8. Elizabeth Bowen, letter to Jonathan Cape, 1948, quoted in Maud Ellmann, *Elizabeth Bowen: The Shadow Across the Page* (Edinburgh: Edinburgh University Press, 2003), 166.

9. Flann O'Brien, *The Third Policeman* (Chicago: Dalkey Archive Press, 1999), 85. Subsequent references to this work are by page number.

10. Beckett, *Letters* 576, 640.

11. W. B. Yeats, *Purgatory*, in *Selected Poems and Four Plays*, ed. M. L. Rosenthal (New York: Scribner, 1996), 225, 227. Subsequent references to this work are by page number.

12. *Purgatory* was published in 1939 together with the eugenicist tract *On the Boiler* (Dublin: Cuala Press, 1939).

13. The original text is Máirtín Ó Cadhain, *Cré na Cille* (Dublin: Sairseal agus Dill, 1949). The first complete English translation was Joan Trodden Keefe, "Churchyard Clay: A Translation of *Cré na Cille* by Máirtín Ó Cadhain with Introduction and Notes" (Ph.D. diss., University of California, 1984). Two recent editions are Máirtín Ó Cadhain, *The Dirty Dust: Crè na Cille*, trans. Alan Titley (New Haven, Conn.: Yale University Press, 2015), and Máirtín Ó Cadhain, *Graveyard Clay*, trans. Liam Mac Con Iomaire and Tim Robinson (New Haven, Conn.: Yale University Press, 2016).

14. Samuel Beckett, "Dante . . . Bruno . Vico . . Joyce" (1929), reprinted in *Disjecta* (London: Calder, 1983), 33.

15. The IRA declared war on England in 1938, leading to internment in both Northern Ireland and Ireland.

16. Ó Cadhain, *The Dirty Dust*, 97. All quotations from *Cré na Cille* in this chapter are from the Titley translation.

17. The pilot gains and loses proficiency in Irish (perhaps selectively) over the course of the novel. Time does pass in the graveyard, but not to any end; it is clear that there is no release and the cacophony goes on forever.

18. Beckett and his partner, Suzanne Déchevaux-Dumesnil, had been given permission to live in the tiny village of Roussillon so long as they did not leave it. See Knowlson, *Damned to Fame*.

19. Richard W. Seaver, ed., *A Samuel Beckett Reader* (New York: Grove Press, 1976), xxx.

20. Beckett's daily life in the isolated community of Roussillon, spent at agricultural labor with little contact with the outside world, must have borne a strong resemblance to life in rural Ireland.

21. Beckett, "Dante . . . Bruno," *Disjecta*, 33.

22. Samuel Beckett, *Echo's Bones*, ed. Mark Nixon (London: Faber and Faber, 2014), 3.

23. Gottfried Büttner, "A New Approach to *Watt*," in *Rethinking Beckett: A Collection of Critical Essays*, ed. Lance St. John Butler and Robin J. Davis (New York: St. Martin's Press, 1990), 177. See also Gottfried Büttner, *Samuel Beckett's Novel "Watt": A Psychological Inquiry*," trans. Joseph Dolan (Philadelphia: University of Pennsylvania Press, 1984).

24. Julian Moynahan, *Anglo-Irish: The Literary Imagination of a Hyphenated Culture* (Princeton, N.J.: Princeton University Press, 1995), 250–51.

25. I refer hereafter to the narrator of *The Third Policeman* as Narrator, to denote the difference between the character and the impersonal concept of a narrator. This is contrary to the convention of calling him "Noman," which I think comes too close to giving him a name.

26. Reprinted in *The Third Policeman*, 200.

27. Michael Rubenstein, *Public Works: Infrastructure, Irish Modernism, and the Postcolonial* (South Bend, IN: University of Notre Dame Press, 2010), 106.

28. Carol Taaffe, *Ireland through the Looking-Glass: Flann O'Brien, Myles na gCopaleen and Irish Cultural Debate* (Cork: Cork University Press, 2008), 64.

29. Michael Robinson, "From Purgatory to Inferno: Beckett and Dante Revisited," *Journal of Beckett Studies* 5 (1979): 69–70.

30. Beckett, "Dante . . . Bruno," *Disjecta*, 33.

31. In the case of *Cré na Cille*, Catriona's quest (to one-up her sister and have a fancy marble cross) is simply pointless, as she has no control over it.

32. In any case, Beckett would have been unable to read Ó Cadhain's novel, though it is likely that O'Brien read it in Irish after its 1949 publication by Sáirséal agus Dill. On the other hand, Rolf Breuer has contended that O'Brien's 1939 novel *At Swim-Two-Birds* directly influenced *Watt*; see Rolf Breuer, "Flann O'Brien and Samuel Beckett," *Irish University Review* 37, no. 2 (Autumn 2007): 340–51.

33. Tyrus Miller, *Late Modernism: Politics, Fiction, and the Arts between the World Wars* (Berkeley: University of California Press, 1999).

34. There are obvious parallels between the purgatorial worlds of *Watt* and *Waiting for Godot*, written in 1948–49. It could be argued that *Godot* is a more highly evolved treatment of Watt's themes, utilizing similar Dantean parallels alongside the major rhetorical trope of repetition. *Godot*'s Didi, however (and to a lesser extent, Gogo), is both more self-aware and more verbally adroit than Watt; he is capable of expressing his situation, but not of solving it.

35. Brian Cosgrove, review of *Flann O'Brien: A Critical Introduction to His Writings*, by Anne Clissmann, *Irish University Review* 6, no. 1 (1976): 123.

36. Terence Brown's essay in *The Cambridge Companion to the Irish Novel*, ed. John Wilson Foster, 205–22 (Cambridge: Cambridge University Press, 2007), is a good indicator of what happens with such a comparison. The chapter title promises "Two Post-Modern Novelists: Samuel Beckett and Flann O'Brien" but examines their work individually rather than drawing implications from the pairing.

37. Keith Hopper, *Flann O'Brien: A Portrait of the Artist as a Young Post-Modernist*. 2nd ed. (Cork: Cork University Press, 2009), 229.

38. M. Keith Booker, *Flann O'Brien, Bakhtin, and Menippean Satire* (Syracuse, N.Y.: Syracuse University Press, 1995).

39. See the following articles in the *Review of Contemporary Fiction* 31, no. 3 (Fall 2011): Robert Lumsden, "Voidance in *The Third Policeman*"; Carlos Villar Vlor, "Flann O'Brien: A Postmodernist Who Happens to Be a Thomist"; Jennika Baines, "Un-understandable Mystery: Catholic Faith and Revelation in *The Third Policeman*"; Maciej Ruczaj, "Infernal Poetics/Infernal Ethics: *The Third Policeman* between Medieval and (Post)Modern Netherworlds"; Anthony Adams, "Butter-Spades, Footnotes, and Omnium: *The Third Policeman* as 'Pataphysical Fiction'"; and Joseph Brooker, "'That Carrousel Inside and Outside My Head': Flann O'Brien and *Pale Fire*."

40. Beckett, *Letters*, v. 2, 55.

41. Jonathan Boulter, *Beckett: A Guide for the Perplexed* (London: Bloomsbury, 2008), 106.

42. Stan Gontarski, preface to *Obscure Locks, Simple Keys: The Annotated "Watt,"* ed. Chris Ackerley (Edinburgh: Edinburgh University Press, 2010), 9.

43. Edna Longley, *Louis MacNeice: A Study* (London: Faber and Faber, 1988), xiii.

44. Robinson's reminder in "From Purgatory to Inferno" is salutary here: "Since they are taken from both the *Inferno* and the *Purgatorio*, the multiplicity of references to the *Divina commedia* frequently provokes a desire to identify individual works with one realm or the other. And yet, if only because references to both realms may coexist in a single work, no direct and consistent parallel can be maintained" (1–2). Attempting to align any of Beckett's allusive texts with a particular moment from Dante, or to claim he is rewriting Dante, is reductive.

45. Beckett, "Dante . . . Bruno," *Disjecta*, 33.

46. Israel Schenker, "Interview with Samuel Beckett" (1956), reprinted In *Samuel Beckett: The Critical Heritage*, ed. L. Graver and R. Federman (London: Routledge, 1999), 147.

47. Beckett, *Letters*, v. 2, 55.

48. Marjorie Perloff, *Wittgenstein's Ladder: Poetic Language and the Strangeness of the Ordinary* (Chicago: University of Chicago Press, 1996), 137.

49. Knowlson, *Damned to Fame*, 282.

50. Beckett's Resistance code name was the astonishingly uncreative Sam Irlandais (Irish Sam).

51. James McNaughton, "Beckett's 'Brilliant Obscurantics': *Watt* and the Problem of Propaganda," in *Samuel Beckett: History, Memory, Archive* (London: Palgrave, 2010), 51.

52. See George Orwell, "Politics and the English Language," *Horizon* 13, no. 76 (April): 252–65, and Theodore W. Adorno, *The Jargon of Authenticity* (Evanston, Ill: Northwestern University Press, 1973) for foundational articulations of this problem. More recently, the new modernist studies has taken war's alteration of language to be axiomatic. See, for example, Vincent Sherry, *The Great War and the Language of*

Modernism (Oxford: Oxford University Press, 2003), Mark Rawlinson, *British Writing of the Second World War* (Oxford: Clarendon Press, 2000); Marina MacKay, *Modernism and World War II* (Cambridge: Cambridge University Press, 2007); James Purdon, *Modernist Informatics: Literature, Information, and the State* (Oxford: Oxford University Press, 2016); and Thomas Davis, *The Extinct Scene: Late Modernism and Everyday Life* (New York: Columbia University Press, 2016).

53. The Galls' name puns on "Gaels," reminding the reader that the entrance of outsiders into the closed world of the Anglo-Irish big house often did, in fact, prove to be the house's "doom." The name is shared by Haemo Gall, the big house owner in "Echo's Bones," whose impotence dooms his bloodline.

54. Cathy Caruth's definition of trauma as "the response to an unexpected or overwhelming violent event or events that are not fully grasped as they occur, but return later in repeated flashbacks, nightmares, and other repetitive phenomena" was fundamental to discussions of trauma in literature for decades (*Unclaimed Experience: Trauma, Narrative, and History* [Baltimore: Johns Hopkins University Press, 1996], 91). In recent years, critics (and especially Holocaust scholars) such as Henry Greenspan, Dominic LaCapra, Greg Forter, Ruth Leys, and Naomi Mendel have revised this definition to account for the ways in which testimony (however belated) suggests that survivors can grasp and remember traumatic experiences. In addition, contemporary cognitive science suggests that the repetitive revisitations that are the hallmark of post-traumatic stress can actually help begin a process of working through and reintegrating scarring events, at least into the individual psyche. See Michelle Balaev, ed., *Contemporary Approaches in Literary Trauma Theory* (New York: Palgrave, 2014) for a summary of the field.

55. Caruth, *Unclaimed Experience*, 5.

56. Knowlson, *Damned to Fame*, 291–309.

57. Donal Ó Drisceoil, *Censorship in Ireland, 1939–1945: Neutrality, Politics and Society* (Cork: Cork University Press, 1996), 121.

58. The Frank Aiken papers at University College Dublin (UCDA P104) contain complete lists of known and censored events.

59. Clair Wills, *That Neutral Island: A Cultural History of Ireland during the Second World War* (London: Faber and Faber, 2007), 8.

60. Moynahan, *Anglo-Irish*, 224.

61. Multiple critics have noted the resemblance of Mr. Knott's establishment to the Beckett family home, Cooldrinagh. See Moynahan, 224–52.

62. R. W. Maslen, "Flann O'Brien's Bombshells: *At Swim-Two-Birds* and *The Third Policeman*," *New Hibernia Review* 10, no. 4 (Winter 2006): 101.

63. Ireland was, in fact, bombed by the Germans several times during the war; the most deadly was a (presumably accidental) attack on Dublin, killing thirty-four civilians on May 31, 1941. In Northern Ireland, Belfast was Blitzed on April 15, 1941, leaving more than a thousand dead; de Valera sent thirteen fire trucks to aid in putting out the flames. For more on the bombings, see Robert Fisk, *In Time of War: Ireland, Ulster and the Price of Neutrality, 1939–45* (Philadelphia: University of Pennsylvania Press, 1983); Brian Girvin, *The Emergency: Neutral Ireland, 1939–45* (London: Macmillan, 2006); Clair Wills, *That Neutral Island: A Cultural History of Ireland during the Second World War* (London: Faber and Faber, 2007); Robert Fisk, "Why the Nazis Bombed Dublin," *Independent* (London), January 24, 1999.

64. It may also remind readers of *Molloy*.

65. Eamon de Valera, *Speeches and Statements by Eamon de Valera, 1917–73*, ed. Maurice Moynihan (Dublin: Gill and Macmillan, 1980), 466.

66. O'Brien's footnote to this episode discusses "the notorious 'Munich Letter' incident involving an attempt to use de Selby as the tool of international financial interests"—a reference, perhaps, to the false promise of the Munich Agreement of 1938 to function as a political victory with no fighting (*The Third Policeman*, 172).

67. Credit goes to my Christopher Newport University Modernism's Ghosts students for coining the term "bikesexuality."

68. Beckett, "Dante . . . Bruno," *Disjecta*, 33.

69. Gnathaí Gan Irraidh (Ernest Boyd), *The Sacred Egoism of Sinn Féin* (London: Maunsel, 1918); available online in a Project Gutenberg reproduction at http://www.gutenberg.org/files/34108/34108-8.txt.

70. Beckett's 1935 essay "Censorship in the Saorstat" excoriated the government's policy as "sterilization of the mind" and called the Register of Prohibited Publications an "advertisement of those books and periodicals in which . . . inheres the a priori excellence that they have annoyed the specialist in common sense" (*Disjecta*, 86). "My own registered number," he notes with a swagger, "is 465" (88). In a January 1940 letter to Joyce, Beckett enclosed—by request—the latest censored list. Enhanced by the Emergency Powers Act of 1939, the wartime censorship managed to quash political dissent while enforcing a Catholic, nationalist aesthetic autonomy favored by Fianna Fáil. Beckett applies a merciless mocking to such Gaelic pieties in *Watt*'s tale of the "Gaelic" savant Nackybal.

71. Seanad Debates, January 27, 1944. Seanad Debates are cited by date and available online at http://oireachtasdebates.oireachtas.ie.

72. Terence Brown, "Two post-modern novelists: Samuel Beckett and Flann O'Brien." *Cambridge Companion to the Irish Novel.* Ed. John Wilson Foster (Cambridge: Cambridge University Press, 2007), 115.

73. The characters' physical lameness is also symptomatic of the general stagnation of their environment.

74. It is no surprise, then, that the worlds of both novels have been read as versions of the Celtic Otherworld. Francis Doherty reads *Watt*'s setting "almost as an analogy to those old Irish stories about lands which lie just beyond the present; Mr Knott's house is lodged somewhere in reality, yet is out of it, too" (Francis Doherty, "*Watt* in an Irish Frame," *Irish University Review* 21, no. 2 [Autumn 1991]: 188). In *The Third Policeman*, the concept of the Otherworld is literalized—and serialized—in the setting: although the Narrator spends only three days in the policemen's strange parish, when he returns home, sixteen years have passed. Likewise, within the parish, the Narrator visits Eternity, an underground world—entered by electric lift—which, like purgatory, is immune from the passage of outside time. Doherty has also noted O'Brien's use of the *sid* and the *immram* as source texts in *The Third Policeman*; see Francis Doherty, "Flann O'Brien's Existentialist Hell," *Canadian Journal of Irish Studies* 15, no. 2 (1989): 63.

75. Because Watt explains this while speaking backward, he is technically left "Nilb, mun, mud" (168).

76. Sinead Mooney. *Samuel Beckett* (Tavistock, Devon: Northcote, 2006), 15.

77. Sam's difficulty in interpreting Watt's various mumblings and murmurings recalls Watt's Dante-esque heard voices on the train.

78. J. M. Silverthorne, "Time, Literature, and Failure: Flann O'Brien's *At Swim-Two-Birds* and *The Third Policeman*," *Éire-Ireland* 14, no. 4 (1976): 73.

79. Benjamin Keatinge, "Beckett and Language Pathology," *Journal of Modern Literature* 31, no. 4 (2004): 92.

80. Hugh Kenner, *A Reader's Guide to Samuel Beckett* (New York: Farrar, Straus and Giroux, 1973), 77.

81. These "fantastic dwellings" of de Selby's foreshadow the Narrator's entrance, on the same page, into Mathers's fantastic big house. Nearly all the de Selby references map directly onto places or occurrences in the parish.

82. John Wall, "A Study of the Imagination in Samuel Beckett's *Watt*," *New Literary History* 32, no. 3 (2002): 547.

83. Many readers have noted that the infinite regressions in *The Third Policeman*, such as the Atomic Theory, appear to parody the theory of atomic half-life, which fascinated O'Brien, and critics have speculated on the likely influence of J. W. Dunne's books *The Serial Universe* (London: Faber and Faber, 1934) and *An Experiment with Time* (London: Faber and Faber, 1927) on both *The Third Policeman* and *Watt*. See Roy L. Hunt, "Hell Goes Round and Round: Flann O'Brien," *Canadian Journal of Irish Studies* 14, no. 2 (1989): 60–73.

84. Michael E. Mooney, "*Watt*: Samuel Beckett's Sceptical Fiction," in Butler and Davis, *Rethinking Beckett*, 166.

85. Stephen Connor, *Samuel Beckett: Repetition, Theory and Text* (Oxford: Blackwell, 1988), 32.

86. Except that he did. Within the parish, the Narrator is sentenced for the murder of Old Mathers, whose belly was ripped in the signature manner of Martin Finnucane. In the parish, the Narrator has an alibi, having been with the police the entire time. But the Narrator did kill Old Mathers—it is the first thing he says in the book—only he kills him in "real life" and is convicted in the afterlife of the parish.

87. Barry Stampfl, "Parsing the Unspeakable in the Context of Trauma," in Balaev, *Literary Trauma Theory*, 22, 30.

88. Arsene's speech closely resembles the "excruciating" language of Beckett's characters in the 1956 radio play set in Foxrock, *All That Fall*; see Samuel Beckett, *The Complete Dramatic Works* (London: Faber and Faber, 1986), 174.

89. Samuel Beckett, *Worstward Ho* (London: Calder, 1999), 8.

90. For more on Beckett and the critical category of the inhuman, see David Houston Jones, *Samuel Beckett and Testimony* (London: Palgrave, 2011); Jonathan Boulter, "Does Mourning Require a Subject? Samuel Beckett's *Texts for Nothing*," *Modern Fiction Studies* 50, no. 2 (2004): 332–50.

91. Again, de Selby's language is mimicked in the sergeant's speech, suggesting, as Doherty argues, that this particular hell is one built by the Narrator himself, and built upon the ideas and fears at work in his mind while alive. As in Dante, the Narrator's punishment fits his crime (Doherty, "Flann O'Brien's Existentialist Hell"). It is worth remembering that the Narrator is already dead, so this death would indeed be an "inferior phenomenon" (*The Third Policeman*, 102).

92. As Stampfl has put it, "Seeming to figure as the ultimate instrument for facing-up-to and coming-to-grips-with, the trope of the unspeakable actually gives permission to turn away" ("Parsing the Unspeakable," 18). The use of the trope of the "unspeakable" can be a form of censorship.

93. Joseph C. Voelker, "'Doublends Jined': The Fiction of Flann O'Brien," *Journal of Irish Literature* 12, no. 1 (1983): 93.

94. M. Keith Booker, "Science, Philosophy, and *The Third Policeman*: Flann O'Brien and the Epistemology of Futility," *South Atlantic Review* 56, no. 4 (1991): 38–99.

95. Although the first twenty-five years of the twentieth century had shown Ireland enough unspeakable violence already.

96. Ackerley, *Obscure Locks*, 14.

97. Naomi Mandel, *Against the Unspeakable: Complicity, the Holocaust, and Slavery in America* (Charlottesville: University of Virginia Press, 2006), 5.

98. Tyrus Miller, in *Late Modernism: Politics, Fiction, and the Arts between the World Wars* (Berkeley: University of California Press, 1999), borrows the term "mirthless laughter" from *Watt* (48) to describe the disruptive black comedy characteristic of late modernist fiction. Miller's taxonomy of late modernism, which includes the presentation of "a deauthenticated world . . . where spectacle and simulacra predominate and characters are near-puppets of external forces," a predominance of grotesque bodies, and "an obsessive depiction of pure corporeal automatism," fits *Watt* and *The Third Policeman* neatly into its parameters (62–63). The novels' "mirthless" or "self-reflexive" (64) laughter is the connective tissue between character and audience in their denaturalized worlds.

Epilogue

1. Alan Shatter, Dáil Debates, Defence Forces (Second World War Amnesty and Immunity) Bill 2012 [Seanad]: Report and Final Stages, May 7, 2013. Dáil Debates are cited by date and can be accessed online at http://oireachtasdebates.oireachtas.ie/debates authoring/debateswebpack.nsf/.

2. Dáil Debates, May 7, 2013.

3. Dáil Debates, May 7, 2013.

4. J. J. Lee, *Ireland 1912–1985: Politics and Society*, 175–270 (Cambridge: Cambridge University Press, 1989), 263.

5. There is a long-standing academic debate about the validity of Irish neutrality. Key scholarly texts are Trevor Salmon, *Unneutral Ireland: An Ambivalent and Unique Security Policy* (Oxford: Clarendon Press, 1989); Garret Fitzgerald, "The Origins, Development and Present Status of Irish 'Neutrality,'" *Irish Studies in International Affairs* 9 (1998): 11–19; Karen Devine, "A Comparative Critique of the Practice of Irish Neutrality in the 'Unneutral' Discourse," *Irish Studies in International Affairs* 19 (2008): 73–97.

6. See Salmon, Fitzgerald, and Devine for more on the common presumption that Irish neutrality is constitutional. In 2003, 2013, and 2016, Sinn Féin introduced bills to create a neutrality amendment in the constitution; none made it past the second stage.

7. Ece Özlem Atikcan, "Asking the Public Twice: Why Do Voters Change Their Minds in Second Referendums on EU Treaties," *EUROPP* (blog), October 19, 2015, http://blogs.lse.ac.uk/europpblog/2015/10/19/asking-the-public-twice-why-do-voters-change-their-minds-in-second-referendums-on-eu-treaties/.

8. Twenty-Sixth Amendment of the Constitution Act, 2002; Twenty-Eighth Amendment of the Constitution Act, 2008.

9. Twenty-Seventh Amendment of the Constitution Act, 2004.

10. Emma O'Dwyer, Evanthia Lyons, and J. Christopher Cohrs, "How Irish Citizens Negotiate Foreign Policy: A Social Representations Approach to Neutrality," *Political Psychology* 37, no. 2 (2016): 173.

11. See, for example, the Irish Peace and Neutrality Alliance (PANA) advertisement for a seminar on World War I, "the Imperialist War," at https://www.pana.ie/. Narratives of Irish "neutrality" in World War I often ignore key elements of history, such as John Redmond's call for patriots to enlist in order to encourage the passage of Home Rule and the U.K. government's long-standing policy of no draft in Ireland or Northern Ireland, which dates to World War I.

12. Since 1996 PANA has been the largest action group campaigning against the integration of Ireland into the U.S., EU, NATO military structures and, in particular, the use of Shannon Airport by the U.S. military for flights to and from the wars in Afghanistan, Iraq, and Pakistan. A poster declares, "Restore Irish Independence, Democracy, and Neutrality: Join PANA."

13. Committee on Finance, National Security—Ministerial Statement, Dáil Debates, May 28, 1940.

14. Dáil Debates, May 28, 1940.

15. Aaron McKenna, "Irish Neutrality Won't Be Respected by the Likes of ISIS, So Why Hold So Dear to It?," *The Journal*, November 21, 2015.

16. Thomas Hachey, "The Rhetoric and Reality of Irish Neutrality," *New Hibernia Review* 6, no. 4 (2002): 38.

17. Quoted in Hachey, 38.

18. O'Dwyer et al., 173.

19. In 2013, TD Lucinda Creighton ruffled feathers when the *Irish Times* quoted her as saying, "We have developed this perception of ourselves that to be neutral and to not engage in any sort of common defence is a badge of honour. That position on neutrality is quite narcissistic: we do not have to worry about its consequences, and we can parade it around the world, go to the United Nations and tell everyone how wonderful we are. But that has become part of Irish identity and it will be very hard to change" (quoted in O'Dwyer, Lyons, and Cohrs, "How Irish Citizens Negotiate," 68). Recent scholarly studies citing the "sacred cow" of neutrality include Róisín Doherty, *Ireland, Neutrality and European Security Integration* (New York: Routledge 2002, 2018); Ben Tonra, *Global Citizen and European Republic: Irish Foreign Policy in Transition* (Manchester: Manchester University Press, 2006), 154; and M. J. Geary, "Irish Foreign Policy and European Political Cooperation: Navigating Neutrality," *European Enlargement across Rounds and Beyond Borders*, ed. Haakon A. Ikonomou, Aurélie Andry, and Rebekka Byberg (New York: Routledge, 2017), 103. The phrase "sacred cow" has become inextricably associated with neutrality in popular discourse; see Brigid Laffan's controversial editorial on Brexit, "Ireland May Have to Sacrifice Sacred Cows to Survive Brexit," *Irish Times*, May 16, 2017.

20. The Thirty-Fifth Amendment of the Constitution (Neutrality) Bill, 2016.

21. "Support Sinn Féin's Neutrality Bill." 2016. https://www.change.org/p/tds-support-sinn-f%C3%A9in-s-neutrality-bill. This petition closed before reaching 100 signatures.

22. Ibid.

23. Dáil Debates, Thirty-Fifth Amendment of the Constitution (Neutrality) Bill 2016: Second Stage [Private Members] (Continued), November 24, 2016.

24. Ibid.

25. Sebastian Barry, *The Temporary Gentleman* (London: Viking, 2014); Dermot Bolger, *The Lonely Sea and Sky* (Dublin: New Island Books, 2016); Mary Morrissey, "Emergency," in *All Over Ireland: New Irish Short Stories*, ed. Deirdre Madden, 27–43 (London: Faber and Faber, 2015).

26. Jo Baker, *A Country Road, A Tree* (New York: Knopf, 2016); Barry Devlin, *My Mother and Other Strangers*, television series, directed by Adrian Shergold (Belfast: BBC-NI, 2016). The favorably reviewed five-episode series was released on PBS in America in 2017.

27. Albert Williams, "Wartime Hijinks, Presented with *Improbable Frequency*," *Chicago Reader*, February 27, 2013. Bell Helicopter is the duo, Irish musicians and composers, Conor Kelly and Sam Park.

28. Arthur Riordan, *Improbable Frequency* (London: Nick Hern Books, 2005), 6.

29. Harvey O'Brien, review of *Improbable Frequency*," *Irish Theatre Magazine*, March 15, 2012.

30. Patrick Lonergan, *Interactions: Dublin Theatre Festival, 1957–2007*, ed. Nicholas Grene, Patrick Lonergan, and Lillian Chambers (London: Lang, 2008), 127.

31. Charles Isherwood, "It's That Old Story: Spies, Physics and Gaelic," *New York Times*, December 5, 2008.

32. Agent Green's name puns on both the color association of Irish republicanism and the Nazis' amazingly unsneaky code name for their (never used) Irish invasion plan, Operation Green.

33. Like Bowen's spies in *The Heat of the Day*, Riordan's spies intertwine the personal and political, but here to comic effect. In "The Bedtime Jig" with Tristram, Philomena gets one of the play's best lines: "Infiltrated by British intelligence / Oxymoronic as well as a sin" (54).

34. See Damien Keane, *Ireland and the Problem of Information: Irish Writing, Radio, Late Modernist Communication* (University Park: Penn State University Press, 2014), and Clair Wills, *That Neutral Island: A Cultural History of Ireland during the Second World War* (London: Faber and Faber, 2007) for more on radio and the Emergency.

35. Arthur Riordan, interview by Peter Crawley, program for *Improbable Frequency*, Rough Magic Theatre Company, 2004.

36. Ibid.

37. Belinda McKeon, "*Improbable Frequency*: O'Reilly Theatre," *Irish Times*, September 29, 2004.

38. Isherwood, "It's That Old Story."

39. McKeon, "*Improbable Frequency*: O'Reilly Theatre."

40. Oscar Wilde, *The Importance of Being Earnest and Four Other Plays* (New York: Barnes and Noble Classics, 2003), 142.

41. A representative sample includes McKenna, "Irish Neutrality"; Editor, "Poll: Should Ireland Give Up Its Neutrality?," *The Journal*, February 13, 2013; Barry Roche, "Coveney Rejects Call for Abandonment of Ireland's Neutrality Policy," *Irish Times*, September 12, 2014; "Ireland Is 'Not Neutral and Never Has Been', Says Eoghan Murphy TD," *Irish Examiner*, March 7, 2015; Ruari Casey, "The Irish Anti-War Movement Says Sending Irish Troops to Relieve and Allow French Soldiers to Fight in Syria, Compromises Our Neutrality," *News Talk*, November 21, 2015; Fergus Finlay, "Not Helping When France Is Being Terrorised Is Not Neutrality," *Irish Examiner*, November 24, 2015; Suzanne Lynch, "Paris Attacks. EU Defence Clause 'Will Not Affect Irish Neutrality,'" *Irish Times*, November 17, 2015; Edward Horgan, "Irish Neutrality Is Breached by NATO and US Military Aircraft at Shannon," *Irish Times*, April 11, 2016; and Julian Gough, "The State Has No Right to Take the Names of James Joyce and Samuel Beckett in Vain," *Irish Times*, May 20, 2014, about the lively controversy

wrought by the Irish Defence Forces' commissioning of naval ships named after James Joyce and Samuel Beckett. In 2016, a third offshore patrol vessel was commissioned *LÉ William Butler Yeats*, to be followed by *LÉ George Bernard Shaw*. As the conversation surrounding the commissioning of *LÉ Samuel Beckett* often referenced Beckett's expatriate status and his service in the French Resistance, it is amusing to imagine what might be made of the contrasts between these writers' exceptionally divergent political views and the work of their namesake ships. The *Samuel Beckett-class* of armed patrol vessels are principally used for humanitarian missions in the Mediterranean. Their primary task, rescuing refugees from inhospitable waters, aligns them with the Irish merchant marine of the Emergency. Their names are a potent sign that Irish modernist writers have themselves become shibboleths of contemporary Irish culture.

42. Irish neutrality comes up routinely (and always heatedly) in discussions of Brexit; by presstime the instances were too numerous to cite. Particularly divisive newspaper columns in 2017 included Laffan, "Ireland May Have to Sacrifice Sacred Cows to Survive Brexit," and Lorna Siggins, "Can We Rely on the EU to Fight our Corner in Brexit Fishing Talks?" *Irish Times*, July 5, 2017. In June 2017, newly elected Taoiseach Leo Varadkar publically defended the policy (Patrick Smyth, "Varadkar Defends Neutrality as EU Steps up Co-operation on Defence," *Irish Times* June 23, 2017), while Fine Gael MEP Brian Hayes's statement that Ireland may need to "reexamine" neutrality in the wake of Brexit caused controversy later in the year ("Fine Gael MEP says Ireland Needs to Re-examine its Neutrality ahead of Brexit," *the journal.ie*, September 13, 2017). Brexit and its aftermath are likely to ensure that the Emergency will continue to be referenced with improbable frequency.

INDEX

Page numbers in **boldface** refer to illustrations.